Praise for *The Law of Averages*

"Frisky, snappy, Becketty pastless, the world of Frederick Barthelme is a good great place full of jolly menace."

Padgett Powell

"*The Law of Averages* reveals the ineptness of the term 'minimalism' when characterizing his art. Despite their modest settings and ordinary people, these tales brilliantly accomplish what fiction strives for: They capture the texture of our modern lives and show how we can transcend incipient banality. . . . In two decades of work, Barthelme has made music from these quotidian details, the detritus of American culture, a fact this collection attests to over and again in ways that are beautiful and true."

John Freeman, *Minneapolis Star-Tribune*

"Tight, beautifully realized stories. . . . Collectively, they chronicle one of the most innovative careers in contemporary American fiction and brim with relevance, breadth, and beauty."

Bret Anthony Johnston, *Book*

"Confirms Frederick Barthelme's status as one of America's most important explorers of the dreadful, banal quotidian and as a unique stylist whose dead-pan minimalist delivery is paradoxically permeated by a heart-breaking strain of pure lyricism."

Fredric Koeppel, *Memphis Commercial Appeal*

"Last year I touted the wonders of the memoir, *Double Down: Reflections on Gambling and Loss,* which he co-authored with his brother Steven. Now this year we have *The Law of Averages: New & Selected Stories.* No one writes like Frederick Barthelme except maybe Raymond Carver on his best day. Every nuance is noted, every small particle that makes up the torn threads of our daily existence is examined and allowed to speak for itself. Do not miss this book."

Robert Segedy, *McIntyre's Fine Books*

THE LAW OF

AVERAGES

New & Selected Stories

▲ ▼ ▲

FREDERICK BARTHELME

COUNTERPOINT
WASHINGTON, D.C.

Library of Congress Cataloging-in-Publication Data
Barthelme, Frederick, 1943–
The law of averages : new & selected stories / Frederick Barthelme.
p. cm.
ISBN 1–58243–115–9 (cloth), 1-58243-157-4 (paper)
1. United States—Social life and customs—20th century—Fiction.
2. Humorous stories, American. I. Title.
PS3552.A763 L39 2000 813'.54—dc21
00–055516

FIRST PRINTING

Book design by Mark McGarry
Set in Palatino

COUNTERPOINT
P.O. Box 65793
Washington, D.C. 20035–5793

Counterpoint is a member of the Perseus Books Group

10 9 8 7 6 5 4 3 2 1

▼

For Dawn

CONTENTS

vii

AUTHOR'S NOTE

I started my adult life as a painter, reading art magazines and trying to figure out what was going on in New York from the relative comfort of Houston. This was the early sixties. I was studying architecture, and my brother Don visited and suggested I become a painter. So I did. I made crude, aggressive, Lester Johnson pictures—lots of paint slapped around some basic human image, a head, a circle with a neck. The painting became more interesting as I ran through twentieth-century painting at about two hours per year, so that by 1965, showing in Houston, I was doing concept art, putting tape on walls, performance pieces. I began writing fiction, doing mostly the kind of Tonka-surrealism that plagues undergraduate writing programs even today. Sand mutants and people turning into pancakes. Soon enough I was thrown out of the architectural school for designing a multimedia performance piece instead of the parking garage my instructor had assigned. So I moved to the art department and started playing music and making sixteen-millimeter films with Mayo Thompson. We started a band called the Red Crayola in 1965, and after touring a little in California in 1967, and recording three LPs (*Parable of Arable Land*, *Coconut Hotel*, and a never-released album recorded in Berkeley in 1967 with John Fahey), I quit the band and moved to New York to be a painter. There I hung around with Don, who was thirteen years older and a successful writer and editor. He was still relatively new to the city, having moved there in 1964 to edit *Location* for Harold Rosenberg and Tom Hess.

Don and I were not peers. He was the mentor I entrusted with my education. He was unfailingly generous and took the job. We went all over New York. He took me to see the mysterious Viking street musician Moondog, aka Louis T. Hardin, and as we left, walking down some moonlit New York street, Don recited his favorite made-up mock-romantic poem—"O Tree / Standing there displaying human hopes and aspirations . . ." It trailed off like that. It was funny. We went for drinks, we went to museums, we went to jazz clubs, restaurants, more museums, the Top of the Sixes. We talked about art, writing, music, politics, consumer electronics—stereos, turntables, speakers, the better to hear the music—and groceries. He wasn't so excited about conceptual art. He was sort of *Art News,* I was utterly *Artforum.* He wasn't thrilled by the noisy and messy Red Crayola LP I brought for him, even though I'd acquired my interest in Cage, and chance music, and noise years before while working for Don as a gofer at the Contemporary Arts Museum in Houston. He ran the museum. I was one of the installation guys. I helped with the crashed-cars set for the Arrabal play, helped hang the paintings, swept the place, chauffeured when luminaries wanted to ride around town. I'd driven Cage and David Tudor when they were there for a concert. I was completely swept away by Cage's music, and *that's* what I'd brought to the band, so the noise and mess were in large measure my contribution, but Don wasn't sold. We had different ideas about art, as it turned out, but I was in the ballpark, so in spite of the odd arched eyebrow, I was encouraged to go my own way.

Two years after I moved to New York, in 1969, someone wanted to commission Don to do a book in a bag—loose sheets, read 'em in any order, that sort of thing. He said it was a silly idea, and he didn't want to do it. So he sent them to me. I said it was a silly idea, and I would be happy to do it. I figured it would be pleasant to have a contract. Daniel Spoerri's *Anecdoted Topography of Chance* had been published in 1966, so there was recent precedent for a book that wasn't quite a book in the conventional sense. And the idea of book-as-container fit nicely with my by now waning interest in conceptual art. That "career" had prospered in a small way—I was in Joseph Kosuth's original conceptual art exhibit at the Museum of Normal Art, and in Seth Siegelaub's first "virtual" show, which was a catalog of sorts, and I'd shown in galleries in New York and elsewhere, a couple of traveling shows put together by the critic Lucy Lippard, and I'd soon show at the New York Cultural Center and the Museum of Modern Art—but concept art seemed terribly *dry*, and I'd come to the conclusion that it might not sustain me.

So I took the commission from Winter House and produced *Rangoon*, a hybrid of stories, faux stories, nonstories, drawings, photos, diagrams, lists, assertions, visual art games, and whatnot. I put in it what was handy, but the thing turned out disappointingly conventional, though I'm still fond of the dumb stories, the diagrams of plumbing, the black pages, and my premiere bad photography show—sixty cheesy, shot-on-the-fly out-the-car-window photographs. I like many of Mayo Thompson's drawings, and I'm proud to have accounted for the first appearance in fiction of Carl Sagan's and I. S. Shklovskii's equation for determining the number of extant civilizations in the universe interested in and capable of interstellar communication. I guess I like the whole thing. It's damned odd. Makes you wonder who put it together and why.

Shortly thereafter I got a deal with Doubleday for another book, eventually called *War & War* because that was the prospective title that got the biggest laugh at Don's dinner table one night (you had to be there). *War & War* was stranger than the first book, a patchwork of lifts from *Scientific American*, Maurice Merleau-Ponty, *Mademoiselle*, and a hundred other sources, a cigar box of little drawings, personal letters, tests, captions, commentaries on the book's construction, found and annotated photos, sketches, diagrams of carnal pleasures, outlines of study-guide philosophy, bits of biography. There was a diary component, as I recall. It's fun to look at now because it induces a kind of data vertigo. It's not held together by much more than the binding, and one is hard pressed to imagine the guiding principles behind its construction.

These weren't literary works of any kind, really. They were books about me at a certain time in my life, excited about a lot of things, interested in everything, unwilling to play by the rules, or even to try to discover what the rules were. The books were Dumpsters for half-digested information, half-realized ideas; they recognized, even revered, the haphazard. Were they good? Probably not, but good was beside the point. They were messages in bottles, loose signals in the night sky, and what they were saying was simple: *Hey. I'm awake. Are you?*

Years later, when I began publishing stories in *The New Yorker*, I started getting letters from an agent in New York. After each story appeared in the magazine a letter would arrive telling me what a nice story it was. In a year I got maybe a half dozen such letters. Eventually came a phone call from the not-yet-notorious agent Andrew Wylie. He was the most remarkable man. He was funny and sweet, sensitive, brighter and better educated than almost anyone I'd ever met, killingly hip, utterly genuine, and completely direct. I think I loved him from that first phone call—his voice, his jokes, the play-savage laughter, the slightly demented cackle. I didn't know who he was or where he'd come from, but I knew instantly that he was smarter and faster than I was, and I wanted him to represent me. Happily, that's what he was calling about. Later, when we were putting together the first book proposal, it was Andrew who suggested we simply not mention these first two books and instead start over with a new collection of *New Yorker* stories. He thought it best not to remind publishers, and eventually critics and reviewers, of the earlier nonliterary efforts—too hard to explain, too easily misunderstood. So that's what we did, and what we've done all these years. Later I would learn that he had his own volumes of concrete poetry discreetly, deeply buried.

So this author's note is the first acknowledgment of the heretofore disinherited mangy first bastard children that now take their rightful places at the beginning of the "Also by Frederick Barthelme" list. They are clumsy art objects and mercifully rare collector's items, but I am happy to have them back with me, brain-damaged or not.

Why am I telling you this now? In part because I have the opportunity, but also to explain something about the book you're holding in your hands.

After the publication in 1970 and 1971 of those first two books, and after another ten years of woodshedding, publishing in literary magazines, writing and not-publishing, having books rejected once written, after returning to school at Johns Hopkins to get John Barth's help, well, the stories gradually became more literary, more like "stories," and it seemed as if I might actually have a career as a "literary" writer. So I sent stories routinely to Roger Angell, Don's editor at *The New Yorker*, and Roger returned each one with a helpful and encouraging word.

In late summer 1980 Roger was away doing his annual baseball work when my story "Shopgirls," which opens this collection, arrived at the magazine. The writer and editor Veronica Geng read the story for Roger and wrote a startlingly genuine hand-scrawled rejection note saying she'd liked the story, though not quite enough to publish it, and would I send more?

That letter was the first rejection I'd ever gotten that sounded more like an invitation than a rejection. "Pool Lights," the second story in this collection, was the story I sent Veronica Geng in November 1980. She bought it and it became, in July 1981, my first *New Yorker* publication.

"Shopgirls" eventually found a home at *Esquire*.

So, at the age of thirty-eight, as a result of the happy accident of Veronica sitting in for Roger, I had my second run at a publishing career. Until then I hadn't really had the pleasure of being thoroughly and carefully edited, and I must admit I was skeptical about it. I was, after all, *the artist*. But working with Veronica was eye-opening. As reader and editor she was the best *The New Yorker* had. She got everything. Send her a story, and she would not miss one single whisper that was in it. It's routine for editors to get a good portion of what you put into stories, but it's unheard of for an editor to miss nothing, to hear every feint, every verbal gesture, every shading, every embedded, even not-quite-understood, suggestion in the work. Every sentence, every line. Every time. Without exception. Working with Veronica Geng over a story was like making love—a delicate, playful, rich, energetic, mutual, and intimate investigation. This was true in the eight years I worked with her at the magazine, and in other editing she did for me as a favor after she'd been forced out at *The New Yorker*. As an editor she was exquisite and without equal. She more or less gave me a new career by reading my stories as well as they could be read, by adding to them, participating in them, making them sites for our mutual celebration of a world by which we were both stunned and endlessly amused. In those early days in 1980, and in the years that followed, her reading of my work, as well as her love and friendship, which I returned in equal measure, made the career that she made possible worth having. It is more than a little less valuable now that she's gone.

But why were the stories themselves good enough to get Veronica's attention? I believe it was that I'd finally dealt with the problem that faces any writer who has a much more famous writer as a brother—I stumbled upon a kind of work that had its own virtues and could not be confused with his. This was no small feat.

At that time Don was everywhere. People were copping his stuff left and right. As his brother, however, I wasn't going to be allowed to do that, and after years of being his student and sharing something of the same sensibility, getting out from under was easier said than done. It happened gradually as I discovered new aspects of writing to be interested in. I came to think that character was a richer kind of language than language itself. I became more interested in representation than fantasy. I grew fond of the mundane because of the way it spoke of us all. These and a score of other thoughts finally came together to make clear a new way of working. The idea came to me in the form of a barbecued chicken of the type you buy precooked at the grocery store. I bought one, one summer day. And it amazed me. I was thrilled by how wonderful and grotesque this prefab, plastic-wrapped, aluminum-panned, shrinking, falling-apart, sweet-smelling chicken was. Somehow it *was* the culture. Delighted, in some kind of swoon about this exquiste chicken, I sat right down and started writing "Shopgirls."

So when you see those chickens that Andrea brings into the Casa del Sol apartment in the story, please be respectful, because from those little chickens mighty "Shopgirls" sprang and from "Shopgirls," the growing realization that I had found an angle on story writing that had not been touched by Don, could not be traced to Don, was not Don-influenced or -suggested, was in no way indebted to him. Ordinary people was just what he was not about.

For good measure, I added this twist—literary types, Don included, always seemed to write about people in extraordinary circumstances. Cultural issues, personal crises, drug addictions, terrible accidents, diseases, wars, deaths, rapes, violence of every kind, magic times, epiphanies, et cetera. My idea—and I can remember the thrill of this even now—was to write about ordinary people in plain circumstances—going to the store, dinner with neighbors, people at the pool, time at the office, camping in the backyard, sitting in the parking lot at the mall. This interest in the ordinary set my stories apart not only from Don's, but also from almost everyone else's as well, and it felt as though, at a single stroke, I had discovered the solution to all of my literary, not to mention spiritual, problems—what I was most interested in, the world as reflected in the details of our routine lives, could be gotten on the page and made literary. Veronica's encouraging rejection letter, and the eventual purchase of "Pool Lights," provided the confirmation I was looking for.

There are in this book twenty-nine pieces that you could think of as stories out of "Shopgirls" by "Pool Lights." There have been other kinds of stories written and published over the years, but these are all from this particular line, though even here the ideas have changed over time, the worlds of the characters have grown and contracted, the problems have sometimes become more pointed, sometimes vanished altogether. And in more than one of these stories, looking at them now, the ordinary part doesn't seem so ordinary anymore.

When I started this note I wanted to say a word or two about why the stories are what they are, how they are constructed, and what they mean to me, but I didn't want to say too much. I wanted to thank you who have read them all these years, and to confess that I sometimes write in disorderly ways. I'll write stories that get folded into novels, only to get extracted again and published as stories years later. In a few cases I'll take parts of novels and turn them into stories after the fact, either reworking material, or pulling it out whole if it seems to me sufficiently sustaining. Often *almost*-completed stories just sit on the hard drive, never bothering to go to market, only to show up later rewritten as sections of novels. I like to get a head start on a novel, and if I have a couple of stories lying about, well, I'll just shuffle them together, change the names and places, and genders, and so on to suit, and suddenly have sixty pages of a beginning draft of a longer work.

It's been this way since the time at *The New Yorker* when Mr. Shawn suggested to Veronica, and she to me, that the story "The Browns" was something new for me and might bear some elaboration. So in *Second Marriage* I stiched together "The Browns" and a couple of other stories to get the foundation for the novel. *Tracer* had something of the same origin. As I recall, the novel *Two Against One* contains a story or two, though by now I'd be hard put to find them, because the pieces become so much a part of the larger work, even if sentence by sentence they are not that different from their story versions. Some other stories, like "Larroquette," "The Great Pyramids," and "Travel & Leisure," were written as stories and not published thus until *after* their use in novels. "Spots" is a rewrite of a scene that was used in a novel but has here been given a new, and twisted, ending. One piece, "Bag Boy," is an all-out after-the-fact rewrite of a novel section. It was originally a story, but an unpublished and unsuccessful one. After I used it in *Painted Desert*, I needed a piece for Ethan Canin's *Writers Harvest 2* anthology, so I took the rewritten novel version of the story and rewrote it again, adding new characters, revising the action, making a new and better piece altogether. This is to say that I feel no qualms about hacking up my work and putting it back together to suit different purposes. If I like something as a story I'll use it as a story, then sometimes redo it for use in a novel. Less frequently I find parts of novels that can "become" stories. Originally, of course, this was economic necessity—if you were working on a novel you always tried to sell parts of it as stories to drum up a little cash.

As for the stories here, they are arranged chronologically, new work at the back. I tried other arrangements, but they seemed artificial. I wanted the second-person stories to appear first, as they had in life, and I wanted the stories to develop again through time, as they had originally, and the changing emotional focus to reveal itself in the book as it had over the years of writing the stories. Ordering the book chronologically seemed eerily powerful, and avoided the dreaded "artful" arrangement. Instead, the show opens in 1980 and closes in the year 2000, and in between we walk the scores of delicately shaded and intertwined paths these particular stories have variously followed these last twenty years.

I don't want to try to characterize the drift of themes and interests in this collection with a single description. Indeed, I have the sense that would be possible only to the degree to which the description would be inadequate, not to say wrong. But just as you will find many small changes in these stories reading first to last, you will also find many similarities between them. A pervasive interest in character, in people, in the tiny glimpses we get of each other in our actions and reactions, in the small expressions that reveal us completely. I've always loved setting and the physicality of place, even if I am never high on the sociology too often associated with them, so by all means take note of your surroundings. I like the way people talk, and the ways they *might* talk, and I adore the dance, the daily tango, the scarce movements we make toward and away from each other as we go about our ordinary lives. These kinds of things you'll find constants here, embedded in glances, gestures, objects, sights, smiles, the looks in people's eyes, the sounds and the silences. You'll also find a polite anarchy here, a deep-background political spine masquerading as disinterest, and a world something like the one you wander around in every day. I hope you will find people who do not despise what has become of America, but who look upon our lives with equal parts astonishment, skepticism, and resignation. And kindness, perhaps most of all. They love this world of maladjusted, inappropriate, wrongheaded, and foolish citizens, all the glop, and tripe, and gunk that make up our everyday lives, and they look on each other, and on us, with fondness and compassion, empathy, affection. These characters take what they're given, and, while laughing at and ridiculing each other and themselves, they love the world as hard as they can. They make me very proud.

NOT MY IDEA

▲ ▼ ▲

SHOPGIRLS

You watch the pretty salesgirl slide a box of Halston soap onto a low shelf, watch her braid slip off her shoulder, watch like an adolescent as the vent at the neck of her blouse opens slightly—she is twenty, maybe twenty-two, tan, and greatly freckled. She wears a dark blue V-neck blouse without a collar, and her skirt is white cotton, calf length, slit up the right side to a point just beneath her thigh. Her hair, a soft blond, is pulled straight and close to the scalp, woven at the back into a single thick strand. In the fluorescent light of the display cabinet her eye shadow shines.

She catches you staring and gives you a perfunctory but knowing smile, and you turn quickly to study the purses on the chrome rack next to where you stand. You are embarrassed. You open a large red purse from the rack and stick your hand inside, pretending to inspect the lining. Then you lift the purse to your face as if the smell of it will help you determine the quality of the leather. The truth is that having sniffed the skin of the purse, you don't know what material it is, and, for just an instant, that troubles you. You look more closely at the purse, twisting the lip a little so you can see the label, on which, in very small print, it says: MAN-MADE MATERIALS.

After what seems like a long time, you glance again at the perfume counter: the girl is not there. You drop the red purse back onto its hook, and stand on your toes looking for the girl. Then you start toward the center of the purse department for a clearer view.

"Can we help you with something?"

It's the salesgirl in Purses. She's thin, a brunette, with stylized makeup that seems to carve her face. She's wearing a thin black silklike dress — a sundress, and her shoulders are bare. She has caught you off guard and presses her advantage by putting a smooth hand with perfect red nails on your forearm.

"Sir?"

"Well," you begin, "I was looking for a gift."

"Of course you were," the girl says. The tone is patronizing. She has seen you staring at the blond girl in Perfumes.

"For my wife," you say.

"Something in the way of a purse," she says. "Or perhaps a nice perfume?"

"I'd better go," you say, but she tightens her grip on your arm and glances over a lightly rouged shoulder at a middle-aged woman who is standing impatiently at the far end of the purse department.

"I have a customer," the salesgirl says. "But why don't you wait a minute and talk to me? Jenny says you're very handsome but painfully shy — are you shy? Will you wait?"

You laugh self-consciously.

"I'll get rid of her," the girl says. "Be right back." As she turns away she draws her nails down on your arm, leaving thin white trace lines.

You watch her show the woman a purse, watch her arms move as she selects a second purse off a treelike stand, watch the way

4

she cocks one foot up on its toe behind the other as she sells. The soft black skirt ripples and clings gently to the backs of her thighs as she moves, and when she goes behind the cash register to ring the sale, one of the straps falls off her shoulder, and she pulls it back into place routinely, smiling past her customer at you.

▼

"Jenny says you followed her everywhere for weeks, is that so? All around here?" Finished with the middle-aged woman, the salesgirl has come back to you.

"I don't know Jenny," you say. But when the girl tugs at your arm and points over the tops of the displays toward the shoe section, you don't need to look. You know the girl she's talking about, the tall girl with the very short hair who works in Shoes. You trailed her around the store and around the mall for a few weeks, watching her shop, watching her eat, watching her sit by the garishly painted fountain in the center of the mall — you trailed her until you got worried. Then you stayed out of the mall for nearly two weeks, and when you returned you carefully avoided Shoes. That's not entirely true. Once you spent half the morning going up and down the escalator so that you could see her over the thickly forested juniors' casual wear.

"She likes you," the brunette says. "I think when you started in on Sally it hurt her feelings, Jenny's, I mean."

You nod to indicate that you have understood, then realize you shouldn't understand, so you say, "Sally?"

"Sally?" the salesgirl says, mimicking you, exaggerating your delivery until it is a high prissy whine. "Sally's the blond you've been staring at all morning while playing with my purses."

"Oh," you say. You think you should have left when you had the chance, but the salesgirl has her hand on you again, her nails biting your skin, and to leave you'd have to jerk yourself out of her grip.

5

"Half the day," the girl says deliberately, "and that's a conservative estimate. That's this morning only. Then there's yesterday, and Saturday — you're quite a regular around here, aren't you? At first Sally thought you were the store dick, but she checked with Mr. Bo — he's our manager for this floor — and found out you weren't. My name's Andrea, what's yours?"

You don't want to tell her that. "Wiley Pitts," you say. It's a football player's name you saw in the morning paper. "I'm thirty-six years old." Instinctively you reach out to shake hands, then abruptly withdraw your hand and lift it to your forehead where a thin string of sweat has broken out along your hairline.

"Are you nervous?" she asks. "You shouldn't be nervous. Come sit with me." She guides you by the arm to a small round-topped stool in front of her sales counter. "I have to stick pretty close to this," she says, tapping the cash register with one bright fingernail.

You take the seat. You are inexplicably docile, obedient. You feel suddenly faint, as if moving about for the first time after a prolonged illness. Andrea is pretty, she smells pretty, she is being kind and gentle with you, and you are enjoying her attention. The sheen of her dress reflects the store light as she moves.

"The others think you're crazy," she says, twirling her finger near her temple and smiling. "I said you were just lonely."

"I suppose I am," you say. You cross your legs clumsily, then uncross them when you find it difficult to maintain your balance on the stool.

"We're all lonely sometimes," Andrea says. "I'll tell you what — I'll get the others and we can go to lunch together, would you like that? That way you can get a really close look at Sally."

"You're very pretty, too," you say. But as soon as you've said it you feel you shouldn't have, and you say, "I'm sorry. I don't know why I said that."

"Of course I'm pretty," Andrea says, laughing, obviously pleased. "We're all pretty. That's why they hire us. Do you think they want ugly girls out here trying to sell this stuff? We have to be pretty because that way the customers buy more so they can be pretty just like us." She tucks and smooths her dress for a minute, for your benefit, then says, "Well? What about it?"

Before you can reply, she's on the telephone. You realize she is talking to Jenny, the girl in Shoes. "Yes," Andrea says, fingering the curled cord and looking at you, "I'm sure he's the same one — you pointed him out, didn't you? No, not at all. Very nice. Yes. No, no — the first thing, yes. Right. Morrison's. You tell Sally — huh? Yes, she will."

You watch a young woman customer in very tight shorts and a lavender tank top glide up the escalator, which is directly across the aisle from Purses. Then Andrea is off the phone.

"Jenny's very excited," she says. "She didn't believe me at first."

You nod again, now staring at the empty escalator.

"Listen," Andrea says, "are you all right? You look very depressed." She tosses her hair over her shoulder and twists around on one leg to look at the store clock mounted on the wall above and behind her. "It'll just be a few minutes," she says. "You won't mind waiting, will you? Is your name really Pitts?"

"Robert," you say sheepishly. "Robert Caul. I'm sorry about the other." But Robert Caul is not your name, either.

"Oh, don't worry about it, and don't look so forlorn, Robert Caul," she says. "You're going to have a great time, really you are. It'll be a dream come true."

"Yes," you say. Then you look away, around the store, seeing only colors and shapes and reflections in columns that've been turned into mirrors. Andrea moves off to chat with a customer, a young man in jeans who explains that his wife is pregnant and needs a new purse for when the baby comes. Finally, accidentally, you look toward Perfumes, and the blond girl is back, sitting primly on a tall stool inside her glass enclosure, talking on a black telephone and toying with the braid in her hair. She is looking at you.

▼

At the cafeteria with Andrea, Jenny, and Sally, you take a thin slice of roast beef, three round white potatoes, a salad, and a shallow cup of peas. The women talk to one another as the four of you slide your trays over the polished aluminum rails attached to the serving counter. They are talking about you, whispering, being a little impolite, but you don't mind. You laugh, too, and smile to yourself as if you are in on the joke.

When everyone is seated at the table by the window, Jenny says, "Why are you doing this?" The window is the size of a bathroom window, small and heavily curtained. It looks out into the center of the mall.

"Never mind that," Andrea says. "He sure is handsome, isn't he?"

"Within certain well-known guidelines," Sally says.

"Posh," Andrea says, smiling at you.

"You really scared me at first," Jenny says. "Following me like that. I didn't know *what* you wanted. But then I got used to it, and I wasn't scared anymore."

"You were going out of your skull," Sally says. "Admit it."

"Sure, at first," Jenny says. "After he'd followed me for a week, I almost went up and introduced myself one day."

"He wishes you had," Andrea says. "Don't you, Robert?"

"I don't know," you say. "Not exactly — maybe." You try to smile, but your lip catches on your teeth somehow, hooks itself there, and your smile feels horrible.

"I like a man who knows his mind," Sally says.

"Oh, leave him alone, Sally," Andrea says. "Can't you see he's nervous?"

"What's he nervous about?"

"You," Jenny says. "He thinks you're beautiful."

"He's right," Sally says. "But that doesn't mean I don't like him. I do like you, Robert. Really."

"Listen to her," Jenny says. "It takes her two hours every day to look like that, and she's so blasé."

"It's worth it," Sally says, wiping a small cone of mayonnaise off her dark lower lip with the tip of her third finger. "It makes me a more sensual person."

"If you were any more sensual," Jenny says, "you'd be an open sore."

"We had to go to school to learn how to look, Robert," Andrea says. "Would you believe that?"

"Some of us did," Sally says.

Jenny bobs her head and mouths some words to make fun of Sally, then turns to you: "We're professionals, like models. We make the women envious and we make the men feel cheated, and that's not as easy as it sounds."

"He doesn't talk much, does he?" Sally says, waving her fork in your direction. "What are we going to do with him?"

"*We're* not doing anything," Andrea says. "I'm taking him home with me." She drops her fingers over your wrist and pats you twice. "We all live in the same complex, Casa del Sol — ever hear of it?"

"I don't," you say. "I mean, I never heard of it, no. Sorry, Andrea."

"It's got a hot tub," Sally says proudly. "More than one, in fact."

"Six," Jenny says, smiling. "By actual count. Of course, some are hotter than others."

The three women laugh at this joke, then Sally says to you, "Jenny would know, she's a real hot-tub artist."

"Thanks, Sally," Jenny says.

"You know who he reminds me of?" Sally says. "He reminds me of one of the Dead Boys — I can't remember which one, though. I think it's the one they call Johnny."

"Jeff," Jenny says. "I saw them last week at the Palace, but he doesn't look much like Jeff, anyway."

You look down at your plate and see that you have cut your roast beef into tiny squares less than an inch on a side, and you have stacked the squares one on top of the other in three small piles. You begin to play with your peas, lifting them onto your plate with the fork and then pushing them across the open center of the plate, encircling the stacks of beef.

Sally says, "You're not going to eat your salad, Robert? I'll eat it if you don't want it." She pulls your salad across the table, then turns to Jenny. "I wish somebody would tell me what we're going to do with him."

"Andrea's going to marry him," Jenny says. "The dear girl."

"Why don't we ask Robert what *he* wants us to do with him?" Sally says.

"We know what he wants," Jenny says, pushing a large square of lettuce from your stolen salad into her mouth. "He wants to lurk around the store watching you bend over."

"Or you," Sally says. "Or you, Andrea."

"We're just friends," Andrea says. "He can watch me at home."

"Well," Sally says, suddenly pushing back her chair and standing up, "I think it's me he really wants to look at. Isn't that right, Robert?" She comes around to your side of the table and leans over you and wraps her bare arm around your head, then pulls back and with her other hand opens her blouse slightly. "See, Robert? Isn't it pretty? Tell the girls I'm the one you really like."

"You're the one I really like," you say, but you don't think Andrea and Jenny hear you because you can hear them laughing, although you can't see them because Sally has your head in an awkward position, her upper arm almost covering your eyes.

"That's nice," Sally says, and she kisses you lightly on the top of your head.

"Doesn't prove anything," Jenny says, dragging a napkin over her lips. "If I showed him mine, he'd swear he'd marry me ten times."

"He'd swear you'd *been* married ten times," Sally says, "if memory serves. You're a little lank through the chest, darling."

"Why, you cat," Jenny says. "You bitch."

Laughing, Sally says, "You guys ready to go?"

"Come on, Andrea," Jenny says, pushing her chair away from the table. "And bring your friend."

"You two go on ahead," Andrea says. "We'll be there in a minute."

Jenny and Sally walk out of the cafeteria together, and you watch them go, you watch the way each careful step causes a particular swing in the hips — they strut, their sleek clothes snapping precisely.

"That was fun," you say.

"Well, I'm sorry," Andrea says, looking at you over the rim of her coffee cup. "I didn't know."

▼

In the living room of Andrea's Casa del Sol two-bedroom apartment identical white rented sofas face each other. You sit on one of these sofas. Andrea is not home. Her television is small, white, balanced on top of a tall straw basket in front of the window. There is a white Princess telephone on the back of the sofa opposite you. The late afternoon sun slants into the room, cutting across the twin sofas and casting dense, hard-looking shadows. You have the feeling that you are the only one home at Casa del Sol.

When Andrea arrives she has two whole barbecued chickens she bought at the grocery store. The chickens are in aluminum foil pans, wrapped in clear plastic. You watch her unwrap the chickens and listen to her talk.

"My father," she says, picking at the skin on the breast of one of the chickens, "was a speedboat racer. Not for a living, but that's what he was really. I have home movies of him on Lake Livingston, if you want to see. I've got lots of movies, in fact, of the whole family — Dad worked real hard editing the movies, putting them all in order by year, you know the kind of thing I mean. He even shot titles and put them in. He wanted so much for everything to make sense."

You notice that the legs of each chicken are twisted together so tightly that the bones have bent around each other.

"He wanted to know how things worked, even the simplest things — the air-conditioning, the movie projector. The first thing he did when he got a new movie projector was take it apart. Then he tried to improve on it, gluing little sticks of foam to the lens mount to cut down on the vibration and, when that didn't work, hooking rubber bands around the lens itself. It was terrible the way all his improvements didn't work. But he didn't notice that, or, if he did, he didn't talk about it. And he always did it, no matter what. He busted the television trying to make a better antenna, and he busted the stereo when he decided he could make a spindle that would drop fifteen records instead of the five the factory suggested. And the older he got, the worse it was. I mean, he just kept busting things and busting things until there was nothing to do but laugh, we all laughed, he even laughed, it was so horrible."

You listen and nod, but she's finished. You don't know why she's telling you about her father anyway. It has gotten dark outside, and the only light in the apartment is a tiny night-light pushed into a socket on the kitchen wall. Andrea is crying.

You ask where Sally and Jenny live, thinking this will help, and Andrea leads you to her front window and points across an open courtyard, empty except for the brilliant green island of the pool, at some apartments in another building. "They don't know you're here," Andrea says. "Do you want to go surprise them?"

"No," you say. "Not tonight."

"My grandmother is ninety-one," she says. "She lives in Palestine, Texas. She runs every day, she was running before everybody else started running, she was ahead. I don't know, around here everybody runs now. You go out at six o'clock, and it looks like one of those sports shows on TV. There isn't any reason to run, but they do it anyway. Bunch of goons. They think just because it's an apartment complex suddenly they're in California.

I bought the shoes, but that's as far as it went. Are you getting hungry? If we don't eat I'm going to scalp this chicken."

She serves you a quarter of a chicken neatly severed between breast and thigh and two slabs of white bread on a bare plate. This makes you very happy. For the first time you stop wondering if you should have taken her key after lunch. Andrea sits on one sofa and you sit on the other, and both of you eat with your fingers, occasionally stopping to tear away a bite-sized square of bread. You smile at each other as you eat. The chicken is tender and spicy, the perfect meal. When you finish, you carry your plate into the small kitchen and drop the bones into the garbage sack under the sink. Then you rinse the plate and turn it upside down on the flecked Formica counter, then you wash your hands with her Ivory soap. As you run the water over your hands, you splash a little first on your lips, then over your entire face. You pull two paper towels off the roll alongside the sink and dry your face and hands. You throw the crumpled towels at the garbage sack, miss it by a full yard. When you return to the living room, Andrea is sitting in the semidarkness, licking her fingers.

▼

"Once, when there was a hurricane coming," she says, not talking directly to you but rather into the room and to herself, "my father required that we make all the preparations, and we checked the flashlights, counted the candles, drew clean water in the tubs and sinks, bought bottled water to drink, taped the huge bay windows in our house with gray duct tape, and nailed plywood over the smaller windows. He carefully plotted the storm's course on a chart he cut out of the newspaper. The storm moved very slowly. My father called the weather service often, cursing and slamming the phone down when he got a busy signal. When the storm finally reached the Gulf it stopped dead in its tracks for twenty hours, whirling itself into a two-hundred-mile-an-hour frenzy, and as the storm got larger and more powerful my father spent his time sitting silently by the radio, his head slightly bent, a coffee cup balanced on the arm of his chair. He wouldn't talk to any of us. He hushed us angrily when we tried to talk to one another. He was intent on the storm, and he sat up all night listening for news bulletins, marking and calculating on the crumpled chart in his lap. The radio spewed instructions about what to do in case of fire, what to do in case of flood, and also history — the great and dangerous hurricanes of the century. We were prepared, and, as far as I knew, the real danger to us was minimal. Nevertheless a silence spread over our house like nothing I'd ever felt before. The kids kept watch at the windows, but the weather outside looked fine and breezy. At eight in the morning the radio announcer read a bulletin from the weather service: Elise had started to move again, but she had reversed her course and was now headed southwest, straight for Mexico. This news did not deter my father from his vigil, and, seven hours later, when the storm made landfall well below Brownsville, my father came to the door of his study and told us the news. He was a big man, a powerful man physically, and I remember him filling that doorway between his study and the living room of our house, I remember the way his voice sounded and how his eyes looked when he told us, and I remember watching him retreat into his study and close the door. He shot himself in the temple with a twenty-two-caliber pistol."

"Killed himself?" you ask, sure that you shouldn't, sure that you already know the answer.

"No," Andrea says. "Crippled himself. In a wheelchair the rest of his life."

"I'm sorry," you say.

"Me too," she says, staring at her red nails.

▼

You notice for the first time that one of Andrea's eyebrows is plucked too much, and that the brows are not symmetrical with respect to the bridge of her nose. Her left brow, the one that is far too thin, also starts well over her left eye. Once you have seen this tiny imbalance, you cannot stop seeing it. Every time you look at Andrea's face you see this odd-shaped patch of skin there above her nose. You stare at it. Her face looks wrong suddenly, almost deformed. You try to think of something to say about her father, but you can't think of anything. You wonder if you should ask Andrea about Sally and Jenny, but decide that that might hurt Andrea's feelings, so you say nothing. You sit with her until well past midnight—hours of occasional sound, occasional movement.

When she decides to go to bed you make no move to follow her into the bedroom, and she makes no special invitation. You sleep on the sofa, fully dressed, without even a sheet to cover you. You imagine yourself leaving the apartment on a sunny day in the middle of the week. Three beautiful women in tiny white bikinis lift their sunglasses as you pass them in the courtyard. They smile at you. You drive to the mall in a new car and spend two hours in Housewares on the second floor. You do not remember ever having been on the second floor before. You buy a wood-handled spatula from a lovely girl with clean short hair. Kitchen equipment is exquisite, you believe.

POOL LIGHTS

THERE ARE things that cannot be understood — things said at school, at the supermarket, or, in this case, by the pool of the Santa Rosa Apartments on a hazy afternoon in midsummer. A young woman wearing pleated white shorts and a thin gauze shirt open over her bikini top introduces herself as Dolores Prince and says, "You have a pretty face." Automatically, you smile and say, "Thank you," but, looking up at her, wonder why she selected that particular word, that adjective.

She is small, already tan, delicate but not frail. Her dark hair is in a braid tight against her scalp. "I mean it," she says, dropping her canvas tote on the pea-gravel concrete apron of the pool. "It's all soft and pink." She steps out of the shorts and snaps the elastic around the leg openings of her swimsuit.

"It's the shirt." You pluck at the collar of the faded red pullover, then point at the sky. "Bounces off the shirt."

"You're at the school, aren't you?" she says. "You're the swimming teacher?"

"Two years, yes. How did you know?"

"Mrs. Scree told me. She tells me everything."

Alongside the edge of the pool, ten feet away, Dolores spreads a black towel laced with salmon, peach, and gray-green flowers, then pulls things out of the tote — a tall red plastic glass and a can of Sprite, a pack of cigarettes in a leather case with a lighter pouch, a rolled copy of *Cosmopolitan*, a ribbed brown squeeze bottle of suntan cream, a thin silver radio the size of a wallet, a pair of square-lensed sunglasses with clear frames; she arranges these items around her towel, on the perimeter of her new territory, at the ready.

"It isn't the shirt," she says after she's in position, on her back on the towel, her knees up, facing the open pagoda next to the pool. "I know enough about color to know that the shirt would turn you brown, not pink."

"Oh." The sureness in her voice is startling. "Then maybe it's the clouds?"

"Clouds are white," she says without opening her eyes.

She's probably not right about the shirt, and she's wrong about the clouds — they're undefined and sulphur yellow.

"You new at Santa Rosa?" she asks, wiping the backs of her lotion-slick hands on her belly.

"I'm in 281 over here." You gesture sideways across the courtyard in the direction of your apartment. "Two months, but I don't come out much — out here, I mean."

She pushes up on an elbow and twists to look. "That's too bad. I'm out here all the time."

"You like it."

"Who doesn't?" she says. She sits up and spins around on her rump, wrapping her long dark arms around her knees. Her fingernails are pointed and chocolaty.

Your sprung metal chair rocks a little. "I imagine all these people looking out their windows at me. It makes me nervous."

"Oh, you can't think about that," Dolores says. She scans the buildings surrounding the pool. "If they look, they look — who gets hurt?" She says this with a coy smile, as if she suspects you watch poolside parties from the apartment window. She wipes more lotion on her thighs. "Some Saturday afternoons in summer the sunbathers are irresistible, I guess, especially through a slit in the curtains."

"I look. Sometimes I start to watch a ball game on TV and then end up watching people out here all afternoon. Don't you do that?"

She adjusts the thick braid at the back of her head. "Not really. I just come out."

"I like watching them talk to each other. The way they move around, gesturing, making faces — it's interesting."

"I know what you mean. And the women aren't bad, either."

▼

Because the floral brocade furniture the landlady had to offer was unacceptable, the apartment looks almost vacant — as if someone is moving out. Buying a round cardtable at Wilson's seemed dumb, but now that it's in place in the bedroom, it seems right. It's sturdy and large enough to hold the twelve-inch Sony, with room left to eat or work. The two pinkish-brown steel folding chairs that came with the table are uncomfortable but serviceable. The only other furniture in the bedroom is a queen-size bed pulled out into the room on the diagonal so it floats, like a great lozenge, on the harvest-gold carpet.

At midnight Friday you go into the small living-dining room and click on the overhead light. There, in neat low stacks along three walls, is the summer project: piles of *Time*, *Rolling Stone*, *Sports Illustrated*, *Money*, *Road & Track*, *Stereo Review*, *American Photographer*, *Skin Diver*, and *Vogue*. All from American Educational Services at a terrific discount. When they started piling up unread, they became a collection. After better than a year, the subscriptions got canceled. And after two moves — one across country, one across town — the project was born: look through the collection, maybe save an article or two, a peculiar picture, a curious headline, and toss the rest. Reading every word seemed at first a possibility, but finally the idea was exhausting.

The project isn't far along. The first thing was to strip the covers off all the issues of *Time* and put them together with Acco fasteners. Then the same for the other magazines. These "books" of covers are on the floor between two natural-wood deck chairs bought at an import store. The chairs and the covers and the magazines are all that's in the living room except for a huge pencil cactus, easily six feet high, which stands just inside the sliding door to a three-by-eight-foot balcony.

Picking up copies of *American Photographer* and the latest *Vogue* in the stack, dated January 1981, you take these into the bedroom, put them on top of the telephone book next to the TV, then go back and water the pencil cactus, straighten the pile of *Road & Track* — looking at the contents of the topmost issue to see what cars were road tested that month — and switch off the light on the way to the kitchen for cornflakes to take into the bedroom. The first issue of *American Photographer* has lots of small ads. The featured pictures seem to be of the edges of things — buildings, cars, furniture, streets. Another portfolio, in color, is of women's backs, taken from down low so that the backgrounds are all blue sky. Some of the pictures are attractive, but fooling with them seems like too much trouble, so you push the magazine back onto the stack and take the cereal to the kitchen, put it in the sink, and run the faucet until the bowl is full of gray water.

Undressing in the bathroom, you watch the mirror above the lavatory, then drop the clothes in a tall plastic basket kept in the hall closet for outgoing laundry. You floss, thinking of the dentist. His assistants wear matching Cheryl Tiegs jeans and T-shirts; he pipes Willie Nelson's "Stardust" into the cubicle; he makes jokes about the color of teeth, and he talks to the mouth when he's working on it. "How's Mr. Mouth doing today?" or "Would Mr. Mouth like a club sandwich?" All this and he tries not to punish. Still, you avoid him.

At one-thirty a movie called *Berlin Correspondent*, starring Dana Andrews, starts on Channel 17.

▼

At noon on Saturday, Dolores is already arranged flat on her stomach near the deep end of the pool, almost directly below your window.

She waves. The phone rings. Your brother in Taos wants to know what has been said to so seriously alienate your father. You tell him you love your father. He says he knows that, but what was said? You just woke up and don't remember. He urges that the family try to understand the father. "He wants us to think he's wonderful."

"He is."

"He's sad. I'm trying to help."

The glistening sliver of Dolores is visible through the curtains. She's wearing a dark Danskin. "I didn't want to upset him. I tried to talk to him. I tried to tell him to take it easy."

"Just be sensible about it. We've got to stop jumping all over him."

This view of the situation is not as correct as he assumes it to be, but when told this, he does not back away from his assertion. You promise to think about it, and ask what is going on in Taos, to which he replies, "Nothing." You agree to call him later, after breakfast.

"Talk to you," he says, and hangs up.

In the kitchen you turn on the coffee, then fill a pan with water to poach eggs, and put the pan on the stove.

Later, when the eggs are ready, shaking gently on crisp muffin halves, you carry plate, flatware, coffee, and napkin back into the bedroom. Getting the one-bedroom apartment overlooking the pool was lucky — so Mrs. Scree said when she agreed to show the less expensive one-bedroom, which overlooked the Santa Rosa parking lot and the Laundromat. "The drain backs up sometimes," she said. "I gotta tell you so when it happens you won't go yelling at me." It is hard to imagine — yelling at Mrs. Scree: after twenty-four years, by her account, managing apartments, she knows how to handle dissatisfied tenants.

By one o'clock Dolores has been joined by several other tenants: a balloonish young husband and his skinny wife, a single girl named Beverly who works at Sears, a plump woman in an emerald terry cloth slit-to-the-thigh bandeau-top sundress, an older man named Wilkins, whose chest is covered with bright silver hair, and on the fringe of the group, standing near the corner of the pool in conversation with a young couple who are obviously apartment hunting, Mrs. Scree, dressed in her usual dark blue slacks and sleeveless flowered blouse.

You stand at the window for a few minutes, watching the party. When Mrs. Scree finishes with the apartment hunters, she pulls a long aluminum pole from behind the redwood pagoda and starts to scoop multicolored miniature plastic bowling pins out of the pool. She is not very good at this, and after she makes several passes at a bright red pin painted with an air force insignia, Wilkins pushes himself out of his lawn chair and, with a flourish, wrests the pole from her. The others are immediately drawn into the action, giving directions, cracking jokes, pointing and laughing as Wilkins tries to capture the bowling pin. He walks to the long side of the pool and eases the pole into the water so its small net dips just under the pin. When he tries to lift the pole, the bowling pin topples off the frame of the net and slides away on the surface of the clear water. Everybody laughs. Even Mrs. Scree, who ordinarily laughs only at her own jokes, punches her tenant playfully on the arm, points at the floating pin, and laughs heartily. Dolores, who sat up when Wilkins took the pole, turns away from the pool, shades her eyes with her hand, and with the forefinger of her other hand beckons you downstairs.

You jerk the two edges of the curtains together, lapping one over the other, certain that she couldn't actually see, that she was just guessing. Getting back into bed, head wrapped in a towel because of wet hair from the shower, you pull up the sheet, lie there, and leaf through the magazines.

▼

Later Dolores catches you by the mailboxes, says she wants to go for a drive, and hustles off to her apartment to change. The afternoon is hot.

"You hid earlier," she says, getting into the car. "I'm ashamed of you."

"I almost came out when Mr. Wilkins was going for the pin."

"I signaled you."

"It was hard to resist."

The interstate takes you fifty miles to a small coast town, Conklin, population 8,528. It's almost five o'clock.

"Let's buy something," Dolores says. "There's a market. Let's get shrimp to take back."

"What's special about shrimp?"

"Nothing." She's got a wraparound skirt over her thin plum suit, and she looks sexy.

The butcher is busy with a customer who looks as if she has never had anything but shrimp in her life — crisp clothes and crisper hair. The butcher holds up a half dozen lamb chops on a piece of white paper for her, and at the same time nods at Dolores to indicate that she's next. Dolores squats in front of his case to get a closer look at the shrimp, which are half buried in ice. The woman wants to inspect the chops; she tells the butcher to put them on top of the counter for a minute. The clock says it's five of five. The butcher drops the paper onto the case and the chops teeter for a second, then tip over the edge and slip one by one down the sloped front, piling up at the lower edge of the glass.

The woman isn't upset. She bends over and sticks her face very close to the meat. Abruptly she straightens and says to the butcher, who is standing behind the case with his hands on his hips, staring at the ceiling fan, "I don't know, Carl. What do you think? They don't smell too good."

"Lady," the butcher says, moving toward the end of the case and wiping his hands on his apron. "They ain't supposed to be gardenias."

The woman turns. "Sir?" she says. "Would you help me with these chops? Would you take a look?"

"I will," Dolores says, popping up from her crouch in front of the shrimp. She takes a close look at the lamb chops, picks up one and squeezes it, then pokes it against her nose. The butcher comes out in front, pulls the paper off the top of the case, and stacks the other chops on his hand again.

"What do you think?" the woman says.

"Yeah," the butcher says. "What do you think?"

"I think they're fine," Dolores says, placing her chop on top of the others. Then she whispers, "Let's get out. It's dog food."

After a wrong turn trying to get back to the interstate, you end up on the old highway, a two-lane job, but it's got signs pointing toward home, and Dolores says she wants to stick with it. An hour later the terrain begins to look familiar.

"See. That wasn't so bad."

She's right. With twilight the temperature goes down fast, and the old highway is more interesting to drive, because of the towns, roadside signs, and animals.

"Better than trees," she says.

At the crossroad that goes back to town she sees a motel, one of those old places with two-room brick bungalows back off the road in a cluster of pines. Its neon sign says GOLDEN GABLES MOTOR LODGE in purple, VACANCY in pink, and BASS POND in lime green.

23

Dolores points at the sign. "You game?" she says. "I've never been in one of these. Let's try it."

"I don't think so." But you brake and pull over next to the entrance anyway, in case Dolores is dead set on seeing the inside.

She is. The office is an Airstream trailer jacked up on cement blocks. The registration desk is a freestanding paneled bar with a thick black pillow of padding around the edge. A man shorter than a ten-year-old boy pushes through a beaded curtain and walks across the small room as if he has a spring on his right foot.

"Can we see a room?" Dolores says.

Only his shoulders and head stick up over the bar. He looks at Dolores, then pokes a knobby forefinger into the collar of his starched white shirt. He tilts his head when he talks. "You staying long? A night? A week?" His voice is high, nasal.

"We don't know," Dolores says, grinning. "First we want to look at the room."

"How come you don't try in town? They got everything in town. Television, food, Magic Fingers — the works." He crawls up onto a barstool with a swivel seat.

"No bass pond."

"Right," Dolores says. "No bass pond — where is it, anyway?"

"You drove over it coming in. Sucker dried up on us last summer."

"How much per night?" Dolores asks.

"You going to use the kitchen?"

"Not tonight."

At this the little man catapults himself off the swivel stool and limps to the front of the trailer, where he steps up on a wooden box draped with a yellow rubber carmat. He looks out the small round window. "This your car?" he says. "Registered in the county?"

"We live in town," Dolores says. "We just want to see what the rooms are like."

He hops off the box and looks hard at Dolores. Sweat as thick as

Vaseline is collecting on his neck just above the tight collar. "You bring your tiger-skin drawers?"

"Let's go, Dolores. I don't think the man wants to rent a room."

"Oh, I want to rent one, all right." He's cleaning the finger-nails on one hand with the thumbnail of the other. "Sure I do. I want to rent twenty. Just don't much want to show one, see what I mean?"

▼

On Sunday at half past ten in the morning, going down to pick up the paper — which the deliverywoman has gotten in the habit of placing, unrolled, on the third step up from the bottom of the stairs — just out of bed, wearing jeans and a terry cloth bathrobe, hair sticking out in all directions, you meet Dolores. She's coming around the corner of the building carrying a cream-colored plastic garbage bag full of sharp-edged objects — boxes, it looks like — that give the bag a set of curiously geometric surfaces.

"That was fun last night," she says. "That guy was really short, wasn't he?"

The morning light in the apartment courtyard is strangely cheerful. The palms around the pagoda shift a little with the wind.

"Sure was." The newspaper slips down two steps.

She laughs and props her bag against the side of the stairs. "Housekeeping," she says, pointing to the bag. "Maybe we can get together later?"

"Sure."

Mrs. Scree follows her dog out of her apartment and, seeing tenants in conversation, rumbles across the courtyard. "Dolores, I forgot to tell you yesterday that they're coming to do your carpet tomorrow."

"Finally. That's great."

"And what's he dressed up for? That your samurai outfit?" She laughs.

"We're discussing cocktails by the pool this evening," Dolores says, smiling lavishly.

"A new romance right here in the complex," Mrs. Scree says. She acts as if she knew it all along. "Well, I'll keep Raymond inside if that'll help—he's such an old gossip." Raymond is her husband.

Then Wilkins backs out of his apartment in tennis shorts and flip-flops. He's got a thick purple towel bunched around his neck, and his sunglasses are balanced on top of his head. In one hand he has a tall glass of tomato juice and in the other a portable radio.

"There you are," Mrs. Scree shouts. "With weather like this I expected you out at dawn. Now, where's that dog got to? Here Spinner, here boy." She crouches down to look across the court for her dog.

Wilkins waves his tomato juice and then points at one of the squat palms around the pagoda. "I think he's in there," Wilkins says. "I see his tail."

"So do you want breakfast or not?" Dolores says.

"Don't go too far, honey," Mrs. Scree says without turning around. She falls forward on her hands and knees, trying to look under the sagging fronds of the palms. She's wearing something like boxer shorts under her black knit slacks. "Making breakfast is serious."

"I had breakfast already, thanks."

Mrs. Scree is crawling about on the grass at the foot of the stairs, occasionally dropping her head to the ground to check another opening in the foliage. Wilkins drags a recently painted steel lounger out into the morning sun, aligning it for balanced distribution of the tanning rays.

"Just let me get set up here, Peggy," he says, "then I'll go in there after him."

"Don't be silly, Fred," Mrs. Scree says. She pushes herself upright on her knees and, with some effort, gets to her feet. "He'll be out of there the instant I go back inside."

An older woman who lives in the apartment directly beneath yours comes out dressed as if for church.

"Good morning, Mrs. Talbot," Mrs. Scree says, brushing at the whitish stains on her pants. "How's the knee these days?"

"Much better, thank you," Mrs. Talbot says. "The hot-water bottle you gave me helps a good deal."

"Your neighbor here been behaving himself?" Mrs. Scree says.

The older woman nods and says, "I'm Irene Talbot." She switches her purse and gloves around, then extends her hand. "I'm very pleased to finally meet you. After all the times we've said hello, I feel as if I already know you." She turns to the landlady. "He's quiet as a mouse, although with my hearing I'm not sure I'd know if he wasn't. Anyway, it's very reassuring to know that there's a man nearby, in case something should happen."

"And a man with such a fine face," Dolores says.

"Now that you mention it," Mrs. Talbot says, eyeing Dolores, "the face and skull *are* very good." She smiles faintly and toys with her gloves.

"A new romance," Mrs. Scree says, winking broadly, making her face a parody of collusion.

"Morning, Mrs. Talbot," Wilkins shouts from his place by the pool. "You look mighty handsome today."

"Thank you," Mrs. Talbot says. Then, when Wilkins turns away, she grins at Mrs. Scree.

Backing up the stairs, you say, "I think I'll go on up and read this," then flap the newspaper a couple of times at no one in particular. "A pleasure meeting you, Mrs. Talbot."

Mrs. Talbot nods, gives a short wave of her gloves to Mrs. Scree and Dolores, and walks off toward the parking lot.

"Well, I'll leave you two alone," Mrs. Scree says. "Raymond's going to need breakfast soon, and I just wanted to get Spinner done." She calls the dog again, and Spinner, so named because he likes to chase his tail, pops his head out from under the edge of the pagoda. "There he is," Mrs. Scree shouts. "Come here, Spinner. Right now."

The dog wipes his nose on his paws but does not budge from the spot under the building.

"Don't forget tonight," Dolores says. She hoists the milky plastic bag onto her shoulder. "He's so pretty," she says to the landlady. "It's embarrassing."

"What's tonight?" Mr. Wilkins says, propping his chin on the carefully folded towel at the end of the lounger.

"Never you mind, Fred," Mrs. Scree says. "You weren't invited. This is a private affair."

Wilkins frowns, and Dolores says, "Oh, sure you are, Mr. Wilkins. We're having cocktails by the pool at six."

"Cocktails?" he says, blinking furiously.

Mrs. Scree pads across the concrete and playfully pushes his face back into the towel. "Fred doesn't need any cocktails today," she says. She reaches behind her, under the tail of her blouse, to scratch her back.

"We could even have a barbecue," Dolores says, following Mrs. Scree. "If we had anything to barbecue."

"I'm going to barbecue that dog if he doesn't come over here right now," Mrs. Scree says. "And tell your young man not to come dressed that way—he looks like Karl Wallenda."

Inside, you drop the newspaper on the kitchen cabinet, go into the bedroom, take off the jeans and the bathrobe, and get back into bed.

▼

The telephone wakes you. "Look," your brother says, "I want to clarify something. I'm not accusing you of being stupid and insensitive about Father, I'm just reporting what it was like there last week. How he sees things. It seems to me at his age we've got to think about that—I mean, how *he* sees things. You know what I'm saying?"

"Yes." Your arm is numb and tingling.

"I'm not saying you're not right. He can be a butt sometimes."

"Uh-huh."

"But that's not even the point. The point is, you have a tendency to jump on him whether he's being a butt or not. I mean, if he wants to play Lord High Executioner, where's the harm?"

"I don't want to humor him." With all the curtains closed, it's dark in the apartment. "Listen, what time is it?"

"Three," he says. "About." He shouts to his wife for the time, then says, "Three-thirty. I didn't mean to humor him. It's just that he isn't always wrong."

"Sure."

"Talk to you," he says.

You toss the receiver at its cradle, miss, shove it into place, reach across the table to switch on the television, and then, when the picture appears, twist quickly through the channels until there's a movie. When the sound is fixed so the actors can just barely be heard, you hunch forward in the metal folding chair, naked, elbows on knees, flexing the left hand and watching. At the commercial you make toast and pour orange juice into a large glass of ice, then go back to the bedroom.

There are shouts from the courtyard. Dolores and the others from yesterday, along with a few more tenants, are gathered in a loose group at one end of the pool. You shut the curtains, sit down at the card table, and eat breakfast.

▼

By five, most of the tenants have returned to their apartments. Mr. Wilkins and Mrs. Scree are the last ones by the pool. They sit at a round green table under the pagoda, sipping drinks from mismatched glasses. You straighten the bedroom, then bathe and shave; at five-thirty the courtyard is empty. In fresh Levi's, a checked shirt, and a black corduroy jacket, you pour a small glass of milk and watch the end of the local news.

29

At six the court is still empty. The lights in the pagoda have come on early, as have the yellow lights at the front doors of many apartments facing the pool. The sun is almost hidden except for a reddish glow reflected from low clouds, which are gray in the eastern sky and shiny scarlet in the west.

Dolores hasn't come out. Mike Wallace interviews a California man who stuffs pet animals for their owners. Harry Reasoner reports on the Florida drug trade. It's not clear whether Dolores intends to come out or was just playing. To be sure, and because talking to Dolores outside in the courtyard might be pleasant, you turn off the television and go down to the pagoda. All the chairs and tables are painted the color of the lighted water in the pool. For the hundredth time, water seems beautiful. The palms around three sides of the pagoda make it feel secluded, even though it isn't really. The apartment windows where there are lights have drawn curtains; the dark windows could hide people. Still, it's comfortable outside, and if Dolores doesn't show, it's not a total loss.

Two young girls go by carrying two plastic baskets of clothes. The overweight young husband and his skinny wife come in from the parking lot — from an early dinner perhaps — and say hello before entering their apartment, switching on the lights, and hastily drawing the curtains. Someone passes between the pagoda and the pool and says, "Aren't summer nights incredible and amazing?" A large tree roach runs along a floorboard. In the distance several dogs howl. Mr. Wilkins, whose front door is almost on a center line with the pool, opens his door and stands on the threshold. There's enough light to see him, even though his porch lamp isn't on. He's wearing shorts and a square-tailed shirt.

"Hey," he says, shading his eyes with a hand. "That you? How's it going out here?"

"Fine, I guess."

"How's that?" he says, moving the hand from over his eyes to cup his ear. "Where's the party?"

"It's a slow-starter."

"Well," he says, waving. "Sometimes that happens." He goes back into his apartment. His porch light snaps on.

Upstairs, you toss the coat on one of the deck chairs in the living room, then take a Coke out of the refrigerator, go into the bedroom, and drink the Coke, thumbing through an issue of *Stereo Review* devoted to minicomponents.

▼

At nine you pull the slim telephone book out from under the stack of magazines and look up Dolores Prince, writing her number on the inside back cover of the book. There is a knock at the door.

Two kids, a boy and a girl, neither older than ten or twelve, are on the landing. Below, on the sidewalk, a man is silhouetted against the pool.

"We're working for Jesus," the kids say in imperfect unison. The boy wears a blue suit and the girl a lilac dress, black pumps, and taut white socks.

"Aren't we all."

"We have Jesus in our hearts," they say. "We have subscriptions to *Spirituality, Aspire,* and *The Beacon,* and we're trying to win a trip."

"Thank you, but no." You hold up your hand like a crosswalk guard in after-school traffic.

They continue, though the young girl, as she speaks, turns and looks toward the foot of the stairs. "Wouldn't you like to have His message come into your home each month? Only twenty-six dollars for twelve issues." Then the girl adds, "Please? Two more and our whole family gets a chance for a trip to Six Flags."

"Yeah," the boy says. "Dad has a chance at a boat, too."

Apart from their clothes, the children are quite ordinary-looking, like kids at the school, or at the shopping center, or on bicycles going down Park Street in the afternoon.

"No, thank you." The man below moves forward slightly to consult a piece of white letter-size paper in his hand, and you call to him, "No, thank you."

The kids turn uncertainly and look down into the dark courtyard. The boy grabs the frame around the door as if he's lost his balance.

"OK," says the man downstairs.

The children turn around, obviously disappointed, and say, "Thank you, sir. May the Lord Jesus come into your heart." Then the girl goes down the steps, her heels clacking on the metal, and the boy, much more cautiously, follows her, his hand a tight fist around the railing.

When the door is closed and the kids and the man have stopped talking outside, and the kids are knocking on Mrs. Talbot's door, the telephone rings.

"Hi," Dolores says. "I tried to call earlier, but you're unlisted. I have to apologize about tonight."

"How'd you get the number?"

"Mrs. Scree. Listen, I got into something I couldn't get out of — you know how it is. Sundays are bad for me."

"We'll do it another day."

"Sure," she says. "I'm out there all the time. Just come on out whenever you're ready."

"Whenever I'm ready I'll just come on out." The telephone book is still creased flat on the table in front of the television.

"Did the kids get to you?" she asks. "They must've thought I was Mary Magdalene, the way I was dressed when I opened the door. But look, are you busy? Why not come for a nightcap?"

The TV is making a curious high whine, even though the sound is off. Outside there are people talking, and there is the sound of a chair being pulled across the pebbly concrete, then Mrs. Scree's loud, sudden laugh, like the bark of a monkey. "I don't think so. Not tonight."

There's another pause, and then Dolores says, "Well, suit yourself. If you want me you know where to find me."

32

"You're in the book."

"Right."

She hangs up. You hold the telephone to your ear until the dial tone returns, then replace the receiver. Some people are running back and forth across the television screen. The voices are coming up from poolside. After a few minutes you go into the living room, put on the black coat, take a Löwenbräu out of the refrigerator, and go outside. You sit sideways on the diving board and listen to Mrs. Scree and her husband, Raymond, and another tenant — the plump woman from Saturday. The subscription kids go out the front gate. Mrs. Scree wags her arms like an explorer in a jungle and introduces you as the king of the crawl.

DOMESTIC

MARIE WATCHES her husband from the porch of their bunga-low, leaning against the open screen door as he digs in their back-yard. The sun is out and warm, although it is fall, and late afternoon. They have been married eight years.

"Albert," she asks, "why are you doing that?" She is not entirely sure what it is that he is doing, but has asked that question already with unsatisfactory result, so she has opted for the question of motive.

"Why?" Albert says. He always repeats her questions.

He has been digging in the yard since eleven that morning, without a break, and his wife has come out of the house to ask him if he would like an early dinner. He straightens and pushes the long-handled spade into the dirt. "Marie, I am doing this because this is what I like, this is something I like, digging this hole. There are too few things in this life that are in and of themselves likable, and for me this is one of them. This is valuable to me and from this

I derive pleasure. You might say I enjoy working with my hands, although that isn't the whole thing, not by a long shot." Albert stops to wipe his brow with a dime-store neckerchief, then turns to look at the hole he has dug, to gauge his progress. "Did you have something in mind?" he asks, turning back to his wife.

"Why don't you come have dinner now," Marie says, waving a fly away from her face.

He points to the sky and reaches for his shovel. "Got some light yet," he says. "Best use it."

Marie suddenly feels stupid for having suggested dinner at four o'clock in the afternoon, and feels angry that her husband has made a fool of her again, in another one of the small ways that he often makes a fool of her, and she snaps, "Well, I don't like it, frankly," and goes back inside.

After watching him from the kitchen window for a few minutes, Marie climbs the hardwood stairs and flops on the king-size bed in the bedroom, on her back, her arms outstretched. Even with her arms and legs spread, she is swallowed up in the huge mattress, enveloped by it, unable to touch the edges. She looks straight up at the ceiling and tries to imagine a great battle from the Middle Ages pictured there — horses, and cannon, and armor — but sees instead a lone knight in black mail astride an equally black horse, riding backward, bent over inspecting the rump of the animal. "Oh Lord," she says, and she rolls off the bed and reaches for the telephone. She calls her mother.

"What're you doing, Mama? How are you? I haven't talked to you in such a long time."

"I talked to you Thursday, Peaches. Is something wrong between you and Albert?"

"Mama! You always think that. And don't call me Peaches, please."

"Marie," her mother says, "you didn't call me two thousand miles across this great continent to ask me the time of day in the middle of the afternoon on the long-distance telephone, I know that don't I?"

"Albert is digging in the backyard is why I called," Marie says. "I don't know why—it isn't even Saturday."

"Your father dug, Peaches."

"This is different, Mama. And don't call me Peaches."

"So you called me now when the rates are high to tell me that your husband and the father of your eventual child is in the back-yard digging a hole? Is that all you have to say to me? And you want me to believe that nothing is wrong in your marriage?"

Marie looks out the upstairs window at the bent white shoulders of her husband, watches as he hoists a small mound of dirt, gazes at the shovel's attenuated arc. "It's a serious problem, Mama, or I wouldn't have called. You know what happened to Papa."

"That was different, Peaches. Your papa went a little crazy, that's all. I suspect it ran in his family. When he bought the P-38 for the neighborhood kids, when he cut the hole in the roof of the den, remember? There were reasons, there were explanations—Papa was always up to some good. And, by the way, have you asked about me yet? How I am and what I'm doing out here all alone on this barren coast? No you have not. Maybe if you had brought that Albert out here last summer like I asked you to, I could have straightened him out, and you wouldn't have this terrible problem you have right now, which, if I may say, doesn't sound all that ter-rible from this distance."

"Thank you, Mama," Marie says.

"Don't start with me, young lady," her mother says. "I'm just trying to help. A mother has an investment in a daughter, as you might well learn one day if that Albert ever gets his head out of the clouds and gets down to business like a real man."

"I have to go now, Mama," Marie says.

"Of course you do, Peaches. You should've gone before you called, if you get my meaning. And, by the way, thank you very much, I'm getting along fine. Mr. Carleton is coming over this evening, and we're going to walk down by the water and maybe take in a show at the Showcase, if you want to know, just by way of information."

"Mr. Carleton?"

"Yes. And if you want my advice you'll stop your whimpering and get out there with a shovel of your own, if you see what I mean."

▼

Albert and Marie live in a small suburb near Conroe, Texas. All of their neighbors own powerboats which, during the week, clutter the driveways and front lawns. Albert and Marie do not own a powerboat, although Albert does subscribe to *Boats & Motors*, a monthly magazine devoted to powerboating. Marie is small, freckled, delicate, blond. Albert is overweight.

That evening, when he finishes digging and comes inside for dinner, Marie presses the question of the hole. "I can't stand it anymore, Albert," she says. "You took a day off from work and you spent the whole day outside digging a hole. If you don't explain this minute, I will leave you."

He looks at her across the dinner table, fatigue and discomfort on his face in equal measures, then pushes an open hand back over his head, leaving some strands of hair standing straight up in a curious peak. Finally he looks at the pork chop on his dinner plate and says, "I love the work, Marie. I love the product. For many years I have been interested in holes — how many times have I pointed out a hole to you when we drive to the store? A hole for telephone equipment, or for a gas line, or for the foundation of a great building? And, of course, I need the exercise, don't I? Marie, there are many wonderful holes in life — dogs dig holes, as do other animals. Pretty women dig small holes on weekend afternoons — can't you understand?"

"I think you're being foolish, Albert," she says, twisting a silver chain around her fingers until the tips of the digits turn purple.

Then she unwinds the chain and twists it again, on new fingers. "You may even be silly. Still, you are my husband, and even though you have not provided me with any children, I love you. What are you going to do with this hole when you get it dug?"

Albert's eyes go suddenly very dark, flashing. "Ha!" he says, thrusting himself out of his chair, his arm at full extension, his fork teetering between the tips of his fingers. "You see? *You* are the foolish one! *You* ask stupid questions!" With that he slaps the fork flat onto the table and rushes upstairs to the bedroom, slamming the door behind him.

Marie sighs deeply and continues the meal alone, chewing and thinking of Albert's fingernails, which looked to her like tiny slivers of black moon.

In the morning, after Albert has gone to work at the airline, Marie takes her coffee to the hall table where she sits staring at the telephone for a long time. The hands of the electric clock on the table fly around the clock's face, making a barely audible whir.

An airplane passes overhead, through the clouds.

In the distance, there is a siren.

Marie begins to cry, falling forward on the table, her arms folded there and cradling her head. Between sobs she whispers, "I don't want my husband to dig this hole, I don't want my husband to dig this hole..."

The telephone rings. It is her friend Sissy, now a secondary school teacher in Vermont. Marie begins to tell Sissy the story of Albert and the hole, but is unable to make her objection clear, and Sissy responds unsympathetically. Marie is surprised that she isn't clearer about why she is upset by Albert's behavior, and instead of listening to Sissy, she gazes at Albert's university diploma which is framed and mounted above the hall table and wonders why she can't explain herself more clearly.

Finally she says, "I don't know why this upsets me so much, it's silly really." But she has interrupted Sissy's explanation of Albert's behavior, and Sissy insists on finishing the explanation.

"A metaphor," Sissy says, "works in a lot of ways to release the feelings of an individual, opening that individual to expressions which are, for some reason, closed to him. Albert may simply be depressed, and the physical digging is for him a model of the emotional digging that's going on, see what I'm saying? Reflects his disaffection, or something. Maybe he's bored?"

"I see what you mean," Marie says, and she marks another minute gone on the pink pad in front of her, a horizontal stroke crossing four vertical strokes.

"Why don't you dig some, too?" Sissy asks. "Seems like that'd be more to the point."

"I've been thinking about that," Marie says.

"Don't think," Sissy says. "*Do.*" Then, her voice rising with relief and new interest, she says, "We're on strike up here, that's why I'm home today. I know it's terrible for the kids, but business is business, right? Besides, they're probably grateful."

"Strike?"

"Yeah," Sissy says. "We're going to bury the bastards if they don't pay up. There've been promises — it's real complicated, but we're up against the school board and an old jerk named Watkins who'd just as soon see us work for room and board. Anyway, we've been out three weeks and no end in sight. I've got a little money tucked away, so it's all right. Maybe you ought to get a job yourself, give you something to take your mind off Albert. I mean, you never worked at all after we finished school, did you?"

"I worked in that hospital," Marie says.

"Oh that. That wasn't work, darling, that was recreation. Try getting an office job these days. Maybe you should take a graduate course? Or pottery, pottery's always good."

▼

When Albert returns from work he goes directly into the yard to work on the hole. Marie watches him from the porch for a few minutes, then goes outside and sits in the passenger seat of their Plymouth station wagon, with the door closed, watching her husband. When, after twenty minutes of sustained digging, he stops to rest, she leans out the car window and says, "You're making this to hurt me, aren't you? I know. I know you, Albert."

"Maybe you're right," he says, looking at the hole. "About knowing me, I mean."

He climbs out of the hole, and Marie gets out of the car. They walk to the house together, side by side, their arms bumping into each other as they walk. He is thirty-nine years old. She is younger.

"I want to watch television tonight," he says. "And then make love. What do you say?"

"You're not trying to hurt me?"

"No, I'm not," he says, and he links arms with her and together they turn to survey the yard.

"But," she says.

"It'll be beautiful," he says. "Just wait."

Marie glances at the neighbor's crisp green bushes, then nods tentatively. "It's hard to understand."

They stand for a moment together on the concrete steps of the porch, then go into the house. Albert washes his hands in the kitchen sink while Marie burns the hairs off the chicken they will have for dinner.

"Why can't we refurbish an old house like everybody else?" she asks. "Or refinish furniture together?"

Albert looks at her and grins. "I lied about the television," he says, and he reaches for her with his hands still soapy, staggering across the kitchen, Frankenstein fashion.

She glares at Albert as hard as she can, then giggles and runs up the stairs very fast. At the landing she stops and leans over the rail and shouts, "I'm not having a baby, Albert!"

She slams the bedroom door, and Albert, who has followed her from the kitchen still acting out his monster role, allows his shoulders to slump, and sighs, and moves on up the stairs. He taps on the bedroom door with a knuckle. "Marie?" he calls through the door.

"What if it rains, Albert?"

"What?"

"My mother doesn't like you," Marie shouts. Then, a little less loudly, "Sissy likes you, but Sissy's ugly."

"What? Who's Sissy?"

"But you can't dig that hole anymore, or I will not do anything you want me to do," she says, still shouting as he enters the room.

"What are you talking about?" he asks.

"Promise me that you won't," she says. "Promise it's over."

"Oh Jesus," Albert says. "Forget the hole for shit's sake. It's just a hole. Jesus."

"Maybe it's just a hole to you, but it's more to me — it's something I don't want you to do — promise, Albert, please."

Marie is on the bed, her knees held tight by her arms up under her chin. She isn't smiling. Albert stands in the doorway with one hand still on the knob. "I just want so see what's under there," he says.

"You don't mean that," Marie says.

"I'm going downstairs to watch television," Albert says.

Much later, Marie tiptoes down the stairs to see what Albert is doing. He is asleep on the couch in front of the television set, and, seeing him asleep, Marie squats on the stairs and weeps.

▼

The following morning Marie eats a late breakfast alone on the porch, staring at the hole through the screen door. It is a cool day, cooler than yesterday, and she feels the closeness of winter, sees it in the graying sky, smells it in the scent of the morning air. The leaves on the trees seem darker to her, as if mustered for a final battle with the season. Taking a fresh cup of coffee in her striped mug, she goes down the steps into the yard. She walks in circles around the hole there, sipping her coffee and surveying the perimeter of their property — the fragment of an old stone fence, a willow, some low bushes with unremarkable fat leaves. The lot is a little more than half an acre — large, Albert has said, for this particular development.

At first she gives the hole a wide berth, almost ignoring it, but as she completes her third circle, she bears in toward it, stopping a few feet from its edge at a point on its perimeter farthest from the house. The hole, she observes, is about five feet in diameter and four feet deep. The sides are cut at ninety degrees to the horizontal, and the bottom of the hole is very flat. Albert's spade is jammed into the spreading pile of dirt that borders the hole on the side away from the driveway. She drops to her knees in the still-damp grass of the lawn and then leans forward over the edge of the hole, looking to see what's inside. "Nothing," she says, "just nothing." She tosses the dregs of her coffee into the hole and watches the coal-colored earth turn instantly darker as it absorbs the liquid. "I don't know what Albert is so smug about," she says. "Just a damn hole in the ground, for Christ's sake." Marie walks forward on her knees and then pivots her legs over the edge and into the hole. Now she realizes that the hole is a little deeper than she had thought, that it is very nearly five feet deep. Standing in the hole she can barely see over its edge and her coffee mug, which is now only inches from her nose, looms very large. She bends to inspect the wall of the hole and finds there only ordinary dirt and a few small brown worms, working their ways across what is for them a suddenly brighter terrain. Above her the sky is going very dark, and the rain is no longer a suggestion, it is a promise. This makes her excited and nervous at once — like a child, she is seduced by the prospect of passing the rainstorm outside, in the splashing mud of the hole, in the cold of the water on her skin. Like an adult, she is apprehensive about getting out of the hole, about tracking the mud into the house, about the scrubbing that now seems inevitable. She looks at her hands, then her arms, then her feet and knees — all muddied — and her pink dressing gown, which is marked and smudged in a dozen places. "Oh my," she mutters. "I suppose I'd better not." But she doesn't make an effort to climb out of the hole, and instead sits down abruptly on the bottom, leaning her back against the dirt wall.

The rain comes. Fitfully at first, the few surprisingly large drops slap into the hole with what is to Marie a charming music. Then the storm is upon her and suddenly her gown is soaked through, showing darker brown where the cloth is stuck to her skin. Under her legs she feels a puddle beginning to form, then sees it, its surface constantly agitated by the rain. She pops the shallow water with the flat of her hand, and the dark splashes stain her gown, and she laughs, and she wipes thick strands of hair away from her face with a wet palm, laughing and splashing the water all about her, and then she begins to sing, in a very wonderful voice, "The Battle Hymn of the Republic," because she has always been a soldier in her heart.

GRAPETTE

Margaret Seaver comes around the corner of the swimming pool, carrying a paper plate in front of her. On the plate is a frankfurter so big it sticks out both ends of the bun. "I was going to fold it up," she says. "I even tried it, but the thing wouldn't stay put." She reaches into her apron pocket and produces a pink plastic knife and fork set, which she presses into my hand. "You can cut off the extra parts if you want." Then she tucks a pink and coral party napkin between two buttons of my shirt. "Okeydoke. That ought to fix you." There's a raised line of mustard along her forefinger, which she wipes on her apron. She's fortyish and built like a seal. We're standing on the combed-concrete apron of the Seaver swimming pool, celebrating the seventeenth birthday of Margaret's daughter, Carmel, who's at the opposite end of the pool, surrounded by her friends.

"Here," Margaret says, grabbing her husband's arm as he passes. "Herm, take your old friend to the garage."

Herman paid seventeen thousand dollars for the water-blue Peugeot, a present for his daughter. "It's a beautiful Peugeot," he says proudly.

"Sure is."

"She's a good girl," he says. "She's earned this."

I nod. The garage is amazingly clean. It looks like a living room — windows and a couch, wall-to-wall patio carpet, and in the corner a huge ficus in a crimson plastic pot. "Nice garage," I say, waving my hand too generously, tossing the frankfurter off the plate and under a rear tire of the car.

Herman is a real estate developer. He's six and a half feet tall, wearing bright orange slacks with a pleated stretch waist and no back pockets. His shirt is white knit. Out the garage window I see the teenagers in their narrow bathing suits clustered around the diving board. "You want me to take that wiener?" Herman points under the Peugeot's rear tire. "You go on back."

He turns along the wall of the house toward the buffet table, and I go between the low, square-cut bushes of the garden to the pool.

Carmel is looking at me over her boyfriend Duane's shoulder. Duane seems to be telling a story. The others are standing and smoking cigarettes and nodding to each other. Carmel's wearing a metallic-finish two-piece swimsuit and jewelry — a tiny gold chain around her waist.

Margaret catches my elbow. "I don't know where she gets those mugs," she says, throwing her head back to indicate the group surrounding her daughter. "Let's have a drink." She leads me to a white iron table with a glass top. "So how's the business?" Margaret says, but before I have a chance to answer, a woman in a black uniform is at the table for instructions. I nod when Margaret points to me and says "Gin?" then look at the lawn, the pines, the shaped bushes that dot the property. Then I look at Carmel.

I've known her since she was two. When she was thirteen and I was thirty-three, we had a little romance. Margaret and Herman wrote it off as a crush, but I wasn't so sure. Carmel looked twenty then; I took her to galleries and movies, and we slept together. One of Margaret's therapist friends wondered if it was such a good idea to encourage this. I told Herman that it was wearing on me, too.

▼

Margaret has to take a telephone call inside — the pool phone is out, and Herman's cordless is upstairs in his bath — so I sit at the white table with my gin. Carmel whispers something to Duane and pats his sleek lavender bottom, then joins me.

"I've got to get out of here," she says, pulling a chair around the table so we're sitting side by side. "It's crazy — Herm's crazy for doing it. I don't think Maggie wanted him to do it, but he did anyway. Did you see it, the car?"

"He showed me. It's very nice."

"Jesus." Carmel thumbs her navel, removing a glossy deposit of suntan lotion. "I've only had my license a year."

Since she was thirteen, I haven't seen her more than half a dozen times, and never alone. We stare at her friends. "How's Duane?"

"Duane drips, to the max," she says. "Duane has discovered his immensely gorgeous body, and he loves it. You look dumb with a mustache."

"That bad?"

"You could manage a Penney's."

"Anything else?" I turn to look at her face, then her breasts. She doesn't look older than she did four years ago, only smoother.

She smiles and rubs some of the oil off her belly, then wipes her palm on my forearm. "I want a birthday present from you. You know Jeremy Stein? In Herm's office? I was seeing him for a while, but he wanted to get married — can you imagine that? He must've been forty."

"I'm close," I say, twirling the remaining cube around the wall of my glass.

"Men are dorks at forty. They don't know what's good for them."

"Thanks."

"Jeremy went to California and took off his socks. A personal breakthrough." Carmel pulls on the soft white string that seems to hold the top of her swimsuit together. The string comes loose, but the halter stays put. "You still like to talk on the phone? Herm put a phone in the car — maybe I'll call you."

She's looking at my wrist, wiping lotion on it and making the hair stick to the skin.

▼

Three engineers share a four-bedroom apartment near mine in the huge Low River complex. The day after Carmel's birthday they're having a Saturday night party. They have lots of parties. They always invite me, but I never go. The engineers are from Michigan. Each owns a new black Toyota Celica — the Supra model — which he keeps in showroom condition. The oldest engineer is Morgan Zwerdling. He couldn't be more than twenty-five.

I'm having a sandwich and reading the newspaper when Morgan rings my doorbell and asks if he can stash a couple of chairs for the evening. "Tonight you gotta come," he says. "Tonight is the end of the world as we have known it."

I help him get four dining chairs and a recliner into my living room. He thanks me, then waves at the chairs and says, "These aren't going to be in your way or something, are they? If they are, just blast 'em to smithereens." He laughs.

▼

I'm trying the recliner when Carmel calls and wants to go to dinner. She's out riding in her new car and she wants some company. I hear car horns over the phone. Then Carmel says, "Up yours, too, Buster."

I struggle to get the recliner upright. "I guess I could watch."

"That's great," she says. "Bring a camera. I'll get you in two minutes."

On the narrow blacktop highway headed for Mobile, she pulls down a metal flap under the dash, revealing the telephone. "Have at it," she says.

"Some girl at your party told me I looked bad. She meant sick, I think. She pointed at my chin."

"I don't see anything wrong with your chin." Carmel's wearing a thin white dress and a silver and turquoise choker; she looks pretty, and she's more comfortable than I am.

"So what's happening since four years ago?" I turn around in my seat, bumping a knee into the phone-compartment door. "All right if I shut this?"

"Sure." She points to the glove box on my side of the dashboard. "Hand me a cigarette out of there, will you?"

I open the glove box and fish around inside for her cigarettes. "I've been to Mobile a couple of times," I say. I hand her the package of Kools.

She pulls the dash lighter out of its socket and plants it on the tip of her cigarette. "Jeremy was a freak for Mobile — the history, everything. You just sit tight."

"Right."

"I might get an apartment. Maybe where you are."

"What about Herm and Margaret?"

"What about them?" She points out the window at an abandoned gas station we're passing. There's a red horse nosing around inside the office of the station. "Sucker's going to get his pretty head bashed if he's not careful. Look at the roof." Carmel snaps her ash onto the straw floor mat, and then turns on the headlights; I stare out the window on my side of the car, watching cows in fields.

Ten minutes go by, and then there's a truck crosswise in the road. The truck is carrying tree trunks thirty or forty feet long, but only a few remain on the bed. Most of the load is spread out over the highway. I put my hand on top of the dashboard and point toward the wreck.

"Not for me," Carmel says. She slows quickly, then turns onto a white gravel drive in front of a sign that says MODERN NED'S CATFISH THIS WAY. She looks at me, and I can tell she's not having fun.

"Want to go back?"

"What, and give up? We've got dinner to eat. We've got to get to know each other again. We've got to do business."

"Right. I forgot."

The gravel stops about a hundred feet off the highway, and then we're on a dirt road with a steeply peaked center. Carmel drives on the right of the road, so I'm pushed up against the passenger door. It feels as if the Peugeot is ready to tip over.

"You OK?" Carmel asks after a couple of minutes.

"Great. You drive in an interesting way."

"How come you never called?" she says, struggling with the steering. "I've been ready." She puts a hand to her neck, and the car dips suddenly to the right, kicking up a spray of whitish dust. Rocks ping against the sheet metal. She grabs the padded steering wheel with both hands.

I brace myself against the dash.

"Sorry," she says. "I have a friend in New Mexico who makes jewelry. You think this collar's too much?"

"Yes."

"I wondered about that. I think I'm still young."

We're a mile into the dirt road. It's dusk, and grayer than it was out on the highway. "You like catfish?" I ask.

"Why, you don't?" She seems satisfied that she can handle the road now and reaches into her lap, where the cigarette pack is lodged.

"No."

She stops digging for a Kool long enough to glance at me. "Here," she says, steering the car up onto the center of the road,

"I'll slow down some and maybe you'll feel better — how's that? Punch that lighter."

She resettles in her bucket seat and drags her dress a little higher over her knees. There's a small square of white on a tree a couple of hundred yards up the road — a sign of some kind. When the lighter pops, I pull it out of its socket and hand it to her.

The sign says POSTED — KEEP OUT. Carmel sighs, filling the car with smoke. "I'm beginning to think Ned's doesn't exist anymore."

"You've been here?"

"Once, with Jeremy. I had white beans." She downshifts, then wipes the palm of her hand up over her forehead and stops the car in the middle of the dirt road. "This road isn't going anywhere. Let's take a walk — what do you say?" Without waiting for an answer, she gets out and slams the door. I follow her. She looks very strange in this setting, like a woman on a hand-painted billboard. I track her for a few steps, then change my mind and sit on the Peugeot's front fender, watching Carmel walk.

▼

It's dark when we get back. Even in the kitchen, which is the part of my apartment farthest from the engineers', we can hear the thump of the bass and the noise of the guests who have taken to the patio. Carmel is eating a peanut butter and jelly sandwich, and I'm searching for the Tostitos. She's taken off the choker. There are thin abrasions on her neck where the silver bit into her skin. I watch her eat.

"Good," she says, finishing the last corner of her sandwich. She points to her plate, which is dotted with bubbles of shining jelly. "Let's go out."

"We just got in. Where do you want to go?"

"Let's get something at the store."

"What store? What kind of something?"

She takes her plate to the sink and runs the hot water. Her skirt is flawlessly smooth in the back. "I don't know — just a store. We'll go to a store, look around, buy something. I always find things I want when I go to the store, don't you?"

"Not every time," I say. Carmel fills a new yellow sponge with water, wrings it out, and starts to wipe the dark wood-grained doors of the kitchen cabinets. "But if you're going to housekeep, I'll go."

She stops what she's doing and looks at the sponge in her hand as if it had suddenly turned into a fish. "Jesus," she says. "I didn't even think — this is your apartment." She drops the sponge on the lip of the sink, rubs her hands together, and reaches for her purse. She removes a small bottle and taps a curl of hand cream into her palm, then screws on the bottle top before rubbing the cream into her skin. "I really do want to go out. Are there any good stores around here? Is that surplus store still open? What time is it, anyway?"

▼

The man behind the platform counter at Fuji News looks as if he should be out buying a Mr. Turtle swimming pool for his kid. He grins when Carmel pushes through the slatted saloon-type doors into the adult-books section.

"We're browsing," I tell him.

"Look at this." Carmel pulls a shrink-wrapped magazine off the rack and hands it to me, tapping the close-up on the cover with her fingernail. "That's love." She hands me another magazine, a tabloid stapled shut twice in the middle of the front cover. "Names and addresses," she says. "You'd be surprised who's in here. Herm and Maggie and their friends. Really. They've got it at home. I've seen it."

The back room of the newsstand is smelly. There are black wire racks for the paperbacks and wooden racks for the magazines. Up on the cashier's platform, which spans the two rooms, there's a glass case of films and sex toys. "I'm going out front," I say to Carmel, bending close to her so that the other customers — a fellow who looks like an Olympic swimmer, a man in a plaid shirt who looks as if he just woke up, and a kid who's hunkered down in an alcove in back — can't overhear. "You be OK?"

"I'm finished anyway. This stuff is sleazoid, isn't it?"

"You want something special?" the counterman says as we go through the swinging doors.

"Nope," Carmel says, smiling at him. "We got what we came for."

A very tan guy in tennis gear looks up from his Italian architecture magazine when he hears Carmel. "Hi," he says. "You on patrol?"

"Oh — Chuck. You win?" She points to his clothes. "I got a Peugeot."

I can see what's on the cover of the magazine he's looking at: an interior, done in new-pastel green satins. Carmel introduces us.

"Chuck's an ex," she says. "He worked on Herm's Omni Centre."

"And look at me now — an old married man with one in the bucket and one on the way."

There's shouting in the back, and the swimmer leaps through the double doors. He grabs Carmel's shoulder and shoves her to one side, then pushes past Chuck and runs out. The plaid-shirt guy catches the swinging doors and shouts, "Try it again, Muscle Face, and I'll teach you mush." He pulls the doors shut, glaring over them at me. "He's a friend of yours?"

"C'mon, Billy," the counterman says. "Ease up."

"We never saw him before in our lives," Carmel says. She grabs my wrist and twists it a little. "Quit shoving, will you? I'm not ready yet."

Chuck has closed his magazine and now he slaps it on his bare thigh several times.

"I'm a welder," Billy says, still looking over the doors. "I work out in Bayside. Nights."

Chuck says, "Oh? I worked on a bank in Bayside, on Dot Street."

Carmel squats down in the aisle and pulls a copy of *Interface Age* off a fresh stack. "Look at this," she whispers to me, pointing to a photograph of an integrated circuit in the magazine.

Billy comes out from behind the doors, his hand pushed at Chuck. "What're you, a designer? You worked on First Bayside? Me and the boys did that lobby fountain. My name's Billy Farrar."

Chuck and Billy shake hands.

"Yep — that's you, all right," Billy says, pointing at Chuck's magazine. "This where you get all the ideas? The boys were laughing all the damn time about that fountain. And it looked good, too." He grabs Chuck's shoulder and gives it a stiff tug. "No, really — it's real pretty." He shakes his head as if he's not certain he'll be believed, then points toward the door. "Little girl tried to grope me. You get that in a place like this." He shrugs and looks at Carmel. "I'm on my way to work. It ain't that bad a drive. All you got to do is come up here and catch the Loop" — he starts drawing a map in the air — "then swing on around by 59 there, and get off at the Dictionary Street exit, there by Cross Tool — it don't take long."

▼

On the sidewalk outside the store Carmel slaps Chuck's backside. "Hey," she says. "Just like old times."

He takes a swipe at her with his magazine, which is rolled tight like a baton in his fist. "My Frank Lloyd Wright imitation."

We walk down the sidewalk together until Chuck steps off the curb to unlock a gunpowder-gray Audi 5000. "So where's this Peugeot?" He stands up on his toes and looks down the line of cars.

"Over here," Carmel says. "Want a look?"

Chuck has to lock the Audi again; then the three of us go for a look at Carmel's car. When Chuck's just about finished examining it, she pushes him into the front seat and shows him the telephone.

"Oh, Jesus," he says. "Sweet everlovin' Jesus."

"Yeah," she says.

We walk Chuck back to his car, and stand on the sidewalk and wave as he pulls out.

"He's OK," Carmel says out of the side of her mouth. "But his wife's a twit."

The newsstand is in a strip shopping center on a six-lane feeder for the downtown freeway and the Loop that Billy was talking about. The street is bordered by silver poles and greenish street-lights and blinking nudie-bar signs, the temporary kind that are always stuck in weedy lots—a red edge outlined with clear blinking lamps and a message that says GIRLS GIRLS GIRLS.

A startlingly thin black woman in skintight lamé jeans and a string top passes us on the sidewalk, headed for the bar next to the newsstand. She says hello to me. She's got glitter all around her eyes and she's wearing some kind of plastic-jewel headdress that comes down her nose and then drapes in shallow arcs over her cheekbones and back above her ears. Carmel pokes me in the arm, then looks over her shoulder at the woman. "I thought you didn't like jewelry."

▼

We got halfway into a parking space in front of my apartment before two young guys who are standing in the space, obviously drunk and having a discussion, look up. They don't move out of the way. One of them, a frail-looking kid with coarse, dark hair and a satin windbreaker open to the waist, waves us away, shading his eyes with a long-neck beer bottle. He's one of the engineers; I don't know the other guy. Carmel rolls down her window, holding the car on the very slight incline of the parking space by alternately engaging and disengaging the clutch.

"Give me a break, hey?" she says, leaning her head out the car window.

The two guys talk another minute, gesturing toward the car, and then step awkwardly out of the way, pressing themselves up against the burgundy Plymouth parked next to the space we're trying to get into.

"Hi there, Peugeot," the engineer says. He bends forward from the waist and rests his folded forearms on Carmel's window. "You want a beer? Good beer — Lone Star." He shoves his bottle halfway in her window, neck first.

"Never heard of it," Carmel says.

He turns to his partner, who's still leaning against the Plymouth, and says, "She never heard of Lone Star."

Carmel opens her door a couple of inches. The engineer jumps back and wobbles.

"Damn," he says. "Scared the pee out of me, woman."

His friend pulls him by the shirtsleeve. "I told you, man, you got to go slow, you got to tattoo her memory pan, slow and easy" — he pokes his friend deliberately on the arm — "bap, bap, bap, bap — like that." Then he reaches forward and opens the door for Carmel. "I'm Vern. Everybody calls me V.O., but my name's Vernon — Vern for short. What's your name?"

"Sugar," Carmel says.

Vern glances at my neighbor, then back at Carmel. "Can I call you Sugar?"

"Maybe," Carmel says. "Good party?"

"The best," the engineer says, stumbling forward. "Light-Emitting Diode City, really. I mean totally killer." He grins at me through the corner of the windshield, then slips and vanishes below the car's fender.

"The women are short," Vern says, looking down at his friend. "All these teeny little women in there." He swings his bottle hand over his shoulder toward the engineer's apartment. "Is everybody suddenly shorter than they used to be?"

"Not me," Carmel says. She gets out and slides between Vern and the front fender of the Peugeot, stepping around the fallen engineer. "Maybe we'll come over."

"Straight?" Vern says. "I mean, you telling me straight?"

"Sure," she says, patting the shoulder of his pale blue shirt. He's wearing red gym trunks and this pale blue shirt with a sail-boat painted on it.

▼

"That's better," Carmel says, her face smushed in a plump off-white cushion. "You've got a great couch."

I turn on the television, crouching in front of the set to leaf through the *TV Weekly* that comes with my Saturday paper. "There's a George Raft movie. You interested?" I spin around on one foot, still in a crouch, and almost fall over backward into the wire TV table.

"George Raft? What else? Why don't we go to the party?" Carmel rolls onto her side and slugs the pillow a couple of times to make it fit comfortably under her arm. "What's all this furniture?" She looks at the dining chairs and the recliner.

"They brought it over to make room," I say. "I may get me one of those La-Z-Boys."

"Sure. I know — I can't go to the party because I'd just get sick after. I hate being sick, really." She stares past me at the television.

I go into the kitchen. "You want something to drink?"

"Cream soda," she says.

I open the refrigerator, then stop and look around the door. "What?"

"Do you have any cream soda? What I'd like more than anything else in the world is a cream soda."

"Sorry." I pull a sixteen-ounce Coke out of its plastic holder. "How about Coke?"

"Gimme a Dew."

"What? Oh—Mountain Dew. Fresh out." I unscrew the cap of my drink, take a swallow, and stand in front of the refrigerator, straightening the cold eggs in the door rack. "You might as well just go ahead and ask for a Grapette."

She turns back onto her stomach, then pushes up on her elbows and presses her forehead into the cushion. "I never heard of it."

She lifts her head and looks across the room at me; her face is shadowed, because the only light in the room is above and behind her, but the pose is familiar. I shut the refrigerator door and go to the recliner, pushing it back until I'm horizontal, floating in the middle of the living room. "No Grapette," I say, scanning the ceiling.

"What is it?"

"The end of the world as we have known it."

"Oh."

"Little purple bottles, six ounces." I wave my hand and twist my head to one side so I can see her on the couch. "Grapette kind of went away, I guess. I hate that."

She's still for a minute, then squirms up on the sofa and pulls the white cushion into her lap, turning to face me. "Are you sure? Maybe we ought to go find some, maybe it's still out there."

VIOLET

KATHLEEN SULLIVAN is back on CNN, a guest on the call-in interview show. She's supposed to be talking about the boom in news, but the callers, who are all men, only want to talk about her bangs, and the new drab-look clothes she wears on ABC. Tonight she's wearing one of her old purple outfits, and her hair's messed up as it used to be when she co-anchored *Prime News 120*. A caller who says his name is Toby, from Tennessee, says that he doesn't think she's the real Kathleen Sullivan, that the real Kathleen must've gone to heaven. "It's still me," Kathleen says, laughing prettily. "I look all right now, don't I?" Her not-quite-coordinated lip gloss, somewhere between grape and burgundy, is a nice touch.

The dinner I'm heating in the oven smells about ready, so I take the telephone receiver out of its cradle and drop it into a crack between the sofa frame and a seat cushion. A lock of Kathleen's hair has gotten crosswise with her part. I crouch in front of the set, tap the glass, and say, "Kathleen, Kathleen," but she goes on talking. I advance the color intensity and twist the hue knob to change the color of her lips to crimson. "That's better," I say to the television.

Somebody knocks at the door. I freeze in front of the set for a minute. When the quick, shy-sounding knock comes again, I decide it must be the landlady, and get up to see what she wants.

There's a girl outside. She's young — she looks about sixteen. Her hair is short, boyish, and she's thin like a stick, smiling at me. "Hi," she says, making a small move with her hand. "May I use your phone? I need to make a call."

"My phone?" It's silly what I've said — as if I had no phone, or didn't know what "phone" meant. I back away from the door and bump into the wall in the cramped foyer. "Sure. Come in."

"What're you burning?" The girl stops by the kitchen door, drops her brilliant green backpack, and stares at the stove. Without going into the kitchen, she bends forward and opens the oven. "I think it's too hot," she says, smiling at my dinner. She twists the temperature knob a couple of notches.

"I was in a hurry."

She goes into the living room. Her pants are Dickies, much too large in spite of the extra darts running from the top of each back pocket up into the waistband. "Oh," she says, seeing the telephone cord stretched out over the arm of the couch. "Are you on the phone?"

"No. I mean, I was, but I'm not now. Go ahead. You'll probably have to hang it up first."

She does a take to tell me I've said something stupid. The living room, which is ordinarily quite comfortable, suddenly seems cramped and shabby. The girl is six feet tall. As I look at her standing beside the couch, dialing numbers on the telephone, I realize that the pants are too big by design, a way to simultaneously disguise and exploit her thinness.

I excuse myself and go to close the front door. My neighbor, a thirty-year-old bookkeeper for Kmart, blond and not very popular with the other residents in the apartment complex, is sitting beside the pool with her Coors in a Styrofoam cooler. She's staring at the front page of the evening paper, the way she does every night. It's the only time I ever see her.

The girl has come up behind me. "Who's that?" she asks. "I can't get through. Do you mind if I wait a minute and try again?"

"Sure." I close the door. "I was watching the news."

"Got any juice?" She backs toward the kitchen. "I love juice. Any kind. My name's Violet."

I follow her to the kitchen, reaching for her hand. "I'm Philip. Let's see what we can hunt up."

"I'm a runaway," she says. "I know it's old-fashioned, but my parents are intolerable."

There's a quart carton of orange juice in the refrigerator.

Violet takes the couch, sitting on it sideways, her back against the arm. I sit on one of the bentwood dining chairs. After an awkward silence, she raises her glass and says, "Cheers," and I raise my glass, too.

"California," she says, anticipating a question. "Northern California, to be precise. It wasn't men or money, and nobody ever laid a hand on me. Not a mark anywhere." She swings a hand in front of her chest to show me where there are no marks, then looks at her glass, holding it up to the fading light outside the double sliding doors. "I wanted to see something, do something."

Her hair is thin, soft-looking, and not much longer than mine. Her face is smooth, the skin tight and the cheekbones exaggerated by narrow scars of blusher. She's wearing a white T-shirt. She seems at ease in my apartment, on my couch.

"So you came South."

"Hitched," she says. "Yeah. It's OK. Sometimes it's fun and sometimes it's scary. But it's not as different as I thought it'd be."

She grabs the phone and starts to dial again, and I stare at the television. On the eighth digit I turn around and watch her dial three more. She covers the mouthpiece with her palm. "I'm reversing the charges. Did you think I'd come in here and use your phone without paying?"

I smile weakly, push myself off the dining chair, and go into the kitchen.

▼

In a couple of minutes she sticks her head around the door frame. "Why don't we go out? We could eat somewhere good."

I've been leaning against the rolled edge of the counter, trying unsuccessfully to hear her conversation, moving pans now and then to make the kind of noise I'd make if I weren't listening.

"Go out?"

She picks up the Swanson frozen-food box from the counter, holds it in front of her chest, and points to the picture of the Salisbury steak, rubbing the cardboard with her fingertip. "See, this is a four-and-a-half-ounce entrée — we can't both eat it. We can go out and get a real dinner. I'll bet it's a month since you saw a vegetable. You can even have hot rolls and a dessert."

"I don't know," I say, looking around the obviously unused kitchen. "I don't think so — not tonight."

She frowns at me. "OK, if that's what you want. What we ought to do is go somewhere you've never been, someplace you always wanted to go but never did." She stands in the kitchen doorway, hands on her hips, the T-shirt pulled tight across her small chest. She's scolding me with this pose.

"There's this funny place on the highway by the Knights Inn — I've never been there."

"See?" She breaks her stance and clicks the oven dial to "Off," all in one move. "Where's your car?"

"I've got to get some shoes first."

"Fine." She's already around the corner and on her way out the front door. "I'll meet you by the pool. Is it too cold for swimming?"

She doesn't wait for the answer. I go into my bedroom and sit in the oak swivel chair by the makeshift desk. I straighten my socks, slip my feet into the loafers I left there earlier, then get up and look at myself in the mirror over the dresser. I bend close to the glass and say, to my face, "Vegetable?"

Going out, I check the oven again, then go to turn off the TV. Kathleen Sullivan is adjusting her lapel microphone, unaware that she's on camera.

▼

The place I had in mind isn't there anymore, so we end up at Shoney's, with oversize, four-color, wrapped-in-clear-vinyl menus in our laps. Behind Violet there are blood-red imitation-bamboo slat blinds that the hostess had to wrestle with to lower. Violet turns the big glistening pages of her menu, making little noises as she looks from picture to picture.

"My treat," I say. "What do you like?"

"Oh, I don't know. Maybe the lobster. I could eat lobster for breakfast. What do you think?" She flattens her menu on the table-top and points to a picture of giant onion rings bathed in thick ketchup. "Look at these," she says. "Aren't they amazing?"

On the windowsill beside her there are two dead flies, one on its back and the other still standing but tipped forward, resting on its nose.

"What about you?"

"I want pancakes," I say. "Ham and hash brown potatoes and a small glass of orange juice."

"No kidding? That's what you want?"

"I wonder if they serve pancakes this time of day."

Violet twists against the diamond-tufted seat and looks across the room at the narrow pass-through between the kitchen and the serving area. "Sure they do. Isn't that what their little man is hold-ing—a stack of pancakes?" She leafs quickly through the menu. "There should be a drawing of him here somewhere."

"Look on the back."

She flops the menu on its face, rattling the silverware. "Nope."

The waitress wanders up to our table already writing something on her small pad. She's wearing a faded brown uniform and a gold, almost oval apron. "You ready to order yet?"

"Hi," Violet says. "Is the lobster good today? I'll have the lobster. Here." She points to the vivid picture on her menu. I order pancakes.

"So," Violet says, straightening her place setting. "How is it so far?"

"Excellent."

The restaurant is crowded with families. "Looks like they're selling a lot of chicken," Violet whispers. She's hunched over toward me with her arm out behind her toward the other diners.

"It's a hamburger. The boy on the sign is holding a hamburger."

"Those too," she says. "Look over here at the guy and his wife in the matching Bermuda-shorts outfits. Is that chicken or hamburger?"

I sit up and look over her shoulder. "Chicken. There was a bunch like that when we came in — all four in matching blue houndstooth shirts with huge collars."

"I don't think people should wear matching clothes," Violet says. "Except maybe at home it'd be all right."

"Even there," I say.

"Yeah. You're right. I don't think so at all."

I move my knife and fork around, then push the sugar rack back against the windowsill. I'm staring at a short, pretty waitress across the room when Violet taps my arm. "Philip? Look — food. Move your elbows so she can put the plates down."

I ask our waitress, who is teetering over the table with a large aluminum tray propped up on the fingers of her left hand, if she has any pure maple syrup. She bats her eyelashes at me and puts the plates on the table. "I'll see what we've got if you can hold your horses," she says. "I've got my hands full here just now."

When everything's on the table and the syrup has finally arrived — abruptly, smacking the Formica and sliding a few inches into the ketchup squirt bottle — Violet says, "Dig in, huh?" The pancakes are coaster-size and lapped on the plate like magazines on a coffee table, topped with scoops of white butter. The handle of the syrup dispenser is sticky. Violet's lobster is a pathetic flat thing, squat on the tan plate.

"Five pairs of legs," she says, catching my eye. "Of course, you don't eat them all. You could, I mean, but you don't have to."

▼

After dinner, at the intersection outside Shoney's, we stop at a red light. Violet has a toothpick in her mouth, and her pale blue running shoes propped up on the safety tray that is part of the dashboard of my Rabbit. A sedan pulls up alongside and the driver honks, two short blasts. The woman driving waves. I don't recognize her. She rolls her forefinger in tight circles to indicate she wants me to lower my window.

"Hi," she says, before the glass is halfway down. "I saw you coming out of the parking lot back there. Who's your friend?"

I look at the woman and point at myself. "What?"

"Hi," Violet says, pressing me back up against the seat. "This is Philip. Philip, that's Crystal."

"Hello, Crystal," I say, raising a hand in half salute. I watch the light for the left-turn lane flick from red to green.

"What've you been doing, Violet?" The woman has to shout to be heard over the engine of a truck turning out of the lane next to her.

"We ate at Shoney's," Violet shouts back. "He had pancakes."

"What? I can't hear you."

"Pancakes," Violet shouts. She makes a big circle with her thumbs and forefingers and holds up her hands for the woman to see.

The light changes. Crystal nods and shouts, "Be careful," then spurts forward past the buzzing sign of the all-night Texaco station, waving up behind her head when she cuts across the beams of our headlights.

I go through the intersection and turn right on the first cross street, Sugar Hill, then pull to the curb, cut the lights, and switch off the ignition.

"You want to walk some?" Violet says. "I don't mind. This is a good street. See, it's even got those new orange lights — look." She leans toward me, touching my arm, and points out the windshield toward the nearest streetlight. The streetlight has a rusty glow.

We sit for a few minutes without saying anything. Finally I say, "Who's that?"

"Crystal? Oh, she's a friend. Somebody I know."

"Somebody you know."

"Well, so what if I'm not a runaway?" Violet says. "So what? I had to say something."

I start the car, make a U-turn and then a left back onto Broadway, and go through a yellow light by the Shoney's. I expect Violet to explain, but she doesn't, and we drive in silence, watching the lights thin out, watching the street change from highway access to old neighborhood to just-built suburb. There are a lot of one-story strip shopping centers along the street, lit and empty. At a light, after a couple of miles, Violet points to a gas station that has been painted solid black and converted into a bar. "Let's stop," she says. "I want to go there."

"The Tip Top Club?"

She turns in the seat to face me. "Please, Philip, I want to see what it's like inside."

When the stoplight changes, I cut diagonally across the intersection and into a space in the parking lot between a silver van and a pickup. "If they ask, I'll say you're my daughter."

She pats my arm. "They won't ask, silly."

The room is dark and cold, and I almost trip on the carpet covering the three steps down to the dance floor. Violet tugs at my hand, pulling me to a small booth in the corner. The Tip Top Club is not crowded. Aside from the waitresses, who are gathered at one end of the bar, we're the only people there. Two empty tables away a stray blue flood lamp lights the surface of a table. A beat-up-looking woman in jeans and a tube top comes over to us and says, "Hi. What can we get you?"

"Scotch, please. Water and ice."

"Tomato juice," Violet says. "Thanks. And can you tell me what time it is?"

The woman bends around from the waist and looks toward the bar. "Nearly nine." She puts two napkins on the table and says, "I'll be back in a sec."

Violet says, "It's so old-fashioned, this place. You're not mad, are you?"

"I don't think so."

"It was the only thing I could think of, you know what I mean?"

The drinks arrive. Violet gulps half of her tomato juice, slides out from behind the table, and quick steps across the room to the space-age jukebox. I finger my glass and listen to her quarters go down the slot. Then she's back at the table, standing beside me, reaching for her juice. With one hand on my shoulder she drains the glass in a single swallow. "Now," she says. She pulls on my arm until I get out of the booth. "This is probably against the law. I know. And it's tacky. But let's do it until they stop us."

The tune is a mournful cowboy song that I've heard a hundred times. Violet puts her arms on my shoulders, leans forward, presses her forehead to mine, smiles, then closes her eyes. I put my arms around her waist, and we shuffle around in a clumsy circle. It's wonderful; I haven't danced with anybody since high school. We go three times through the song without stopping. Then I notice the waitress standing by our table at the edge of the dance floor, obviously amused. I pull away, and when Violet opens her eyes, I raise my head toward the waitress. Violet looks over her shoulder. "We're fine," she says to the woman. "We don't need anything."

▼

There's a guy the size of a tree peering in the driver's window of the Rabbit when we get outside. "Oh, hi," he says, straightening and slapping the roof a couple of times. "This yours?"

Violet puts a hand on my shoulder and presses close. I say, "Yes." Now that he's standing up, the guy is at least a foot taller than I am. The car only comes up to his elbows. He has huge hands, and fingers like breakfast sausages.

"I want to try it out," he says. "I want to go around the block."

I look at my watch. "We've got to get to the airport. My daughter's on her way back to college."

"She doesn't look old enough," he says. "I thought she was your girlfriend when I saw you dancing."

"Looks like he's got us," Violet says. She dances a little more in the gravel of the parking lot. "Let's give him a ride."

"That'd be real nice," the big guy says. "Maybe I could even drive."

He's standing alongside the driver's door. Violet and I are still in front of the car. "What do you want to drive for?" I ask.

"I never get to," he says. "I like to drive."

I shake my head. "Well, I'm sorry, but we're booked up. Sorry." I don't know what I'm going to do if he insists.

"Is he drunk?" Violet whispers, her lips pushed into the shoulder of my jacket.

He hears her and wags a meaty finger. "No, ma'am. Not in the slightest. I don't drink at all, as a matter of fact."

Violet moves forward a little, still holding my shoulder. "Look," she says, "why don't you go to a dealership? We could take you to a dealership" — she turns back to me — "couldn't we? Do you know where one is?"

"I don't need to go to a dealership when I've got this Volkswagen right here."

Violet backs up a step and says to me, "He doesn't need a dealership."

"I heard."

The guy takes a swipe at the door mirror, knocking it off the car. "Oops," he says, looking down at the ground and then back at us. "I busted it. I didn't mean to do that, honest."

There's no traffic, and I can hear the flicking of the electric switches in the box that controls the stoplight. The sky is muddy — no stars. We're in a standoff with this huge guy. He doesn't seem bent on violence, but he's very definite about wanting to drive the car. I don't want to give him the car unless I absolutely have to, so I say, "Let's go back inside, Violet," and start for the door of the Tip Top Club.

"Why don't you just let me have the keys for a minute?" the guy says. He isn't following us. I figure, at worst, he'll wait until we're inside and then take the car.

"Can't do that," I say, holding the door for Violet.

I wait just inside the entrance, looking out the diamond-shaped glass panel in the door. Violet says, "You want me to call the police?"

"I don't know. Hold on a minute." The guy is staring after us. He can't see us through the glass. He puts the door mirror on top of the car, then bends down and rests his head on the top, too, like a man listening to railroad tracks. "I think we're going to get lucky."

"What's up?" It's the waitress in the tube top, stepping back and forth on her tiptoes, trying to get a look out between the beer decals of the glass. I back away and let her look.

"This guy's drunk, or crazy, or both. He wants my car. We're going to have to get the cops."

"Oh, Jesus, Mary, and Joseph," the waitress says. She starts to say something else, then puts a hand to her forehead and pushes out the door. "Sidney," she says sternly. "You get right back in the van. Now." She slaps her thigh and stamps a foot for emphasis. "Go on." She lets the door close about halfway and hisses something I can't hear. Then she opens the door for me. "Come on out. It's just my brother Sidney. He won't hurt you."

When we get outside, Sidney is climbing into the side door of the van next to the Rabbit. My mirror is gone.

"He's gentle as a lamb," the waitress says.

Violet and I get into the car. The waitress is standing by the front of the van, holding her brother at bay. He's sitting there in the open door, staring at us. Violet says, "I think we should take him with us."

"Oh, yeah?"

The waitress waves. Violet waves back and says, "We could at least take him around the block — that's all he wanted, really."

The waitress comes up to Violet's side of the car, hits on the window, and says, "What's wrong?"

Violet rolls down the window. "We were just talking about taking Sidney for a drive. We didn't know he was your brother. We thought he was a creep."

"Oh, you don't need to do that," the waitress says. "He gets plenty of rides with me. I take him everywhere I go."

"But we want to, don't we, Philip?" She pats my arm like a wife.

"Sure," I say, thinking maybe the waitress will kill the deal. "Can he drive? I mean, does he know how? He seemed to want to drive, for some reason."

"Sometimes I let him steer," the waitress says. "That's all. He likes your car because of the basketball-player commercial — have you seen that one?"

"Yeah," Violet says. "Sure. Maybe we'll just take him for a spin around town — you know, twenty minutes, no more. Would that be OK?"

The waitress bends farther down to look at me. "There's nothing wrong with him," she says. "He's just a little slow in the head. I don't know — what do you think?"

On my left, Sidney is sitting back in the seat of the van, smiling. I think he knows what we're talking about. "OK," I say. "He can ride in the front here. Violet, you get in the back."

"I'll tell him," the waitress says. "This is real nice of you people."

As Violet is getting into the back, she pulls herself forward and kisses my cheek. "It'll be fine," she says. We watch the waitress give Sidney his instructions as she walks him around the front of the car. He nods vigorously.

Sidney comes into the front seat headfirst. He grins at me. "Hi, Sidney," Violet says from the back. "I'm Violet. He's Philip."

"Hi," Sidney says, struggling to get all the way into the car. "I'm sorry about before. I wasn't really going to take the car, really."

"We know," Violet says.

The waitress, who is standing in the parking lot waiting to shut Sidney's door, says, "Now, you tell me when you get back, you hear? Just come in and tell Mike or Bub to fetch me. Are you listening to me, Sidney?"

"Yes," he says, reaching for the armrest. "I'll come in first thing."

Sidney's wearing black high-top sneakers and dark green work pants. With the door closed, he has to sit with his knees apart, and his left knee is in the way of the gearshift. "I've got to get at this," I say gently, tapping his leg with the back of my hand.

"Oh, sure," he says. He wraps a huge arm around the leg to keep it out of the way. "Where are we going?"

Violet sits up, leaning between the seats. "Where do you want to go, Sidney? We can go just about anywhere."

Sidney thinks a minute, while I get the car out of the parking lot. "Which way?" I say. Close up, he's not so menacing. He points to the left, knocking the rearview mirror out of whack.

"Oh, I'm sorry," he says, starting to reset the mirror.

Violet reaches forward and tugs on his arm. "Don't worry about it," she says.

"There's a lot of room in here," he says. "Don't you think so?"

He flattens his hand and wedges it between his head and the white padded headliner of the Rabbit. His knee falls on the gearshift and knocks the car out of third. "What happened?" he says when the engine revs noisily.

"Nothing," Violet says. She pats his shoulder. "How'd you like a big piece of cherry pie?"

He shakes his head. "I don't like cherry pie," he says. I shift into fourth gear.

"Do you like any kind of pie?" Violet asks. "I can get us all the pie we want, any kind."

"How's that?" I say.

"No," Sidney says. "I really don't like pie very much." He turns around in the seat. "But thank you anyway, Violet. You're being very nice to me."

"You're being nice, too," she says. "I work at the pie store on Palmetto Street. I'm a pie girl."

I turn around to look at her.

"That's what they call us."

We drive around for half an hour seeing the sights. Sidney spends a lot of time inspecting the car — asking about the tires and the seats and the gas mileage, running his thick fingers over the dashboard covering and the carpet, trying the horn and the air-conditioning and the radio. Finally he says, "Can I drive now? Trish never lets me drive."

I look in the rearview mirror at Violet. She nods quickly and mouths "Please," so I make a turn onto an empty residential street and stop the car.

"OK, Sidney. It's all yours."

"Really?" he says. "Now?" We switch places. He takes a few minutes practicing his shifting, and says, "Don't worry, Philip. I can do this." After a couple of stalls he gets us going, and he does fine. He has to bend his neck awkwardly to see out the windshield, and it's hard for him to release the clutch pedal, because his knee jams up under the steering wheel, but he gets it figured out, and we drive around some more. Violet compliments him lavishly on his driving, pats his shoulder and pushes his hair back off his forehead. She seems genuinely pleased for him. She asks him how tall he is, and he says, "Real tall," and laughs, looking up at her in the mirror.

"More than seven feet, I'll bet," she says, curling his hair back around his ear with her finger.

"I'm taller than Kareem, too," he says proudly. "Seven-four."

"I think it's nice," she says. "I'd like to be seven-four."

▼

At the club he parks in back, next to a chicken-wire cage and a bank of six steel trash cans. "Will you wait a minute?" he says, pushing himself backward out of the car. "I want to tell Trish we're here." He lopes around the front of the car and into the club through the kitchen door.

Violet punches the back of my seat. "See, that wasn't so bad, was it?"

"What's all this pie business?"

"That's where I work," she says. "Pie Country — you've been there." She's sitting forward on the rear seat, but we're not looking at each other — we're both looking out the windshield.

"I know I've been there. I go there all the time."

"After work," she says. "Usually." She punches the seat twice more. "Come on, let a girl out, will you?"

I unlock the door and open it, then turn sideways in the seat so that I can see her. She's got her hands on the seat's headrest, ready to pop out of the car. "Pie Country?" I say.

"You probably wouldn't know me out of uniform," she says. She shakes the seat back the way an infant shakes the sides of a crib. "Move it."

We're standing beside the car when Sidney and the waitress

come out of the club hand in hand. "Did he really drive?" the waitress asks.

"Yes, ma'am," Violet says. She gives Sidney a quick little hug, which he returns awkwardly. "He drove real well."

The waitress looks at me. "Perfect," I say. "Didn't miss a trick."

"See?" Sidney says to his sister. "I told you."

INSTRUCTOR

Southwestern Alabama advertised a one-year, non-tenure-track instructorship in biology, and, more or less routinely, I sent my vita to the chairman of the department. When he called and asked me to interview for the position, I was surprised and pleased. I flew down on Wednesday, rented a Chevette, and signed in at the Tropic Breeze Motel, as he'd suggested. Thursday I spent the morning with him, the search committee, the dean of the college, two vice presidents, and the president, and after lunch I sat in the department lounge talking with whoever happened in. That's when I met Sonia. She was an associate professor from Kansas, three years in rank and ready for promotion because of a book contract with Plinth. She had wavy red hair and a long, almost defiant stride, and she came in late, close to five. She introduced herself, asked who was taking care of me, then invited me to dinner with her and her brother Jack.

We went to a fish place down by the channel, and when we came back into town the rain that had been on and off all day let up. Everything was shiny and bright — the pavement, the stoplights, the violet and green neon from shopwindows that lined the street.

"So much for science," she said as we drove past the university. "Let's get some beer — what do you say?"

"Maybe one," I said. "I have my presentation to the faculty at ten tomorrow."

"They shouldn't make you do that for this kind of a job," she said. "Anyway, you'll be perfect, don't worry."

"He's insecure," Jack said, glancing at me in the rearview mirror. Jack was an electrical engineer and apartment developer. He was a small man to start with, and looked smaller because he was driving Sonia's 1955 Buick. His hair was springy, also red, and floated around the sides of his head. We pulled into a 7-Eleven parking lot alongside a police car.

"Yum yum," Sonia said, pointing to the cop who was in the store drinking coffee out of a polka-dot cup. He was a young guy with a little-boy haircut and a black leather jacket, and he had his hat cocked back on his head. "Oh," she said. "It's Burt."

Jack lifted up in the seat as he reached into his back pocket for his wallet. "Burt?"

"Ex-student," she said. "Look at him. He's so sweet."

"My sister needs a boyfriend," Jack said, looking at me over his shoulder.

"My brother thinks I'm a one-woman sexual revolution," she said. "But I tell him we all need boyfriends." She went inside and got two six-packs of Coors out of the cooler. Then she said something to Burt. They talked while the skinny girl in the red jumper covered with 7-Eleven patches worked the register and put the beer in a sack.

"I kid her," Jack said. "But she's a good sister. You have a family?"

I slid down on the backseat and stuck my hand out the open car window to feel the rain. "Four brothers," I said.

"Sisters are different," he said. "We have a brother in Kansas, but we never talk to him."

The 7-Eleven overhang was wrapped with white fluorescent tubes, and beyond them the sky was medium gray, the tree limbs black.

"She does need a boyfriend," Jack said. He leaned over the seat back. "What are you doing back here?"

"She shouldn't have any trouble," I said.

"That's what I thought," he said.

Sonia and the policeman came out of the store together, still talking. He walked her to the car and opened the door. The interior light came on, and Sonia said, "Meet Patrolman Burt. This is Jack, and that's David in back. Jack's my brother."

"Howdy," the guy said. He leaned over so that he could see into the car. His jacket creaked.

"He's off duty," Sonia said.

Burt smiled.

Sonia patted him on the back. "So tell them how things are, crime-wise."

"Not much happening," he said. "It's quiet."

"Burt and I are going to drive around awhile," Sonia said. "I love police cars. Are you coming by later?"

"I could take David to Blister's," Jack said.

"That'll be fine," Sonia said, smiling. "Then I'll tell him what Chairman Stibert really thought about him. OK, David?"

"You don't want to go to Blister's?" I said.

"I hate it," she said. "We'll meet up shortly."

Burt adjusted his gun belt, and, while he wasn't looking, Jack and Sonia made faces at each other. Then she dropped the sack on the passenger seat.

"An hour?" Jack said. "You figure to get your driving done by then?"

"That'll be superior," Sonia said. She turned to me. "Are you all right, David?"

"Fine," I said, waving.

Sonia rolled her eyes and made a playfully impatient face. "Oh, get up here in front, will you?" She slapped the back of the seat with her palm.

▼

Blister's was full of students and young faculty types. The music was loud. Everyone seemed to be having a good time. Two guys signaled Jack from a table near the bandstand, and, when we got to where they were, they both started talking right away, completing each other's sentences. The club was dark. The waitresses wore smart yellow tights. I took a seat at one end of the table and said hello to the guy with extraordinary sideburns, glasses, and a black T-shirt that had "COBOL" block-lettered across the chest.

Jack said, "This is David." He pointed at the guy next to him, then at the one next to me. "Mitch, and Hacker. Mitch, you have to do the women."

"I already did the women," Mitch said, and everybody laughed.

There were three women. One of them said, "Mitch is the art department, so you can forget him. I'm Carmen. That's Mamie, and this one" — she patted the head of the woman sitting next to her — "this one with the blue hair is Lucy."

"Hello, Lucy," I said. Lucy had bright eyes to match the hair, which was brushed back and up in a rooster cut.

"Her name's not really Lucy," Carmen said. "Everybody just calls her that."

"Right," Lucy said. "And I don't mind it, either, because my real name's Alma."

"That's not such a bad name," I said, but when everybody started whistling and hooting I held up my hands and said, "OK, it's horrible."

Mitch leaned across the table and kissed Lucy on the neck, just inside the collar of her shirt.

"A territorial thing," she said, stroking the back of his head.

The waitress brushed her hip against me. I ordered a Stroh's and then listened to two of the women talk about a guy both had had in class. Mitch sat down and put an arm around Jack. Hacker rubbed his nose in tight circles with his knuckle. "I hear you're interviewing. How'd you do?" he said.

"All right, I guess." I wiggled my beer bottle. "The president had some trouble remembering what I was here for, but outside of that it was fine."

"He has trouble remembering what *he*'s here for," Hacker said.

"Laughs," Carmen said.

"He's all right," Lucy said. "So what if he likes plaid? That's his job."

Carmen and Hacker both did slow double takes, and I got the idea that this was their routine.

"You're not biology, are you?" I said to Lucy.

"Poetry," she said. "I teach poetry and comp. Mamie's in social work, and Carmen—what do you do, Carmen?"

"I show the little coeds how to tear up men."

"I think she means phys ed," Lucy said. "How come you're with Jack? Where's Sonia?"

"She's probably doing a little biological research," Carmen said. "She does more research than anybody I know."

"Take a hike, Carmen," Mamie said.

"Carmen doesn't know Sonia," Lucy said, bending the edge of a beer coaster. "Carmen thinks Sonia should be a good little girl like the rest of us."

"At least I don't envy her," Carmen said.

The musicians, who had been sitting at the next table, went onstage, and Carmen and Mamie got up to dance, taking Mitch and Hacker with them. Jack came around to my side of the table and sat next to Lucy. We watched the customers trot out onto the tiny dance floor. A willowy blond guy in a tight emerald muscle shirt and baggy white pants started dancing alone, his eyes closed. The other dancers pulled back to allow him room.

"Who's this?" I asked, bumping Lucy's arm.

"That's Paul. He tried to hang himself from the diving board at the pool next to student housing. He used an electrical cord — one of those big orange ones they sell at the grocery stores now. Some swimming coach got him down. Paul's a very intense kid."

"He looks it," I said, watching him do some kind of wobble-knee step.

"Sure he does," Lucy said, glancing at me and then at the Schlitz clock over the bar. "Everybody says that."

▼

On our way to Sonia's, Jack told me Hacker was a computer whiz. "He does all my financial work for half what I'd pay otherwise. He was Sonia's boyfriend when she got back from Rhodesia. She married this black guy and they moved over there, but he got killed, I think. Something like that. Anyway, he didn't come back. He was an exchange student."

Sonia's apartment was at Palm Shadows North, one of Jack's properties. He told me he had apartments in every major architectural style. These were Tudor — brown wood crisscrossing stucco buildings that were bathed in white light. When we got into the central yard, he pointed at a group of buildings partly hidden by a Japanese rain tree. "Her light's on."

The living room looked like a model in a department store. There was a humpbacked sofa with a matching chair, a big red Oriental urn, a rattan basket with tall dried weeds inside.

Sonia and Burt were in the kitchen.

"Still warm," he said, pointing to a pile of french fries on the counter. He was big, thick through the chest and shapeless from the shoulders down, and young. The tail of his blue police shirt was out, and his black belt was slung over the back of one of

Sonia's bar stools. He stuck out an arm to shake hands. "Burt," he said. "You're David, right?"

"He prefers David," Jack said.

Sonia kept pushing the french fries around in a hat-size pot of cooking oil.

"David," Burt said, repeating himself uncertainly as he shook my hand.

"Either one," I said. I grinned at him. "Doesn't matter."

"We got tired of driving around," Burt said, gripping my shoulder and turning me toward the counter. "We thought we'd make some homemade french fries."

"The first ones burned," Sonia said. "I don't know what I did wrong."

"I told her it was her oil," Burt said. He came up in back of Sonia and patted her rump. She jumped and gave him a look. "Oops," he said. "I think I'd better get the beer. Where's that beer you got?"

I offered to go out to the car, but Burt said he wanted to, and took the keys from Jack. "Which way is it again?" he said from the apartment door. "Out this way?" He pointed off in the wrong direction.

"Straight across the courtyard and make a right past the mailboxes," Jack said. "In the first row, about twenty down."

"Back in a flash," Burt said.

Jack leaned against the counter, staring at Sonia, but she ignored him. "Hi, David," she said. "You doing OK?"

"Fine. We went to Blister's. I met the faculty."

"Oh, yeah? Who?"

"The regulars," Jack said. "So what about Burt?"

"Burt's a vet," Sonia said. "Vietnam. He learned a whole lot about human nature over there. He builds model trains. He likes bicycling, and he's not good in bed."

"Oh, Jesus," Jack said. "Is he married or what?"

"His wife was Rose Queen in his high school pageant. No kids. He says she's OK."

"Is this peanut oil or regular oil?" I said.

"Crisco," Sonia said. She removed the newly browned french fries and rolled them onto paper towels on the countertop. "Salt those, will you?" she said to Jack.

"Just curious," I said.

Sonia patted my arm. "It's a game we play. Actually, I have no idea about his wife, not to mention how he is in bed. My brother, however, likes to think of me as a lady of darkness. So I do the best I can."

"That's cute," Jack said. "Poor kid's probably steaming by now."

"He's doing fine," she said. "Anyway, what about that Puerto Rican girl you liked so much? What was her name—Felicidad?"

Burt opened the front door and shouted, "Beer run." He came into the kitchen carrying the sack with the top rolled over like the top of a lunch bag. His shirt was patterned with coaster-size spots. "I sat in the car a minute waiting for the rain to quit. Then I listened to it on the roof—you know, that old car, the way old cars smell, and here's this rain—thunk, thunk, thunk—you know? It's dark. Nobody's around. So I sit there for a minute, just listening. You know what I'm saying?" He put the bag on the counter and unrolled the top. "Maybe not. Who's thirsty?"

"I'll have one," Jack said, pulling a can out of a six-pack.

"Take off the shirt," Sonia said. "We'll put it in the oven again."

"I'm OK," Burt said. He flapped the tail of his shirt. "It'll dry quick enough."

"Oh, go ahead," Jack said.

Burt shook his head. "Nope." He handed out beer.

Jack took a Kleenex out of the dispenser on top of the refrigerator and wiped off the top of his Coors can, bunching the tissue to clean the can's rim, then put the beer on the counter and wadded the tissue into a ball, rolling it between his palms.

We drank the beer. Jack kept looking at me as if I was supposed to do something. Finally he said, "We still have to get your Budget car out at the school, right?" He pushed off his stool, drained his

THE LAW OF AVERAGES

beer, then flattened the can on the counter. "Right. It's getting late. Time to move."

"It's ten o'clock, Jack," Sonia said. She fluffed his hair. "Although I do have class at eight. I used to like early classes, but I sure don't now."

Burt stuffed his shirttail back into his trousers, wrapped the gun belt around his waist, and put his cap on his head, the visor low over his eyes. "I've got to get on, myself," he said.

We went to the door together, the four of us. Burt was the first outside. "Looks like it's quit again," he said, holding his hands out at his sides.

Sonia followed him out and wrapped her arms around his neck. "Thanks, Burt," she said. "I had fun. Really." She gave Jack a high five as he walked past. "So long, Brother." Then she whispered something else to Burt and let him go. I started to follow them, but Sonia said "Wait a bit" and tugged my coat. Jack and Burt were fifteen feet away. Both turned in our direction.

"You coming, David?" Jack said.

"I don't know," I said.

Burt adjusted his cap, then put his hands on his hips, staring at Sonia, then at me. He was still for a minute, then abruptly turned, waving over his shoulder. "'Night," he said.

"Meet you at the car?" Jack said.

"Take yours, Jack," Sonia said. "I'll run him out to school."

Jack caught Burt halfway across the courtyard, and by the time they made the turn to go past the mailboxes they were laughing. The sound echoed in the yard, which was full of lights bouncing off the wide blades of the yuccas, off the wet bushes. Everywhere there was the sound of dripping water. Sonia put an arm around my waist, and I put an arm around hers, and we stood there watching Jack and Burt. "I like them," she said. "Isn't that strange?"

▼

My presentation to the faculty the next morning went well enough. When an old guy I hadn't met got nasty in the question period, Sonia reminded him, gracefully, that a lot of new work was being done in regenerative plant tissue. "We all understand how hard it is to keep up with the literature, Dr. Holdt," she said. He huffed, and then the meeting broke up. I got a polite round of applause.

Sonia had to stop at the bank on our way to lunch. When we got in line for the Auto Teller, she bumped into the back of a Dodge Polara. "How about seafood, Professor?" she said, watching the driver in front look at who'd hit him.

"How about insurance?" I said.

"I'm sorry about that business with Holdt, but I despise the old balloon."

"He doesn't seem to like you much, either," I said.

"They're used to me," she said. "I'm that way in all the faculty meetings. They don't care, or they're scared, or they just think it's funny. I don't know."

We went to a restaurant called Seafood in the Rough, where the drinks came in glasses shaped like telescopes. She looked at the menu and decided on crab claws.

"If they do the chicken and the fish in the same oil, I want fried chicken," I said.

She called the waiter over and asked about the chicken. He was eighteen and looked like John Travolta, with the wet eyes and the jaw. He liked the trout, only they were out of trout. He was mixed on the chicken and didn't know anything about the oil.

I said, "I thought it was traditional in a place like this."

"No kidding?" he said.

Sonia ordered for both of us and asked him to send the cocktail waitress back. "I've heard of it," she said, when he was gone.

▼

My plane wasn't until seven, so after lunch Sonia took me to Jack's apartment. "I wanted you to see it," she said.

Jack had gone out of town for the weekend. His place was two studios converted into one big apartment, and it smelled like cinnamon and had a lot of furniture. Everything was jumbled together. There was a coffee table with a glass top and an Indian sand painting under the glass, and there were oil paintings of horses — horses standing alongside red-jacketed girls, horses staring into the cramped room, horses with blue ribbons pinned to them. At one end of the living room, there were two sliding doors covered with satiny curtains that almost glowed. Two low, shaded lamps provided a grimy light. I made a face by way of appreciation, and Sonia said, "You like it, right?"

"Yes," I said. "It's dark and mysterious."

She tugged on the curtain so she could look outside. There was some thunder and a flash of lightning, and she jumped away from the window. "It's great out there," she said.

I looked at a brass pot stacked with some other pots next to the wall, then settled on the floor and leaned against the couch. "I don't think I slept enough last night," I said.

She sat on the couch and flicked my hair around with her hand. "Yeah, right. You left really late — maybe ten, ten-thirty. You don't like night, you told me."

"Dumb," I said, nodding at her. "I was exhausted."

She nodded back at me.

"Dumb," I said.

She left her purse on the couch, then stood up right in front of me, close, for a minute. I stared at where her knees were under the skirt, then looked at her shoes, which were red with an open toe and a heel shaped like a funnel. The cinnamon smell was strong. I touched her shoe and she took a step closer, then backed away and went into the bedroom. After a few minutes she appeared again wearing a floor-length black silk robe decorated with red piping and a Chinese dragon — antique and stunning. "You want some

84

space candy?" she said, tearing the top of a bag. She flipped her hair out of the collar of the robe. "I'm nuts for the stuff."

"Me too," I said. "What is it?"

She poured some kernels of the candy into my palm. The candy looked like small gray rocks. "Put them on your tongue," she said.

I did that, and the candy seemed to explode inside my head. "Umm," I said.

"Kids used to have this all the time," Sonia said. "I think they took it off the market or something. Jack's got cases and cases."

She went across the room to a lacquered dressing table that was built out from a huge round mirror. She sat with her back perfectly straight and studied her makeup, and when she combed her hair she did it the way women do in shampoo commercials, dreamily, as if the hair were precious. She was watching me watch her in the mirror. Finally, she slid the comb into a drawer, swiveled around, dropped the robe off her shoulders, and made a little flourish with her hands.

I did a short laugh and said, "Yikes!"

"Yikes?" she said. She raised an eyebrow at me and then, when I didn't move, she looked at herself, brushed her fingers across her breasts, and bent down for the robe, which she folded over her hands in her lap.

"Just something that came to mind," I said. "You're real pretty."

"Thanks." She waited another minute, then shook the robe out and started to put it on. "My idea of a friendly gesture," she said, turning to face the dressing table again.

I got off the floor and went over to her, and we looked at each other in the mirror, and then she laughed and said, "So you want to go to a movie or something?"

"What a wonderful idea," I said.

She slid to one side of the stool so I could sit down, and then she put her head on my shoulder, then kissed my arm, leaving a pair of shiny red lips on my shirtsleeve.

▼

Sonia dropped me off at the Tropic Breeze. She said she'd come back at six to take me to the airport.

"I can get a cab," I said. "I mean, if you're busy."

"I'm not," she said.

The motel was run by a guy named McCoy, who'd told me that his father built it in the fifties. The wood siding had a fresh coat of aquamarine paint, and the trim was done in coral. My room was floor-to-ceiling wood paneling. I spent the afternoon reading a book called *Guide to Coastal Alabama*, which I'd found on the nightstand.

At four I went for a walk. The motel was on a street lined with fast-food restaurants and gas stations, so I didn't go far. It was cool, and there were winds — quick bursts that bent tree limbs and rattled signs. There was a big live oak in among the buildings, next to an abandoned Roy Rogers Roast Beef place, and in it there was a platform tree house with three low walls made out of auto hubcaps. The cars going by had their parking lights on, and the tires still hissed on the road. I wondered how I'd done in the interview, and if I would get the job. A red pickup went by, and the driver honked. I waved, even though I didn't know who it was — it could have been someone from the bar, or somebody who thought I was somebody else. I sat down on a concrete bench at the bus stop and watched the cars.

When I got back to the motel, Sonia was leaning on the wood railing outside my room. She was wearing an ice-blue leotard, a leather flight jacket with a fur collar, and a pair of bulky silver pants like some I'd seen in *TV Guide*.

"I'm early," she said, as I crossed the parking lot toward the stairs.

"I'm lucky," I said.

When I got upstairs, she was standing by the door holding a miniature dumbbell in each hand.

"What's this?" I said.

"I've been working out," she said. "I always carry these things in my car." She did a couple of demonstration curls, first one hand and then the other, her breasts popping under the thin fabric. "This place looks like a golf course. I've never been here before." She lifted her head to indicate the colored boards McCoy had around his flower beds.

I nodded and pointed toward the office. "I think the owner likes it here."

She held the dumbbells over her head and then slowly lowered her arms until they were fully extended straight out from her shoulders. "You lift?"

McCoy came out of his glass office wearing caramel-and-white saddle oxfords and high white pants with a thin cordovan belt that seemed to be twisted in the loops. He looked as if he'd just shaved —his skin was smooth and sunburn-red. He had moles that looked like erasers on his left cheek. "What's this?" he said. He looked at me, then licked his finger and tapped it on the burning tip of his cigar.

"This is personal stuff," Sonia said. She dropped the weights onto the balcony. "We're talking about getting you a rocket ship for your place here."

He beamed and looked at the grounds of his motel. "I wanted to bring in some living animals, something like that, but the city wouldn't let me. They got rules."

She nodded, and he wagged a hand, got a newspaper from the orange rack by the door, and went inside.

"He likes you," I said.

She rolled her eyes, then grabbed me by the lapel of my jacket and pulled me inside. "C'mon. I'm a knockout with a motel room."

"Right," I said.

I unlocked the door, and we went in. "How come everything's in the middle? Open plan making a comeback?"

I'd moved the bed away from the wall. I always do that when I stay in motels. It hadn't seemed strange to me until she came in and started looking at it.

She walked a circle around the bed. "Maybe you should get some spotlights in here." She sat on the couch that was covered with a Mexican-style rug. "So where were you? Did you call me?"

"I went to see the sights."

"Smooth," she said. "That's the professor in you. Me, I was lonely." She dropped the leather jacket on the seat beside her, then straightened the Danskin over her belly. "I almost hit somebody in a parking lot." She turned to look out the window. "Shut the door, will you? So are you taking the job? You've got it. I talked to Stibert."

I said, "I'll take it." I shoved the door closed and sat on the edge of the bed, facing her.

We grinned at each other for a minute, and then she grabbed a handful of the silver material bunched around her knee and said, "You ever see these things? They make you look so stupid, but they work. I lost two pounds. I had to send away for them." She pressed the fabric into folds that she traced up and down her thighs. "I usually go through pants pretty quick, but these dudes are endless."

NOBODY LEFT TO TELL

▲　▼　▲

EXPORT

"RIGHT NOW you're what I'd call marginal," Mariana Nassar said. We were standing alongside a Dumpster she was painting yellow. It was about noon. I had spent the morning cleaning my apartment, and I'd come out with a plastic bag stuffed with garbage. She poked the bag with her brush. "That about a week's worth?"

"Breakfast," I said, pulling the bag away from her.

Mariana was forty, and looked half of it. She owned a small apartment complex where I'd lived with my first wife, so when the second marriage went I rented an apartment from her. She was wearing khaki shorts and a lime-green tube top, and she was prettier than I remembered.

I angled my bag into the mouth of the Dumpster.

"We're painting this thing yellow," she said. "We think that'll make it more attractive to passersby. On this thoroughfare here." She looked up and down the alley, then balanced her brush across the lip of the can. "You ready for our big talk?"

We went into the courtyard and sat down by the pool. She sat on the edge, dangling her legs in the pale blue water. I took a chair.

"So, Henry," she said, watching her feet distort in the ripples. "You got trouble. Just like old times. Have I got it straight—your first wife stole your second?"

"And my child," I said. "You don't know Rachel, do you?"

"No," Mariana said. She rocked her hips and edged backward a little, then lifted her legs out of the water. "So we're working on tactics right at the moment."

"Right," I said.

The water glittered and shone as breezes got its surface. Mariana sighed and slapped the water with her feet. "What's our worst case?"

"I get a new start."

"Whoopee," she said, turning to look at me over her shoulder.

I grinned. "You busy or anything?"

She laughed and pulled her knees up, putting her feet on the pool ledge. She wiggled her toes. "But what are you doing to these women? How come they like each other better than you? Looks like you need some high-quality advice." She got up, stretched, then slid her hands into her back pockets.

I got up, too. "I remember. You gave me a lot of high-quality advice when Clare left. You told me to go get her."

"My John Wayne period. Doesn't work in the new world." She slapped my stomach with the back of her hand. "First, we got to lose a little of this. Then, something about the hair—what is that, a Bruce Dern makeover? And the pants, Henry. It's the eighties, right? We don't have to wear jeans anymore. We can get some regular pants. Maybe a shirt with some kind of color, or pattern, or something. And we can get our things dry-cleaned, you know? Give us a crisp look. There's a lot to do here." She walked in circles around me, pulling at my clothes, poking me with stiff fingers.

"This touching stuff—is this part of the treatment?"

She pinched a section of my shirt. "You're still doing all cotton, right? Right. But—what color is this, anyway?"

"White," I said.

"Just kidding. Just playing around. Actually, you don't look bad at all." She stopped right in front of me and tapped my lips with her fingers. "Spread 'em."

"What?" I started backing away from her.

She came after me, matching my steps, laughing and clicking one of her long, clear fingernails on her front teeth. "Gums," she said. "Open up. Open up."

▼

We drove to the mall, the fish market, then a shop across town that was having a sale on French shoes. As we were leaving the shoe store, a deaf-mute came up selling ballpoint pens. I gave him a dollar and got a red pen with a small flag attached to its clip. Mariana said, "There's your problem right there, Henry. Couldn't be more clear."

"Habit," I said. I watched the guy go down the sidewalk toward the A&P. "You don't want to make too much of it."

"Question of style. You're a born pussycat."

"I'm gonna pussycat you. You want me to get the dollar back?" I turned around and took a couple of steps toward the guy with the pens.

"Eek, eek," she said, putting her hands on her hips. She gave me her bored-to-death look and then spun around and started for the car.

I followed her across the faded blacktop. "I was going to take my dollar back from the pen guy," I said, getting into the car.

"We noticed that. They got you coming and going, don't they?"

"Who?"

"Never mind. Forget it." She reached across and knocked on the dashboard in front of me. "Hand me that pistol out of the glove box, will you?"

"I'll *bet* you've got a gun in here." I released the latch and peered into the compartment. There was a gun in it.

"Just kidding," she said. "It's not loaded. It doesn't even work. Don't worry."

I rolled my eyes, but she wasn't looking, she was backing the car out of its slot, so I waited until she turned around and I rolled my eyes again.

"Saw it the first time," she said. "Why don't you just take it easy here awhile, huh? Kind of ride along, enjoy the scenery — you know, relax. I don't think you're doing so bad. I mean, you could've lost an arm instead of a wife, somebody could've been killed, big shootout over to the One Hour, you know what I mean? You could've been caught with some little Twinkie friend of your daughter's — "

"Never touched her," I said. "I swear."

"There it is again," Mariana said, taking her hands off the wheel and holding them up, palms forward, in front of her. "Maybe you should have jumped her, showed her who's boss. Show the wife. Might be fun."

I found a St. Christopher medal behind the gun in the glove compartment. I brought the medal out to look at. Mariana stopped too close to a traffic light and had to lean forward to see it out of the windshield. "So can we change the subject now?" I said.

She grinned and slapped me on the thigh. "We're just getting started, Bucko. We've got restless nights in the apartment. One after another in a long, endless parade — get that? Long and end-less, both of those. We got daytime in the kitchen with four red plastic pebble-finish glasses that you bought because they seemed sensible. We got light in there looks like it's trying to kill you. It's ordinary light, coming in windows and stuff, but it's so dusty and dry it's gonna soak you right up off the face of the planet." She switched lanes very quickly, slipping in in front of a mustard-colored BMW. "So then you put on the radio and what comes out is high school, real soft and sexy. You switch on the lights just to get some red into the room. You get a lot of cupped-up breasts in your mind, from the music, so you put on a record. But the record is old and reminds you of something, or it's new, and hip, and you bought it at Eckerd's drugstore."

"But I've got the light going," I said.

"The light's no better," she said. "You burn up the TV, trying to get some color into the place, but nothing works. It's a desert in there. You're a thousand miles away, like the song. You ache. You get a woman in, and she smells funny. I mean, she doesn't really smell funny, she just smells funny to you. You tell her that, and she gets mad."

I pointed to the speedometer. "We've got a thirty-mile zone here."

She took her foot off the accelerator and let the car coast until the orange pointer got down to forty.

"So this woman packs up and leaves in a hurry. The apartment looks like the inside of a Bake-O-Matic body shop at full tilt, and you're in the bedroom with this smell in the sheets and the light looking medical, and you got in your head this picture of a sweet-smelling girl you danced with about twenty years ago on the lawn of a rich kid's house. It's a misty night, fall — cold and sparkly, with the patio lights putting tree-trunk shadows across the grass — and this soft girl is up close, her mouth in your neck, and she says something, or you think she says something, so you ask her 'What?' and she rocks her head back and forth, pulling her lips up over the lobe of your ear, and says 'Uh-huh' in a voice that feels like a little bit of warm water going down your legs — "

I put a hand over Mariana's mouth. "I get the picture."

She struggled a little, then playfully slumped forward onto the wheel. The car veered off to one side, narrowly missing a blue mail-box that seemed to come out of nowhere. Mariana spun the wheel, yelled a muffled "Jesus," and sat up, all at once. "Don't mess with the driver," she said when we were going smoothly again.

"Sorry," I said. "I had to stop you."

"Stop me what? I was dramatizing your plight. I was working."
She looked at me, and I looked at the car's headliner. "So what are
you telling me — that you don't want to go back?"

I rolled down my window and adjusted the outside rearview
mirror. "Not a good question," I said, closing my window again.

"Yeah, yeah, yeah. You want to answer anyway?"

Her blouse had come unbuttoned. I could see the curve of the
bottom of her breast and the line above it where her tan cut across
the pale skin.

She caught me looking. "So what's the answer, Henry?" she
said, buttoning the shirt with one hand.

"Don't know," I said.

She nodded and pushed the hair up and away from her fore-
head. "I thought so. All the men say that. The women don't say
that at all, see — that's the thing."

I shook my head.

"Sure it is," she said. "You got girls flying away in droves, cat-
erwauling — going away as if shot from guns is what I mean." She
illustrated by wagging her hands in circles and then batting them
into each other. "Love doesn't know your name, fella. You've got a
serious problem here, and you're thinking levelheaded's gonna
get it." She turned to inspect a guy who had pulled up alongside
us at the light in a GMC truck. I watched him realize she was look-
ing him over. He was rubbing his neck, and when he saw her he
raised his eyebrows a fraction and, at the same time, dropped his
head, acknowledging her attention.

I couldn't see what kind of look she gave the guy, but after he'd
done his hello there was a pause, then a smile spread slowly over
his face. He looked away, then past her to me, then at her again.
His smile turned into a chuckle.

"He's about a two," Mariana said, still looking at the guy.

"You'd better quit, or he'll run that truck up on the back of here
and start two-ing you," I said. "What are you doing?"

She turned around. "Practicing." She twisted the wheel back

and forth. "Where was I?" After the light changed she started fast to get the jump on the guy in the truck. "Oh, yeah. I was helping you. I was being seductive."

I squinted at her. "That's very flattering," I said, but it didn't sound right, so I said, "That's nice."

"You're welcome," she said.

She propped her elbow on the door and her head on her hand, and drove more slowly. I looked out the window at the hamburger places, fried-fish places, barbecue places. An old guy with a bicycle decked out like a five-and-dime wheeled by on our right with one of his two overcoats tied up into a cowl over his head and a small TV strapped with duct tape to the handlebars on his bike. I reached over and touched Mariana's shoulder.

She shrugged my hand off and then laughed, a lovely short laugh that flickered over her face and ended in a small, tight smile for me. "Yes," she said. "We have decided to take your case. Our people will be in touch with your people. Not to worry."

▼

We took an eighteen-passenger flight to Brownsville, then rented a car at the airport and drove over to Port Isabel, a coast town in extreme south Texas. We went for the weekend. There were palm trees lining the highway. People pulled carts in the dirt alongside the road. Very quaint. Mexico was about twenty-five minutes away. The rain was thick and blue, falling constantly, relentlessly, as it had done since we left home. I had called Rachel to tell her I was going out of town to think things over. Rachel said, "That's what I'm supposed to tell Mom?"

When we got into Port Isabel, we dropped our bags in the lobby of the Alamo Hotel and went for a drink at a club called the Tim Tam, which was full of prostitutes. They were dancing together, circling clumsily in dots of light from a fifties beer-advertising display. We drank Superior and watched the women dance.

Mariana said, "How about this one?" She indicated a woman in a black sheath slit over the hip. "You want us to wrap her up for you, Henry?" She fiddled with the thick chips in a gold basket on the table.

"Maybe we should walk around, see the town," I said. I glanced out the yellow saloon-style doors at the rain. "No, I guess we shouldn't."

"We can run to the hotel, if you want."

One of the women we had been staring at, not the one in black, came to the table and leaned on the third chair. She had on elbow-length gloves and a T-shirt with no sleeves. Her nipples were large circles against the shirt. "This your first time?" She glanced around at the little bar, which was dark and used-looking. "Ain't much, is it? Good against rain and not much else. I'm saying we got a perfect roof, though. Tight as a drum." She waved at the ceiling.

"Just taking a look," Mariana said.

"That's what I see. I'm Felice." She winked at me. "I figured you weren't — you know, customers, in the usual sense of that term."

Mariana said, "My name is Mariana. This is Henry. We just got here. For the weekend."

"Uh-huh. And you ain't Texas, are you? I can tell Texas-born. Except Houston. Those folks always sound like they're from L.A., or either Michigan. One of the two."

I said, "We're at the hotel a couple of blocks over here." I pointed toward where I thought the hotel was.

"Are you, now?" Felice said. "The Alamo. I've been in there. Seen some of my better days there, matter of fact. You kids having another beer?"

We thanked her and said no, and she thanked us and said to keep her in mind, business-wise. We said that we would, and then all three of us laughed.

▼

The hotel was a six-story brick building on a square that opened on its fourth side to a seedy little dock where people got boat rides. The trees in the square were tall, but they had thin trunks. The man behind the hotel desk was Hawkins. He had a built-up black shoe on his left foot, and a back about twenty degrees off the vertical. We had used Mariana's card to register, so he called me "Mr. Nassar."

Alongside the desk, a sleepy-looking girl about twenty was shaking a clear plastic rain hat. She said, "Sweet Jesus. He's really after me this time."

"Who is?" Hawkins was staring at the wall of slots behind the desk, trying to find our key.

The girl grinned at Mariana, then at me. "Him," she said, pointing up. "Big Guy. It ain't rained like this since I was a kid in love with Rodney Beauchamp. I did naughty things for Rodney Beauchamp in his pickup — he was the football captain at my school. The Big Guy rained on me nearly a month. On that occasion."

Hawkins introduced us. "This is Mr. and Mrs. Nassar. Mariana and — is it Henry? Henry. Meredith Rotel. Meredith does the night work on the desk here. She's a local girl."

"Eighty-percent local," Meredith said. "The rest of me's entirely rayon."

I signaled hello, and Mariana stepped around toward the side of the desk to shake the girl's hand.

Hawkins wiggled his head back and forth as if to dismiss Meredith's remark. "She'll run you ragged if you give her a chance. Won't you, Meredith? Don't ask her about hot spots, whatever you do."

"I'm the hottest spot I know," Meredith said. She flapped the collar of her printed shirtwaist. "Only at the moment I ain't so hot. More wet, like."

"Well, I guess we'll be talking to you," Mariana said, grinning at the girl. "I want to hear more about the pickup."

"Me too," I said.

Mariana slapped my chest. "Settle down there, pard."

We got the key and squeezed into the elevator. The trim was brass and badly stained, and there was some kind of AstroTurf on the walls. We got off on the third floor and found our room, which was large and sour-smelling, with two windows overlooking the square. I took a chair by one of the windows and cocked my feet up on the radiator.

Mariana sat on the bed. "We shouldn't have gone to the bar first thing, right? So I think what I'll do is shower and take it easy for a bit." She unbuttoned the front of her blouse, then its cuffs. She pulled her suitcase onto the bed and popped it open, bringing out a plain leather travel kit. She loosened her belt, then stood by the bathroom door, one hand on the frame. "Well," she said, straightening her blouse with her free hand. "We could just forget it if that's what you want. I think it'll get better, but it's no big deal."

"It's a fair-size deal, isn't it? It's not routine — maybe for you, not me."

"Oh, heck yes," she said, turning away, entering the bathroom. "I come here all the time. I always come here. I was here last week with this guy who plays pro hockey."

"Sorry," I said.

She looked back into the room and waved off the apology, then closed the door.

I sat in the chair and scanned the square, listening to the water sizzling in the bathroom. Somebody knocked at the door. I answered, and a big guy in a khaki uniform introduced himself — C. E. "Fred" Corbett, sheriff of Olympia County. He was six-five, easily. I nodded at his badge and then invited him in, but he stayed in the hall. "You Joseph Butcher?" he said.

I said I wasn't. When he asked for identification I gave him my wallet.

"Vacation?" he said. "Or business?"

"We're having a small vacation. Just a weekend."

He was like a giant William Bendix, with the slablike jaw and the limp mouth. He glanced up and down the corridor. "You met any people here, staying here?"

"We met the desk guy and a girl who works nights — Meredith. That's all."

He handed me my wallet and stuck his hands in his jacket pockets. "Fine. Thanks. Sorry to bust in."

I said, "I wish I could help you," then waited for him to move away from the door before closing it, only he didn't move. "Is there something else?" I asked.

"Nope. You can go ahead and shut her down. We appreciate your cooperation." He smiled but didn't move.

It was awkward closing the door in his face, but there wasn't anything else to do, so I did. When it was shut, I locked it and stood there, listening. For a minute I heard nothing, then I heard his boots shuffle away, and then the sound of his knock next door.

Mariana stuck her head out of the bathroom. "Who was that?"

I was still facing the door, bent forward. "He said he was the sheriff. I sure was glad to see him, too. I'm just glad I'm not Tuesday Weld, or I'd be in real trouble right about now." I went back to my chair. "How did we dig up this place?"

She stepped into the room with a hotel towel pressed against her chest. "Sheriff? I don't believe you."

"He had a badge and everything. I checked it out. I was tough on him, studied the badge. It was a star on something that looked like a horseshoe — it wasn't a horseshoe, but it was shaped like that." I drew the shape in the air. "It had those balls on the star points."

"So he wouldn't hurt himself." She lifted her wet hair, pushed it back above her ear.

"Well," I said, slapping the arm of the chair and then standing. "I'm ready for the big checkout. Find a Holiday Inn or something. Down by the beach — which way is the beach? Over here?" I pointed toward the square.

"Don't be silly. Just because a single sexually potent peace officer knows where we are?" She made a face and came across the room. "Wait a minute. I didn't mean that the way it sounded."

When she was ready, we went out hunting for a restaurant. Meredith suggested Motor Bill's, a seafood house two or three blocks away, along the harbor. "It's my type of a place," she said. "Kind of a more natural atmosphere."

It was a pretty evening. There were people in the street, even though it was still sprinkling. They were walking in twos and threes, enjoying themselves. The sky was a breathtaking silver. We were about half a block from the hotel when the square suddenly filled up with police cars. They slid around corners and out of alleys, without sirens, engines sounding like wind as they accelerated, then stopped hard and diagonal in the street, their top lights flicking the buildings with reds and blues. People started gathering in a circle around the Alamo's entrance canopy. The streetlamps were already on, dropping freezing green circles of light on the pavement. Across the small square, pleasure boats pulled dully at their ropes.

We went back and joined the people in front of the hotel. I heard someone say that somebody was the daughter of a Latin who ran the largest rancho in Panama. Two other guys were talking about a business deal. One said, "Hey, the deal is cut, I'm just down here for the signature," and the other said, "Sure you are. And they're talking about sending you to Cairo. That must be swell."

The cops stayed on either side of the hotel, next to their cars, lights still swiveling, flashing. They seemed less concerned with us than with the park and the street. We were in a circle, but there wasn't anything at the center, so I guessed we were waiting for somebody. I said to a small man in a gray chalk-striped suit, "What's the story?"

The guy turned and looked at me, then at Mariana. I put my arm around her. He said, "Out of town?"

"Right," I said. "What's this about?"

"Nothing for you to worry with," he said. His tie had a gold clip in the shape of a musical note about three quarters of the way down. He fingered the clip as he talked to us. "It's a local situation. You're visiting, so you've got no reason to worry." He took a business card from his vest pocket and handed the card to Mariana. "I am Muhal Richard Cisco. Export. If I can help, please call me. Don't hesitate."

I peeked over Mariana's shoulder at the card, which had on it his name and a ten-digit phone number. Nothing else. Then a tall Mexican guy whispered something to Cisco, who eyed us as he listened, nodding and patting the tall guy's arm. A squinchy kid in high white pants and sparkling red shoes pushed his way out through the hotel's revolving door. He stayed close to the building. Several people from the group pressed forward, closing around him. They talked nervously, several at once, until the tall guy who had been with Cisco handed the kid some folding money, a lot of it, and the kid managed a toothy grin and slipped back into the hotel.

Mariana said, "I'm thinking maybe you were right about this place. Shall we go?"

We crossed the square and walked down along the dock until we found the restaurant Meredith recommended. It was a tiny wood-frame building with a tile floor, bum furniture, and plastic tablecloths decorated with farm animals. We sat in a corner under a hanging jade plant that was on its last leg. Our table butted up against a window that had been painted brown, but a couple of fist-size peepholes had been scratched in the paint. Outside, there was a timber dock that had three white rowboats tied to it. A guy wearing a full-length apron over an undershirt came out of the back of the restaurant and said something to the girl who had seated us, then brought over two bond-paper menus sleeved in plastic.

Mariana ordered fried scallops, and I said I'd try the snapper. The guy took our menus and disappeared back through the swinging doors, each of which had a half circle of dirty glass in it.

There weren't any other customers. On the opposite wall there was a kind of altar — a black sombrero surrounded by photographs, palm leaves, statues, a rosary made of nuggets of red glass, airplane postcards, other stuff. Mariana got up to take a look. I watched the boats through the scratched brown window. Coming back, she said, "So what do you say, Henry?"

"It's sweaty for my taste," I said. "Colorful, but sweaty. We could go out where the rest of the tourists are, wherever that is."

"It's not like I remember it, that's true. That guy was probably just a lottery guy — the kid, I mean."

She slid her jacket off her shoulders onto the spindles of the ladder-back chair. Outside, I saw the man in the apron trot past the boats and around the corner of a rusted steel shed. I waited for him to come back. When he did, he was carrying a stack of white containers like those used for takeout food. Two Mexican kids wearing khaki pants and open shirts ran alongside him, talking and gesturing. I said, "I think Motor Bill just ran out and picked up dinner."

Mariana leaned across the table to see, but the guy was out of sight.

The kids were about thirteen, Rachel's age — maybe a little older. They came in from the kitchen laughing, then saw us and got very quiet as they sat down at a wobbly table. The guy who had taken our order came out and said something in Spanish to the boys, and they screeched their chairs across the floor and followed him into the back.

The food was served on colored plates — mine was peach, Mariana's was lime — and it wasn't bad. She kept telling me to slow down, that I was eating too fast. Out the window I saw the Mexican kids running along the pier away from the restaurant carrying garbage bags twisted down to the size of footballs. The undershirt guy came out to see how things were going.

"Very tangy," Mariana said. "I love the butter sauce."

"Thank you," the guy said. "You would like to have a jar of

pulque? I have a pulque that you would never forget in a thousand years."

"He's going to get us on the flies," I said, half muttering.

The guy heard me and didn't think it was funny. He swatted at the next table with a dish towel he carried over his arm, then put on a too-polite smile. "You do not have to drink the pulque, my friend. I have only offered it to the lady who you are with. If she does not want the pulque, then I am sure that she will not have it."

"I think I won't, today," Mariana said, smiling at the guy. She dabbed at the corners of her mouth with her napkin. "But thank you very much. It's kind of you."

"You are welcome," he said, and he bowed at the waist, giving us a view of the top of his head, where a scab the size of a quarter was tucked in under the damp hair.

When he was gone I apologized. "Uncontrollable urge. The flies, I mean. It was stupid. It just leapt out. I'm covered with embarrassment."

"You're gonna be covered with pulque if you don't settle down."

The guy put a guitar record on an old turntable propped up behind the bar, but the music was hard to listen to because a CB radio cut in and out. Mariana turned around and smiled at the guy anyway.

We finished dinner pretty quick and went back out into the drizzle. Mariana had her hair pulled back tight to her scalp. Drops of the mist settled in the wiry hair above her forehead, making her younger and prettier. She took my arm and steered us down a crooked street lined on either side with buildings painted hot, chalky colors. The cars were parked crazily, in the road and up on the sidewalk. At first, we climbed around them, then we gave up and took to the middle of the street. I was watching my feet when the two Mexican kids appeared out of a low doorway and asked us if we wanted to buy vegetables. Very fresh, they assured us.

I was all ready to say no when Mariana said yes. She got out her wallet and gave one kid a five-dollar bill, while the second kid ducked back into the doorway and fetched one of the garbage bags I'd seen them with earlier. The bag was green and a little bit transparent, and through it I could make out carrots and round things that might have been peppers or red onions. Mariana took the bag and peered down into it, then grinned at the kids. "Terrific," she said. "Wonderful. Thank you."

They thanked her in Spanish and vanished through a royal-blue door.

We went on walking, arm in arm, along the curving, sloping road. The rain was so light I could barely feel it, but I was getting cold. "This goes down to the Gulf. That's what we want?"

"I want to play cards in bed tonight," Mariana said. "I love to do that. It slows everything down."

My heel skidded on a badly set paving stone, and I would have fallen on my face if she hadn't held me up with her arm. "I'm ready when you are," I said, freeing myself. "I need to get me a pink suit and duck shoes to walk around down here."

▼

Saturday morning I went down to the lobby and called Rachel. She didn't sound happy to hear from me. I asked about her mother, and about what was happening, and so on, and her answers were terse — single words. Finally, I said, "What's wrong here? What are you mad about?"

"Oh, nothing. Only, where are you? What are you doing down there? Who's with you?"

"Texas, nothing, and for me to know," I said. "I'm just taking some time off." Hawkins was about twenty feet away, behind his desk, stealing glances at me.

"You're taking a ride on the Reading, is what you're taking. I suggest you get your story together. What am I supposed to say to Mom?"

"I told her what I was doing," I said.

"Yes. And she told me, but she's not dumb about it."

I waited a second, then said, "This is great. I feel lousy, so I call you up, and what I get is worse than what I started with. Thanks a lot."

"So jump a plane. I'll set it up for you."

I found a wad of grape-colored gum somebody had stuck to the wooden wing of the telephone enclosure. "I'll be back tomorrow afternoon," I said. "You can take me out to dinner."

"What if I don't want to?" I didn't answer that, and she waited for a few seconds, then said, "OK. Sorry. Tell me how big a deal this is. I mean, what's the correct level of anxiety for a child like me?"

"You could probably guess. I'm calling you up in the middle of it. Not high."

"Good," she said, her voice softening. "In that case, go ahead and have a really wonderful time."

"Thanks, amigo," I said. We hung up, and I sat there for a while, feeling better.

It was still raining when we got the car out of the shed-like garage and drove out to the beach for lunch. Mariana was driving and being quiet. I stared out the window. I liked the desolate, broken-down look of things. The land was empty, and, in spite of the rain, I could see that it stretched miles in all directions. We passed a big shallow hill that was a field full of wrecked cars, and around the cars there were black-and-white cows grazing and birds strutting quickly in the rain. I knotted my hands together and grinned at how lovely that was. We made a turn onto a road that was straight and thin to the horizon. The palms that staked either side were a hundred yards apart and forty feet tall, curved by the wind.

Mariana glanced around, then turned back to the highway. "Feeling better?"

"I called home. Rachel wanted to know about you. I didn't tell her."

"Oh. Not feeling better. I see." She changed her position behind the wheel, then curled her fingers around her hair, dragging it away from her face. "Do you want to go back today?"

I watched a truck in the rearview mirror on my side of the car. "No. I don't think so. We've got cards to play. You think I'm letting you get away with the big winner?"

"No," she said. "I don't."

She turned and smiled at me—a wry, sad smile that made me long for her and for other things. I started to cry and covered it by looking out the window at the stiff trunks of the trees and the delicate grass and the helmet-like sky. The tires ran on the highway, and the windshield wipers clacked, and I waited a minute before I faced Mariana again.

"Easy," she said, reaching to circle her hand around my wrist.

PUPIL

EACH SUMMER I teach a course in BASIC at the junior college. This year Tracy Whitten is my favorite student. She's eighteen — bright, handsome, cheerful all the time. I like her braces. She's self-conscious about them, always remembering a minute too late to keep her lips tightly closed. She comes to class in shorts and a T-shirt, perspiration glinting at her temples, and we talk, her eyes darting around as if we ought to be more discreet.

By the fourth week of the session I'm so taken with her I'm ready to break the rules. In the hall, after class, I say, "Maybe you could come for dinner? I'll ask some other people. We can cook out."

"Oh, sure," she says, giving me a look that means maybe I'd better think again. "That'd be real suave."

We walk down the corridor without talking, then go outside and stop near the bike rack. "I'm sorry I mentioned it," I say, making a show of looking for my car in the parking lot. "Well, not really sorry."

She smiles, wires glittering, then turns away and looks out over the baseball practice field. Today she's wearing pale pink running shorts, the shiny kind, and a thin Jack-in-the-Box T-shirt, and she's tapping her key on the rack, so there's a pinging sound in the air.

Finally, she turns around and gives me a squinty look. "I wouldn't mind coming, if you're serious."

"I am serious." That sounds too serious, so I try for a Chevy Chase joke with some stupid faces, wondering how I could have been silly enough to start this.

"Take it easy, will you? Calm down. Let me think." She watches me and does some faces that look good on her. "We know it's not a great idea. We both know that, right? It's destructive and impossible, and you're too old, and it's bad PR."

"My specialty," I say.

She studies me for a second, then she's all smiles — patting my arm, straightening her hair, ready to walk away. "I like it. I'll come. We'll have a good time. Where is it?"

▼

I have two bedrooms, a large living room with lots of glass, and a small garden — a side-by-side duplex, one of a hundred and ten similar units in a development that has four pools and no cleverly winding paths. I'm used to it. Not so much that it feels like home but enough so that I can overlook, most of the time, the utilitarian way of things. Sometimes I even think it's pretty.

Saturday I go out and buy a barbecue cooker and the tools that go with it — tongs, a giant fork, hot-pad gloves that look like alligators. For dinner I decide to go with chicken, so I spend some time at the A&P, figuring out chicken. By late afternoon I'm set up on the deck at my apartment, watching the cooker and waiting for Tracy. There's a lot of smoke around, because I've used too many mesquite chips.

I've only been out a few minutes when the doorbell rings. I go through the house to answer it, and Tracy's there with a guy about forty who has a clean face and pink skin. He's wearing black jeans.

"Hi," she says, moving her hand in a robot-like way between me and her friend. "This is George, and this is Ray. Ray's my brother, but he's really more like a pal, aren't you, Ray?"

"Sure am," he says, and we shake hands. Ray's got a soft, smooth hand and a putty-like grip.

Tracy's hair looks as if it's still wet from washing. She's got on baggy linen pants and a yellow Hawaiian shirt. She comes in first, almost bouncing, and Ray follows, giving my apartment the once-over.

I go into the kitchen to get them drinks—beer for Ray, Tab for Tracy, glasses for both of them—and I cut my finger on the pop-top of the Tab can, so I have to excuse myself while I go get a Band-Aid. When I return they're already out on the deck. Ray waves at the yard. "Pretty," he says.

I look at the yard, which is small and brown.

He says, "I didn't know there was so much socializing—you know, teachers and students—out at the college."

"Sure," says Tracy. "All the time."

"There isn't much," I say. "It's frowned on."

"Yeah," he says, nodding. "That's what I thought. I saw this thing on TV about some trouble they've been having out in California. Arrests, you know..." He gives Tracy a glance that she, bless her heart, refuses to share. She's smiling, taking in the scenery.

"I like this," she says. "This is a nice apartment." She wipes the bottom of her Tab can down the thigh of her pants.

My neighbors are in the yard working on their bulb garden. They're a young couple with a new baby, and they have a dime-store coat of arms—a painted wood shield with "THE HERNDONS" across the top, "ESTABLISHED 1977" across the bottom, and a duck in the middle—displayed next to their front door.

"Not much privacy," Tracy says, motioning toward the couple. "What are they doing there, anyway? Looks like they're burying something."

"Bulbs," I say.

They've been working on the garden since midwinter. It's a mound, like a grave—a dog's, or a child's. They roughed up the ground and then dumped a foot of bag-dirt on top. That's where they put the bulbs. None of the flowers ever showed up.

Ray says, "Listen, we don't need to be real nervous about me coming over here. It's just a formality. She's a full-grown woman. You're both grown. That's my feeling."

"Oh, Raymond," Tracy says. She turns to me. "Ray's worried about me growing up and all that. He feels bad about it." She looks at her watch, a heavy gold Timex. "How long have these chickens been on here?"

"Well," he says. "You're my sister."

The chickens are reddish brown. I'm ready for Tracy and Ray to leave, to call the whole thing off, so I stare at the chickens and say, "I'm probably out of line." I look at him, asking for some understanding. "I slipped up, OK? Maybe we ought to—"

"Hey!" Ray says. "Hold on. Don't get me wrong. I don't mind. She's a girl, you're a boy—you look OK. Hell, you look like a million to me." He does a broad smile and pats my forearm.

Tracy shakes her head. "Oh, jeez. Raymond? I mean, we're not at home, OK?"

Ray shrugs, waving his hands around. "No more king of the dorks, huh? Well, I can't go anywhere. Helene's picking me up."

"Helene's about twelve," Tracy says.

She wraps her arms around his neck, and he pretends he doesn't like it, picking them off. "How can a person function with you all over him?"

"You wish." She grins and pushes off. "Ray's always ready to do some pretty powerful functioning."

Ray blushes, says, "That's your idea, you and Billy Hunter. He tells everybody he's helping out his secretary, and then he helps her a lot in his office."

"Billy," Tracy says, explaining to me. "One of Ray's close, close friends. He's a happening guy. I hope he catches his rear on a linoleum knife." She rattles the ice in her glass. "Anybody want soda?"

She goes in, leaving us staring at the cooker. "She's touchy," Rays says. He looks over his shoulder, trying to see into the house. "But at least she doesn't think as soon as anything bad happens it's because men run things. I told her it's ideas—all you have to do is have the good ideas. Right?"

"It helps," I say.

"Sure it does," he says. "I mean, if it ain't great, who cares who's running it?"

"Right," I say.

"Take you, for example. You've got something going. I mean, she's pretty, she's young—all that time in front of her, all this stuff to learn. Listen, I understand you college boys. You got women out there in Kmart underpants, guys belong in the zoo—you can't make much of that. I mean—" He waits a second, thinking about it, scratching the back of his head. "I mean, if you're going to have a romance it ought to at least be lovely."

He thinks some more, smoothing his hair where it's standing up from the scratching. "This deal's sweet. It's a little bit stupid, but it's sweet."

I take off the cooker top and wave it back and forth trying to clear the smoke. Flames jump up under the chickens.

"Know what I'm saying?" he says.

I nod at him, then turn back to the cooker. "I'm doing these by the book, the 'indirect' method. Every time I open it I get all this fire."

"So close it," he says, taking a look at the chickens, which are getting black and crusty. "You better get those suckers off before they turn to dirt." He reaches out to wiggle one of the drumsticks, and it comes off in his hand. "If I were you I'd submerge 'em for half an hour."

Tracy sticks her head out the door. "Ray? Your wealthy friend is here. This car goes by about three times, checking out the place. You want me to get her?"

"Why don't you work the chickens," Ray says. "George can get her."

▼

Outside, the sky is thunder-gray except in the west, where there's a ribbon of coral at the horizon. There's a fresh breeze, and the streetlamps are on, and there's a dampness about the way everything looks. Helene is easy to spot. She's in a brilliant red 318i about half a block down from the apartment. I signal to her and, when she pulls up, introduce myself.

"Ray's inside," I say. "He asked me to come get you."

She's in her twenties, wearing a sleeveless knit cotton top and white shorts, and her arms are tan, muscular. I notice a blue vein that runs over her biceps and down her inner arm. It's prominent, easy to see.

"You must be kidding," she says. "Where's his truck?"

"What truck? He has a truck?"

"Sure does," she says. "A purple eighteen-wheeler. Lots of yellow lights."

I'm standing in the street alongside her car, scanning the parking lots as she describes these lights.

"They're great at night," she says. "He's always leaving the truck going, and you can hear it, even inside, and you look out and all the lights are sparkling—you've got to see it."

I look up and down the road. Nobody's out, but there are cars jammed up behind other cars in the head-in parking spaces. Everybody's having company. I stretch out my arms and say, "I don't know, but Ray *is* inside, with his sister Tracy."

"How do I know you're not woofing me? Maybe you're the kind of a skunk-guy who'd do a thing like that." She gives me a look as if she's sizing me up. "Naw, I guess not. Let me park this job."

I back away and wait for her to pull the car into a slot. She gets out and walks the curb as if it were a tightrope, coming toward me. "We were at the Tubes last night, me and Ray," she says, watching her feet. "You ever been there?" She shakes her head and does a little snort of distaste. "One of the great places. Really."

Out of the car, Helene's a tiny girl, easily under five feet, shaped like a bodybuilder. She says, "Ray's kind of a polecat. I don't meet many men that aren't, know what I mean? All of you got some polecat in you." She smiles at me as if she's pleased about that, then looks up ahead of us. "You live in here?"

"Yes, ma'am," I say.

She flips open the purse she's carrying and pulls out a business card, which she hands to me, holding it between the tips of her first two fingers. "This is me," she says.

The card says "SMALL PLEASURES," in chiseled-looking type, and under it there's a printed signature — "Helene," in red — and a telephone number. I read the card, then hold it close to look at the signature. "This looks real," I say. "The signature part, I mean."

She reaches out and pats my hip. "It's a store, boyo. My own private store. Things for women." She smiles playfully. "Well, so maybe it's not only a store."

I do a little wave with the card as we go up the steps to my apartment.

"I almost called it No-Man's-Land," she says over her shoulder. She pops the door and it opens, then she turns around and grins at me. "But we gotta be careful."

Tracy has the chickens on top of the stove. "So what do we do with these?" she says as we come in.

"Eat 'em," Ray says. He grabs Helene and lifts her up, high, in the air, then puts her down by the window in the living room.

"Hey!" he says, pointing out the window. "A possum just went by out here. Hey! Did anybody see it?"

▼

The dinner is quiet and quick. Helene has to have the single-volume *Columbia Encyclopedia* to sit on so she can reach the table. Tracy finishes first and moves to the brown recliner across the room, staring at the TV. Ray's watching Helene and, at the same time, talking about a hot-rod Chevrolet he persuaded his father to buy in 1957. He raced this car a lot, made his high school reputation with it.

"This one kid used to call me Rhinestone Ray," he says. "His mother bought him a Thunderbird. He hated my guts and figured this was his chance, so one night we went out and he did a triple flip into an A&W Root Beer place, and I ended up going sideways across a four-lane highway, staring at headlights. Nobody was killed, but he lost a hand in the windshield. I went to see him in the hospital a couple of days later."

"This happened twenty-five years ago," Helene says. "Just to put things into perspective."

"He said he thought maybe I'd jumped the flag," Ray says, softly thumping the table with his forearm. He waits a minute, then says, "I don't know why they bought that Chevy. I mean, it was *fast*."

Ray fidgets with his glass, then turns to look over his shoulder at Tracy. "What're you up to? You're either out the door like a shot or you're sitting around staring at things."

"I'm rolfing my feet," she says. "I figure it's time to rediscover the seventies."

"Didn't we do that already?" He lifts his glass and wags it at her. "Hand me some ice, OK?"

Tracy gives him a look that means she'll do it but he's a jerk for asking, then comes to get the glass. He watches her go into the kitchen.

"Short legs," he says. "No way around it. Give her another cou-ple of inches and her whole life'd be different. The teeth you fix, but you file the legs."

"You're cute," Tracy says from behind the open freezer-compart-ment door. She looks at me and says, "He gets this way after dinner."

"I can testify to that," Helene says.

I nod, as if I know it too.

Ray is drawing circles on the wood-veneer tabletop. "Two nights ago, I take Tracy to dinner at this steak place we always go to, and we're sitting there and this guy I knew ten years ago, a guy named Stewart, slips up behind her and starts mouthing her neck. I'm not kidding — the guy's making a mess. You figure she's going to jump or something, right? Not this one. She leans into it."

Tracy is in the kitchen doorway, listening. She's got Ray's ice ready. "I liked him," she says.

"He's greasy," Ray says. "But it's *Miami Vice* grease so it's OK."

"Ray's afraid of *Miami Vice*," Tracy says, slipping his glass in front of him. "He says it 'devalues light,' whatever that means."

Ray pours beer into the glass. "It means the guys are anchovies, the pictures, the music — it's *The Anchovy Show*."

"I don't agree," Helene says. "Besides, anchovies have certain desirable aspects."

"Like what?"

"Like they're silver, and if you want to you can slice them up into little tiny pieces," she says.

"I think it's silly to be afraid of a TV show," Tracy says.

"He wants to love it," Helene says. "You like the *Blade Runner* guy, don't you, Ray? He's on there. The gum-wrapper guy?"

"Yes," Ray says. He takes a drink, then fills the glass again. "I hate being on this side of the argument. I'll learn, OK? But first I'm going to finish this story. Please?" He turns to me. "So this guy at the steak place likes Tracy. Guys are always poking at Tracy."

Tracy makes some can-you-stop-this gestures to Helene behind Ray's back, then retakes her seat across the room.

117

"Poking is central to Ray's world," Helene says.

He gives her a steady look and continues his story. "So I watch and smile at all this kissing, then I wave, trying to get their attention." He demonstrates waving. "Stewart's got the leather jacket, the peach pants. He's probably got perfume going in there—"

"Smelled good to me," Tracy says.

Ray freezes and stares at her. She does a little curtsy, then pulls her foot into her lap and studies her toes, ignoring him.

Ray turns back to the table and pulls both thumbs over his shoulders in her direction. "See?" he says. "Just like that. She shuts me down like a garage door." He points at me. "Are you listening? I'm trying to say something here."

"I'm listening," I say.

Helene sighs. "Speed it up, will you, Butch?"

He gives her an instant smile. "So I'm out there in this restaurant jerking around like I'm dodging a fly. I mean, I might as well be alone."

Helene does some whimpering like a hurt animal, and then Tracy does it, too—there's a chorus of whimpers.

Ray waves both hands, giving up.

"Thank you," he says. "I want to personally thank each and every one of you for your kindness and compassion."

"Aw," Helene says. "That's real sweet."

"It's OK," Tracy says to me. "The place is known for flies, fat boys—green, shiny wings and everything. They make this rattling noise when they go by you. They must go a hundred or something, hundred and twenty easy. Scale speed, I mean."

I get up and start for the kitchen. "So what happened?"

"We had dinner with him," Tracy says.

Ray puts his head down on the table. "We had dinner with him," he says. "Way to go, Tracy. Way to hit the long ball out of the park."

"Well? We did."

"Yes. I know. We heard all about his life. We know where he

works, we know about his wife and his kids — we saw pictures, I swear to God."

"He's a med tech," Tracy says. "He works at the pathology lab. He sits there in a room the size of a Volvo putting stuff on slides. I didn't believe him until he showed me his badge. He has to wear a badge around, to show that he belongs there."

Helene says, "Is that it?"

Ray looks at her. "See, she doesn't care if this guy crawls on her, but it's painful for me. I mean, I don't want her learning on just anybody."

"You don't want her learning," Helene says.

"That's my pal Helene," Ray says. "Casualty of the sexual revolution."

"Hey," Helene says, "I'm the big winner."

"Yeah. You and Joan of Arc."

She gets up from the table. "OK. Time for Mr. Ray to say good night."

Tracy comes across the room and puts an arm on Ray's shoulder, standing behind him. She leans over and whispers something, then nuzzles his neck.

He looks up, pressing his head into hers, brushing her hair with his fingers, his jaw set. He gives me a wry smile.

Helene says, "Well, I, for one, had better go out and get me some dessert before I go blind."

I say, "I've got ice cream."

"That," Ray says to me, "is terrifying." He shrugs Tracy off his back and gets out of the dining chair, comes around the table, puts a hand on my shoulder and gives me a squeeze. "A fine boy." He pats my back and follows Helene to the door.

Tracy stays on her side of the table.

"What's this *blind* business?" Ray says. "I like the concept. I like the concept very much."

"Thanks," Helene says, taking a bow. "It's nothing. I do whatever is humanly possible, and if that's not good enough, why — "

She pauses midsentence, pretending to have forgotten her thought. "Why, then I just do something else."

"Right," he says, looking in my direction.

▼

I go out with them. It's cool and stars are shining. The light from the full moon is like a veil on the neighbor's Pontiac, which is in my parking place again. Somebody goes by in a bright Ryder truck. There's a faint scent of gas in the air as Ray and Helene move across the lot toward her car. It takes them a minute to get it started, then they roll off down the road, taillights burning. I watch until they make a slow left at the stop sign, then go inside.

Tracy's holding a green ceramic bowl, into which she's put the leftover chicken. She says, "We want to save this, right?"

I take the bowl and dump the chicken into the paper bag under the kitchen sink. Then I get a plastic trash bag from the closet and put the paper bag in the plastic bag. I scrape the rest of the plates into the paper bag, and put the dishes in the sink, then turn on the tap full blast and use the built-in spray nozzle to rinse the plates and glasses and the silverware. Tracy's watching me do all this. I get some paper towels and wet them, wipe the countertops and the top of the stove, then the dining table. I shake the place mats over the sink, rinse everything again, then lead her out of the kitchen, hitting the light switch as we go.

"So now we start stuff, right?" she says. She grins after she says it, reaching for one of the buttons on her shirt.

She's so beautiful. Her braces are shining. On one of her front teeth there's a tiny reflection of me and of the living room behind me. I think about touching the down on her face. I move her hand away from the button.

DRIVER

RITA SAYS the living-room lights keep her awake when she goes
to bed before I do, which is most of the time. The light comes down
the hall and under the bedroom door, she says, and in the dark it's
like a laser. So on Sunday, after she'd gone to bed, I started to read
Money in semidarkness, tilting the pages to get the light from a
book lamp clipped onto the magazine. That didn't work, so I gave
it up and watched a TV program about low riders in San Diego.
They put special suspensions in their cars so they can bounce them
up and down. That's not all they do, but it's sort of the center of
things for them. I'd seen the cars before, seen pictures of them
jumping—a wonderful thing, just on its own merits. I watched the
whole show. It lasted half an hour, and ended with a parade of
these wobbling, hopping, jerking cars creeping down a tree-lined
California street with a tinkly Mexican love song in the back-
ground, and when it was done I had tears in my eyes because I
wasn't driving one of the cars. I muted the sound, sat in the dark,

and imagined flirting with a pretty Latin girl in a short, tight, shiny dress with a red belt slung waist to hip, her cleavage perfect and brown, on a hot summer night with a breeze, on a glittering street, with the smell of gasoline and Armor All in the air, oak leaves rattling over the thump of the car engine, and me slouched at the wheel of a violet Mercury, ready to pop the front end for a smile.

In the morning I left a note attached to the refrigerator with the tiny TV-dinner magnet, telling Rita what time I'd be home from the office, then got in the Celica and headed for the freeway. I'd been in traffic for half an hour, most of it behind a bald, architect-looking guy in a BMW 2002, when I saw a sign for Kleindienst Highway Auto Sales. This was a hand-painted sign, one quarter billboard size, in a vacant lot alongside the freeway — a rendering of a customized 1949 Ford. I got off at the next exit and went back up the feeder to get to this place, which was a shell-paved lot with a house trailer at the rear, strings of silver and gold decorations above, and a ten-foot Cyclone fence topped with knife wire.

A guy jumped out of the trailer the minute I got onto the property. He followed me until I parked, then threw an arm around my shoulders before I had my car door shut. "Howdy," he said. "Phil Kleindienst. Hunting a big beauty, am I right?"

"Just looking," I said.

"We got the classics," he said, making a broad gesture with his free arm. He swung me around toward a Buick four-door. "Mainstream, high-profile, domestic, soon-to-be-sought-after classic road machines for the world of tomorrow."

"That's a big amen," I said.

He liked that. He laughed and walked me around the lot, keeping his hands on me the whole time — on my shoulder, my forearm, my back. He didn't have any cars that weren't huge and American, and he didn't have any custom cars. "Take a gander at this," he said, opening a brown Chrysler sedan. "This baby's Autorama clean."

We went up and down the rows together. He was citing virtues, giving me histories, and I was looking for the hot rods. Finally, I said, "What about this sign?"

"What sign?" Phil said.

"Out there on the freeway," I said. I pointed back up to where the sign was. We could just see the back of it.

"Aw, you don't want to mess with that stuff. Lemme show you an Eldorado I got."

He started to move again. I said, "I'm a little late. I guess I'll have to come back another time. Thanks anyway."

"Hold your hanky there," he said. "I got one. I'll show you one. A Lincoln, pretty old."

He took me around beside the trailer to a corner with a banner that said "BARGAIN CORRAL" strung over the top. There was one car there, and it could have been in the TV show I'd seen. No price was soaped on the windshield, so I asked.

"Oh, hell," he said. "I don't know. Too much. Let's go back up front, lemme show you some sweethearts." He turned me toward the front of the lot. "How about this Caddy? About a '77, a honey-dripper. Purrs like a pistol."

I stopped him. "You don't want to tell me what you're getting for this one? What's the deal?"

"Whew," he said. "You're too tough. You're kidding me, right?" He waited a minute, looking me over to see whether or not I was kidding him. "You don't want that porker, do you?"

The Lincoln was pale blue with black and green pinstripes, front wheels smaller than the rear, and it was low, maybe two inches off the ground. There was an airbrush illustration on the side, between the front and rear wheel wells—a picture of the Blessed Virgin, in aqua-and-white robes, strolling in an orange grove, behind each tree of which was a wolf, lip curled, saliva shining. The glass in the windshield and in the doors was dark green, and the steering wheel was huge and white. A head-bobbing metal Bambi—I think it was supposed to be Bambi—sat on the shelf behind the backseat, staring out the rear window.

I said, "I'm just curious. What's it worth?"

He let go of me for the first time since I'd arrived, backing away, putting a little distance between us as he studied the car. Finally, he slapped his hands together and said, "I don't even want to give you a price on that there. See, that's my boy Pico's car. Was anyway. Pico got shot up in 'Nam. He was this kid used to hang around, then worked for me. Built the car himself — did all the custom work, put in the hydraulics, stereo. All that in there's rhino skin. I don't even know where he got that."

"Looks professional," I said.

"Oh, yeah, heck yeah. He was good. He's got D. & H. Reds in there. It's real clean. It's about a thousand percent clean. He's got so much chrome under the hood you could put the hoses in your bathroom, use 'em for mirrors. I don't know why he's got these tiny wheels up front here, I guess that's a cholo thing..." Phil gazed at the Lincoln. He was half fat, maybe forty, with prickly blond hair, double-knit pants, a short-sleeved white shirt with a spread collar. "Pico cut her himself — know what I'm saying? Build a car like that today costs a fortune." He grinned and held his hands up as if giving me the bottom line. "I figure we're talking six, in the six area."

"What about the Toyota?" I said.

"OK. Fine. That's all right," he said. "I can work with you on that." He locked an arm around one of mine and gave me a quick pull toward the office. "Let's boot some numbers around."

▼

His trailer smelled like Pine-Sol. Everything was covered in knobby fabrics, earth tones. There was a dining booth, a tiny kitchen, a living space with a six-foot ceiling and a bubble skylight. He had four TVs, all consoles and all turned off, lined up against one wall. When we sat down, he said, "Let's verify our situation here. What's your line?" He was shuffling around, looking through a wood-grained-cardboard file cabinet.

I said, "I'm in sales. Pools, pool accessories, like that. Above-ground stuff. Is that what you mean?"

"Naw. I mean how come you want this car? Is this a kick-out-the-jambs thing for you, or what?" He waited a second, then went on. "OK, so don't tell me. What's your telephone? I'll check your wife on the deal. You got a wife, don't you?"

"Rita," I said.

"I mean, you tool in Nipponese and you want to leave a Flying Burrito Brother, and I don't buy it. What's the better half gonna say? How do I know you got the bucks? How do I know you're in your right mind?"

"I don't know, I do, and I am," I said.

"Ha," he said. "That's good. What's the number? Better gimme the bank, too."

I gave him the numbers. He said, "Great. Get you something in the fridge. I got some Baby Ruths in there, if you got Olympic teeth. Help yourself."

He wiggled out from behind the table, went through a narrow hall to the rear of the trailer, shut a door between that room and the one I was in. There was a Plexiglas panel in the door, so I could see him in there, black telephone receiver to his ear, staring at the ceiling as he talked, swatting his hair with the papers from the file cabinet.

He was in there only a minute. When he came back he said, "The woman's not home, but the bank thinks you're aces." Then he gave me a long look. "Now listen," he said. He reached up under his shirtsleeve to scratch his shoulder. "I'm thinking you don't genuinely want this car. I know I'm supposed to be breaking your leg to sell it, but I figure you got some kind of momentary thing going, some kind of midlife thing — you look like you're about midlife."

I shrugged. "Not yet."

"Yet don't matter," he said. "My brother had his at twenty-seven. By twenty-nine he was putting toast in milk during the

local news." Phil brushed something off the table. "Tell you what,"
he said. "I'll rent it. You take it maybe a day or two, leave yours on
a collateral basis, take this guy, drive him a couple of days. Then,
you still want it, we come to closure. How's that? I don't want you
down my throat next week begging to undo the deal, right?"

I said, "I'll rent it right now."

"Sure you will," he said. "And I don't like it, but now and then,
hell — what's it hurt?" He started through the file cabinet again. "I
got a form here saves my heinie when you go to Heaven in it."

Phil had to go to his house to get the form. He lived right down
the street, and he asked me to mind the store while he went, so I
sat on the steps of the trailer and watched the highway. Traffic had
thinned out a lot. He was gone forty minutes. When he got back I
took the Lincoln.

▼

I stopped at an Exxon station and filled up with gas, then drove to
my office. I had just gotten into my assigned parking space when a
young associate of mine, Reiner Gautier, pulled up in the drive
behind me.

"What, you went overboard on chimichangas?" he said. "What
is that? Where'd you get it?"

"Just trying her out," I said.

"You got a built-in Pez dispenser on there?"

I waved the remark away and pretended to search my brief-
case, hoping Reiner would move along. Finally, I had to get out.
He'd left his car door open and was giving the Lincoln a careful
look.

"That's Mary," he said, pointing to the picture on the side of the
car. "She's got wolf trouble there, doesn't she?"

I shrugged. "She'll make out."

He looked at the picture another minute, turning his head back
and forth. "That says it all, know what I mean? I like it. I go for this

cross-cultural stuff." He walked back toward his car, giving my shoulder a pat on the way.

I let him leave, then got back in the Lincoln and pulled out of my space. I went to the shopping center near the office, stopped in the parking lot, and tried out the lifts. I looked out the door, and I was better than eighteen inches off the ground. That got the attention of a black woman who was standing outside the ice cream store, leaning against one of those phone-on-a-pole phone booths.

She said, "That some kind of trick car?" She was a young woman, in her twenties, and good-looking except that she was snaggletoothed. She was holding a clear plastic shopping bag with yellow rosettes on it.

I said, "Yeah. I guess it is."

She looked at me, then at the car, with a kind of amused curiosity, tilting her head back, squinting her eyes as she sized me up. "Well," she finally said. "What else do it do? Do it dance or anything?"

I grinned at her, shaking my head, then put the car in gear and left. At a bar called Splasher's, which I pass every day on my way back from work, I pulled up and went in for a beer. I'd never been in this bar before. It was one in the afternoon and the place was deserted except for a woman with feathery hair who handed me a wet bottle of Budweiser. She was cleaning up. The ceiling was falling in on this place. The walls were black, and the only illumination came from back of the bar and from the beer signs you always see, the kind that sparkle and throw little dots of light. One sign had a waterfall that light rushed over. I took my beer to a window table so I could watch the car through the stick blinds.

The woman played Country Joe and the Fish on the jukebox. I thought that was amazing. I spun my coaster, listening to this music I hadn't heard in twenty years. Between tunes I went to get a bag of beer nuts from a metal rack next to the cash register. The woman watched me search my pocket for change, then nodded when I put two quarters on the bar.

Two kids on trail bikes stopped outside to give the car a look. These kids were about fourteen, with dirty T-shirts and minimal hair. They straddled their bikes and stared in the car windows, and I smiled about it until I saw that the kid on the driver's side was prying off the door mirror. Then I rapped on the glass and went out. "Hey! Get off of that, will you?"

The kid who had been doing the prying gave me an innocent look. "Great car," he said. "We're checking it out. Right, Binnie?"

Binnie was already on the move, standing on the pedals of his bike, rolling away. "Pretty good," he said. "For a dork-mobile."

I said, "Sorry you're leaving."

"Whoa..." he said.

The first kid started moving, too. Then he stopped his bike and turned to me. "Hey," he said. "You know that mirror on your side? It's real loose. I can probably fix it up. Ten bucks."

I gave him a nasty look and shook my head, then got in the car. I stopped at a drugstore on the way home, went in to get cigarettes. A college-age guy with blue eyes and pretty brown hair was in back, sitting at a folding table, eating his lunch. It didn't look like takeout food — it looked homemade. He had a dinner plate, a salad plate, a jelly glass with red and green swirls on the side. There was milk in the glass. He asked if he could help me.

"I need a pack of cigarettes," I said.

He came across to the cigarette counter, wiping his mouth with a yellow paper towel. "What kind?"

I said, "True. Menthol."

He looked at his cigarette rack, one end to the other, then turned around and said, "I don't see 'em. You see 'em out there?" He pointed to the front of the counter, where more cigarettes were displayed.

I'd already checked, but I looked again. "None here."

He came out from behind the counter rewiping his mouth. "I don't guess we have 'em. I was sure we did, but I guess I was wrong. I can order you some."

I waited a second or so, looking at the guy, then picked a pack of Kools off the counter. "How about these?"

"We got those," he said.

▼

Rita came to the window when I pulled up in the driveway and honked. It took her a minute, but then she figured out it was me and dropped the curtain. "What's this?" she said, coming out the front door.

I held up a hand and said, "Wait a minute. Stay there. Watch."

She stopped by the gas lamp at the edge of the drive. I jumped the front end of the Lincoln a little, then as far as it would go. Then I raised the rear to full height, then the front. I kept the car up until she was coming for a closer look, then I let it down, left front first, like an elephant getting on its knees in a circus show. That stopped her.

I got out of the car. "How do you like it?"

"Whose is it?" she said.

"Ours." I put an arm around her and did a Phil Kleindienst sweep with my free hand, covering the Lincoln front to back.

"What about the Celica? Where's the Celica?"

I reached in the driver's window and pulled the hood release, so I could show her the chrome on the engine. "Traded it," I said, leading her around to the front. "Guy gave me a whopper deal."

She stopped dead, folding her arms across her chest. "You traded the Toyota?"

"Well, sort of. But this is a killer car. Look at the engine. Everything's chrome. It's worth a zillion."

Rita looked at the sky.

"C'mon," I said. I tugged her arm, leading her to the passenger side, and put her in the car. I went back around, latched the hood, then got in and started the engine. I waited, listening to the idle. "Amazing, isn't it? Can you hear that?"

"The motor? I hear the motor. Is that what you're talking about, that rumbling?"

We toured the neighborhood, then I started to go downtown, but Rita remembered she needed some lemon-pepper marinade, so we stopped at the supermarket. I sat in the car while she went inside. A lot of people walked by wearing shorts, and all of them looked good.

We picked up a family bucket of fried chicken on the way back, ate most of it in the car, then finished up inside. Then we had bananas and ice cream. After that Rita switched on the VCR and put in a tape. "I want you to see this," she said.

It was a PBS documentary about China—about a peasant family. The grandmother ran things and got carried around on the back of a bicycle through this gorgeous countryside of misty, contoured land. Her son didn't know much about communism but felt things were a lot better now, with the Four Modernizations. His wife cooked, his daughters helped in the field, and his son wore a leather motorcycle jacket when he went out to help with the harvest. At the end they cut to the father, alone in some room, sitting by a big vase with thin branches in it, dusty light slanting in. He talked about the family, his voice ricocheting around the high registers while out-of-sync white translations popped on the bottom of the screen. When he got to his son, what he said was that the boy had been "stunned by the West."

That was it. Rita stopped the sound and we watched the credits go by, then the network logo, then some previews of WGBH shows. She poked me and pointed to the *TV Guide*, which was on the coffee table on my side of the couch. I gave her the guide and then watched her look up listings.

When she finished, she tossed the magazine back on the table. "Well?" she said.

"It's a rent-purchase thing," I said. I showed her the paper I'd signed for Phil Kleindienst. "I can give it back anytime."

She laughed and said, "Hey! Not so fast. I may love it. I may want to go for a spin."

We went out about ten o'clock. It was cool, so we slouched down in the seats and left the windows open. We went by an apartment project we used to live in, and then we went over to the other side of town, where there is a lot of heavy industry — chemical plants and refineries.

Rita said, "It rides pretty good, doesn't it?"

"It's stiff when it's down," I said.

"So pump her up," she said. "I wonder what it'd be like to keep."

"People would stare."

"Great," she said. "It's about time."

She looked terrific in the car. She had on a checked shirt open over a white Danskin, her feet were up on the dash, and her short hair was wet and rippled with wind. Her skin was olive and rough, and it was glowing as if she were in front of a fire. When I missed a light next to Pfeiffer Chemicals, a couple of acres of pipes and ladders and vats and winking green lamps, I leaned over to kiss her cheek, but she turned at the last minute and caught me with her lips.

"Why, thank you," she said when I sat back again.

"Yes," I said.

On the way home we stopped at the mall. The stores were closed, but there were kids roller-skating in the parking lot, and a couple of cars parked nose to nose under one of the tall lights. We pulled up next to a palm tree in a planter about fifty yards away from the kids.

Rita said, "It's amazing out here, isn't it? How can this place be so good-looking?"

"Beats me," I said.

She put her head in her hands. "It's awful, but I have a craving for tamales. Really. I'm not making a joke, OK?"

One of the kids, a girl in shorts, pointed a finger at us and skated over. "How come it stays up like that?" she said.

"Just magic," I said. But then I opened the door and showed her, letting the car down real easy, then jumping the front a little bit for her.

"You've got her now," Rita whispered.

The girl stood back with her hands on her waist for a second. "Boy," she said.

She was pretty. Her shorts were satin, with little specks of glitter on them, and she had on a tiny undershirt-style top. Some trucks sailed by on the highway. I offered Rita a Kool. She took it and held it under her nose.

"What's your name?" I said to the girl, rolling my cigarette between my fingers.

"Sherri," she said. "With an '*i*.'"

I nodded. "You out here a lot?" I wagged my hand toward the other kids, who were sitting on the hoods of their cars watching us.

"Sure," she said. She rocked back and forth on her skates, rolling a little, then stopping herself with her toe. "Make it go up again, OK?"

I did that, getting it wrong the first try, so that I had one side up while the other was down. Rita was laughing in a lovely way.

The girl watched, then shook her head. "Boy," she said, smiling and skating two small circles before starting back toward her friends. "You guys are weird."

"Howdy," Rita kept saying all the way home. "Howdy, howdy, howdy. Howdy."

▼

She went to bed at one. I couldn't sleep, so I watched a movie we'd rented a couple days earlier. When that was over I rewound it, paged through an issue of *Spin* that she'd picked up at the grocery store, then watched the end of a horror show on HBO. By then it was after four. I tried to sleep but couldn't, so I got up and went outside. It was almost light enough to see out there. I sat in the Lincoln and thought about how nice it was that Rita could just sleep whenever she wanted to. After a while I started the car and went for a drive. I stopped at an off-brand all-night market and bought some liquid refreshment in a sixteen-ounce, nonreturnable foam-sleeved bottle. I wondered if the glass was less good than glass in regular bottles.

The scent of countryside in the morning was in the air. The rear window was smeared with condensation, and the storefronts were that way, too, and it was hard to focus on the stoplights, because of the way they made rings around themselves.

I went downtown, and it was like one of those end-of-the-world movies down there, with somebody's red hamburger wrapper skittering across a deserted intersection. The sky was graying. I made a loop around the mayor's Vietnam memorial, then took the highway running west, out past the city limits. The mist got thicker. Close to the road the trees looked right, but farther away they just dissolved. In the rearview mirror I could make out the empty four-lane highway, but above that it was like looking through a Kleenex.

Finally, I turned around and drove back by my secretary's apartment, saw her car with its windows solidly fogged, then passed the mall again. Some overnight campers had turned up in the lot, and their generators were chugging away. There were two Holiday Ramblers, cream-colored, squarish things, and an Airstream hitched to a once-green Chevrolet. I pulled in and stopped. The air was so wet you could feel it when you rubbed your fingers together. The sky showed bits of pink behind a gray cloud that was big above the eastern horizon. A bird sailed by in front of the car, six feet off the blacktop, and landed next to a light pole.

These two dogs came prancing into the lot, side by side, jumping on each other, playfully biting each other's neck. They were having a great time. They stopped not far away and stared at the bird, which was a bobwhite and was walking circles on the pavement. They stared, crouched for a second, then leaped this way and that, backward or to one side, then stared more. It was wonderful the way they were so serious about this bird. These dogs were identical twins, black-and-white, each with an ear that stood up and one that flopped over. I made a noise and their heads snapped around, and they stared at me for a minute. One of them sat down, forepaws stretched out in front, and the other took a couple of steps in my direction, looked for a sign from me, then twisted his head and checked the bird.

The dash clock said it was eight minutes to six. I wanted to drive home real fast and get Rita and bring her back to see everything — the dogs, the brittle light, the fuzzy air — but I figured by the time we got back it'd all be gone.

The lead dog took two more steps toward me, stopped, then stretched and yawned.

I said, "Well. How are you?"

He wagged his tail.

I said, "So. What do you think of the car?"

I guess he could tell from my voice that I was friendly, because then he did a little spasm thing and came toward me, having trouble keeping his back legs behind his front. I opened the car door and, when he came around, patted the seat. He jumped right in. He was frisky. He scrambled all over the place — into the backseat, back into the front — stuck his head out the passenger window, ducked back in and came over to smell the gearshift knob. The other dog was watching all this. I called him, then put the car in gear and rolled up next to him. He didn't move for a minute, just gave me a stare, kind of over his shoulder. I made that kissing noise you use to call dogs, and he got up and came to the door, sniffing. Finally, he climbed in. I shut the car door and headed home. They were bouncing around, and I was telling them the whole way about the girl in the parking lot and about Rita and me, how weird we had been. "We aren't weird now," I told them. "But we were weird. Once. In olden days."

RESET

PEOPLE AT THE office assumed Ann and I had been having an affair for the five years she'd been working for me. We hadn't, though we hung around together all day, every day, and we fought and bickered and made fun of each other the way husbands and wives do, so I guess it's only natural everybody thought we were in some kind of love. We probably were, though we hadn't pushed it. Recently things had cooled off quite a bit between us. She was rarely around at lunch, and the daily play had turned a little more bitter than it had to be. Still, it was a shock when she came in to quit. She gave me ten minutes' worth of reasons — her recent divorce from a professional golfer named Carl; that there weren't any good men around; how great it would be to get a new start somewhere; what fabulous job opportunities she'd heard there were in Texas. About halfway through the list I started feeling kind of lost, as if what I had to say, what I wanted, didn't matter at all — she had her mind made up. We'd talked about her leaving now and then, but it hadn't occurred to me that she'd really do it, and now that she was in front of my desk, on one foot, her pale blue eyes high and bright, the irises clipped by the upper lids, and she was cool, clear, and definite — well, I felt as if the bottom had dropped out.

I said, "I'm real sorry. I thought we'd just stay together. You know, onward and upward."

"Me too," she said. She was looking down a lot.

I said, "Let me try that again. I don't want you to go. We're a team. We've been together a long time. Why do you have to quit?"

"It's just the way it goes," she said. "I really don't want to do it. I've been sweating this one for a long time. It's much worse, thinking about leaving here, than the thing with Carl. You helped me with that."

"Nope," I said. "I was clean, remember? I stood for patience and reconciliation."

"You wanted him out, didn't you?" she said. "I knew what you wanted."

People kept coming in congratulating her, asking questions about her plans. I didn't like it much, so I asked her to shut the door. She gave me a look, then closed it just enough so that the edge touched the jamb.

"I'm serious," I said. "I want you around all the time. I think about you."

"I think about me, too." She nodded, then took a breath and held it, exploding her cheeks like Dizzy Gillespie.

"Great," I said. Out the window some city workers in orange overalls were tearing up the street. There were ten guys out there working on a hole the size of a sink. They kept going over to their trucks for water or something.

"I don't like this," Ann said. "Doing this." She made a little wave at me and at the room, then stood there with her hands at her sides. She toyed with her mother's wedding ring on her right hand, rolling it around her finger with her thumb. Her mother had bigger fingers than she did. And then she sat down, folded her hands in her lap, and looked at her knuckles.

She was very still, upright in the blue chair facing my desk, the hands now quiet in her lap. Her skin caught the summer light in this fashion-magazine way, became luminous, delicate, soft. The look she gave me was about the loveliest thing I'd ever seen — fierce, full of determination.

"You're real pretty," I said.

She got up. "Hey! I'm trying," she said. "I'm giving you the A stuff." She opened the window. Our building is old and has windows that open. She crossed her arms over her chest and sniffed the air, watching the guys in the street. I went around the desk and stood beside her, smelling her hair. I always told her how nice she smelled, and she always laughed and said it was Dial.

"Maybe you don't have to do this," I said. "No kidding. It'll kill me if you go."

"That's weak," she said. She put an arm around my waist. "Anyway, you deserve to die." She giggled at this joke and then stared some more at the workers. After a couple of minutes she turned her head a little and said, "Wouldn't it be nice if you could make me stop? I mean, wouldn't that be something?"

▼

Robin Romer, an account rep who worked on the other side of the office, poked open my door and asked Ann if she wanted to go out and celebrate. "You're going to Austin, right? Perfect town, great town." He stared out my window for a minute. "This place reminds me of a place my brother Desmond would like. He's over in 'Nam working up an import thing."

"He must be the interesting brother," I said.

Romer did a shrug and went right on. "Yeah, you know, the usual crap they bring in from places like that. Grass crap and stuff. Baskets. Those people can do baskets." He did a kind of leer at

Ann. "I might go over there and learn the business, but first I've got some stuff to learn around here."

She patted his shoulder. "Mr. Romer has a problem with his chickens."

"Anyway," he said. "No point hanging around, is there?"

"Hey!" Ann said, hooking a thumb at me. "What about him? I have to take care of my boss, don't I?"

"He's cool," Romer said. "Aren't you, boss?"

He was a small man, always neatly tucked into a little suit, and I didn't like him. She used to make fun of him, but since the divorce she'd been making a lot of new friends, and he was one. A couple of days before, when I'd made some tasteless crack about Romer, she got mad and gave me a lecture on tolerance. I liked him less now that she was defending him.

I scratched two fingernails across my forehead. "I'm cool," I said.

"He can come with us," Romer said. "We'll loosen him up, show him a good time. We're going to Blood's." Blood's was a bar a block away in the basement of a butcher shop. People from the office routinely went there for drinks after work. I'd been a couple of times.

Romer swung out of my office, pivoting on the hand he had on the doorjamb, but no sooner was he out than he was back. "What's he going to do without you?" he said to Ann. "How will he function?"

"Rehire," I said.

She gave me a tight look, then smiled at Romer. "You can go now, OK? We'll be there."

He stayed gone this time, and Ann shut the door again and came around behind me. She traced the hair over my ears with her fingertips.

"I'm sorry," she said.

"You can pick 'em," I said.

"I picked you," she said. "First. Anyway, that's not what I'm talking about. I meant I'm sorry I'm so polite. I think maybe I've got a self-esteem problem. Let's go get the drink."

We went to the bar. Romer must have got lost along the way. We were the only people there from the office. It was dark and cold, and there were pockets of customers around. We got a corner table. While we waited for the woman to bring our drinks, Ann said, "My family used to take these holiday trips. Dad got bored with retirement and decided we needed quality time together. A couple years ago it was Florida — Gorilla World Headquarters, famous for the petting zoo."

"I love those places," I said.

"Me too, me too. They're so seamy. It's like you can barely believe them, know what I mean?"

I looked at the snack menu, which was a hand-done sheet in a plastic sleeve. I was wondering what she'd think of stuffed mushrooms.

"He was a priest," she said. "Episcopal. He really didn't like women very much. He was always putting them down, saying they'd do anything in a thunderstorm." She glanced at me, then checked the rest of the room.

"So," I said, craning toward the bar window. "What's the weather?"

"You're a mop," she said. She studied my face, her eyes doing a tiny box-step. It was a way she always looked at me, something I figured was proprietary, something I liked.

"Thank you," I said.

She hunched over the edge of the table, looking earnest and innocent. "Why's somebody so upset? I mean, a girl'd think we were talking major love here, the way you carry on."

"We're talking," I said. She toyed with the saltshaker, moving it in chess patterns on the checked tablecloth. First, the knight, then the rook. Our drinks came. Ann gave me a nice look while the woman was getting the napkins down, then watched her go and spun the ring. When the woman was out of the way she said, "So maybe I'll just stay here with you forever."

I said I thought that was a good idea.

Ann was on the phone when I stopped at her office door the next morning around nine. "Hey," I said.

She held up a finger telling me to wait a minute, then finished on the telephone. When she hung up she said, "You want coffee? I can get us some coffee."

"Not for me," I said. "I want love only."

"Got no love," she said. "You've got a choice of genuine emotion of unspecified type, ordinary friendship, or . . . that other stuff. Any combination. But you're taking a ride on the love."

"Big offer," I said.

"We try," she said.

Her office was drab. She'd brought plants and a Diebenkorn poster, but the effort was halfhearted. The poster was still leaning against the wall, where it had been leaning for over a year. She held the point of her pencil while she watched me get into a chair across from her.

"It's personal," I said, reaching to close the door.

"I'm still going," she said.

"I know," I said. I couldn't get the door, and I was all twisted up — legs out in front, one over the other, body turned ninety degrees at the waist, left arm out at full length toward the door. My shoulders were perpendicular to her desk, and my head, which ought to have been facing the wall of her office, was twisted back toward her. "You probably don't recognize this body language," I said. "It's foreign. Dutch, I think it is. Colonial. Celanese, maybe."

"Celanese is a fabric," she said.

"That's what I mean." I shut the door, then sat straight again. "So. This is a great office. I like the poster — what is that?"

"Hard to believe?" she said, examining the mess she was making between her fingers with the pencil. Pretending to be tough was a routine. I played soft, she played hard. It was fun. It had always been fun, from the first day. I thought about that.

I said, "Can you go to Tennessee? I'm going to Tennessee today. Our client—Mr. Romer's client—Starlight, Inc., wants a new headquarters, and they have, as you know, discovered Knoxville. Or someplace near Knoxville. I leave in an hour. You don't have to go. I just thought it'd be nice to have some company."

She nodded. "Company's nice. Is this, like, a date? I mean, twenty-third-century version?"

"I don't know," I said, drumming my fingers on my knee. I looked at the empty parking lot outside her office. It was empty because the entrance was blocked by the men working out front. "I guess. Maybe it's a bad idea."

"I didn't say no," she said.

"Thank God," I said. Then I held up my hands, smiled, tapped my head. "Sorry. The heart's saying what the brain wants unmentioned. I'm supposed to be playing close to the chest through here, right?"

"You're doing fine."

"Thank you," I said, picking a stick of gum out of the pack on her desk.

"There's a lot of thanking going on this morning," she said. "I don't like it. Makes me nervous." She put her feet on the corner of the desk closest to the window, away from me, and gave me a friendly smile. "Now, how long a trip we talking?"

I put the gum back. "Forty years, tops."

▼

It was noon when we got to Vesco's Motor Lodge & Weekender, in a town called Review, Tennessee, outside of Knoxville. The registration desk was knotty pine, decorated at one end with an inflated heart tied to a straw. The owner was Charlene Vesco, a woman in her fifties, squat and mannish, with rough hands, short fingers, square-cut nails. She was some relation to the notorious Vesco, she told us, and her mother had run the Weekender in the fifties, when it was the Blue Ridge Motor Court. Charlene signed us in, complaining about a couple she'd just signed out. "They were some bozo individuals, I promise you. I hope and pray never to see them again crossing my line of vision." Charlene gave me the eye. "That's a joke, son. But don't you worry about it."

I smiled at her.

"He never worries," Ann said. "He's worry free."

The motel was eighteen wood-frame bungalows bunched on two acres next to a stream the brochure called "Vesco Falls," though no falling of more than six inches was anywhere in evidence. Up the hill behind this place, stuck up in the trees, was a plywood flamingo that must once have been painted but was now plain, weathered, streaked with pink at the edges.

Charlene caught me looking out the window at the sign. She said, "I was doing that in '62, when I took over. I figured to go with it, you know, tourist art—birds on the ground, the whole thing. So then I started hanging around with the sign guy—he wasn't local —and, well, we did a one-eighty on the plans." She winked at Ann and handed over the keys. "I'm guessing you understand, right?"

"Right," Ann said.

I was in number ten, surrounded by tall pines. I had two rooms and a kitchen the size of a confessional. Ann was in seven, in a tiny clearing thirty yards away. The bungalows were war era, white, trimmed brown around the windows and at the eaves.

We put up our stuff, and then I called Ketchum, the town-council guy we'd come to see about Starlight. The first thing he wanted to know was if Ann was with me—he'd talked to her a lot on the telephone. I told him she was. "Then I'm buying lunch," he said. "You had lunch? We got motel or drive-in. Or local color, but it's kind of sticky."

I chose the latter and he told me how to get to a place called Raindrop's, and then we hung up.

Ann and I drove into town, following his directions to the letter. At a stoplight we pulled up next to a giant Volvo driven by a guy with hair combed to a point in front. He grinned, then dropped his visor, and looked into a mirror on the back.

"Pretty damn thrilling," Ann said, seeing the guy.

We watched him work his teeth. Then his mustache. Then he brought out some tiny scissors. I turned away, but he was hard to ignore. When I looked again he was on the telephone *and* working the scissors. He was laughing into the receiver.

"Maybe you could get a job with him," I said.

"Will you stop?" Ann said.

We followed the Volvo right to Raindrop's. The driver turned out to be Ketchum.

We spent the afternoon with him. I'd hoped to be able to get by on lunch alone, but he was so happy to see Ann, and she was so nice about it, that at five he was still showing us the sights. We got to see the tar pits, the train depot, the rushing brook that sliced the town in half. We saw the land south of downtown that he had a piece of.

"I can get you in on this," he said. He did a slow-motion punch on the top of my arm. "Blind, of course. No problem."

"Looks mighty handsome," I said.

He went back to Ann, slinging an arm over her shoulder. "We're going for the whole 'new town' thing," he said. "Maybe work out a lake over beyond the bank. Wipe all that out, of course." He waved at a two-block stretch of single-story brick buildings. "Nuke those dudes and swing back with the wood-siding thing, you know? Very upscale, West Coast—nothing modern, just nice middle-of-the-road shops, family-oriented."

Ann was smiling hard, pointing some.

▼

I took a nap when we got back to the motel, then cleaned up and went to find Ann. She was with Charlene in the office. They were drinking coffee, sitting at one of the three tables in the alcove that was the Weekender restaurant. They were looking at a magazine open to a picture of a model with bruise-colored cheeks, black lips, eye sockets like anodized aluminum. She was wearing a lace top, a zebra skirt with a red belt, burgundy stockings, shoes with silver flames. The jewelry was big wood, and the hair was stiffed up in a wedge.

"Well, she ought to be out trying wieners," Charlene said. She smacked a knuckle on the open magazine. "I'm telling you."

I said, "She's probably real lovely." I had come up behind them and was leaning over Ann's shoulder.

"Well, looky here," Charlene said. She gave me a pat on the shoulder. "You want some eats? Just don't ask for no lobster bisque, hear? I ain't seen lobster in forty years. You want something like that you're gonna roll on down the road."

"I asked for lobster bisque," Ann said.

"That's true," Charlene said. "Now, if you want toast, I can handle toast."

"The toast is great," Ann said.

Charlene, already on her way toward the kitchen, stopped and did a suspicious look.

"Honest," Ann said. "It's incredible toast, really." She started to cross her heart with a finger, but stopped halfway through.

The phone was ringing in the next room. Charlene did an eye roll and cut across toward the registration desk. In a minute she was back, dragging the telephone with her. She got about halfway to us before she ran out of cord.

"It's your office," she said, wiggling the receiver at me.

I took the phone. "Hello?" I said.

It was Romer, calling to tell me Starlight had changed its mind. "I guess you'd better forget it," he said.

"Are you sure?"

"Sure I'm sure," he said. "What, I'm making it up? We just got a call ten minutes ago."

"OK," I said. "Thanks."

"Hang on," he said. "Uh . . . " There was a pause, and that closed sound you get when somebody on the other end of a telephone call puts a palm over the mouthpiece. Then he was back. "Listen," he said. "Is your friend Ann around there?"

I said, "No, she's not around. I think she's at the pool."

"That's all right," Romer said. "I guess I'll catch up with her later. Don't worry about it. You OK?"

"Fine," I said. I hung up and carried the phone through the arched doorway and put it on the desk, then sat down again. I started rubbing my eyes, because the lids were clinging to each other, but then it seemed like I couldn't stop rubbing. Finally, Ann tugged my arm. "Are you OK?" she said. "What's the deal on the phone?"

"Starlight's down the tubes," I said.

"No kidding?"

"That's it," I said. "Romer asked for you." I was working on my eyes again. "You have a change of heart or anything?"

She pulled away, reaching for her coffee mug.

"Sorry," I said. "It's just that I dreamed about you in my nap. We were in a parking lot. There wasn't anything there but this pink asphalt and the blue sky. We were naked, lying out there. You didn't have any legs, and you had one arm. I mean, you had the legs and the other arm, but you'd taken them off or something. I asked why, and you said you were saving them."

She sighed and dropped her head into her hands.

"Yeah," I said. "I know. I didn't want to dream it, either. Tonight I'm going to dream about bowling." I looked at her eyes, which were tired and watery.

Charlene came through the kitchen door with a ten-inch stack of toast. She noticed Ann's eyes right away, then mine, and stopped short of the table, pulling the plate back and to one side as if she might withhold it. "What've we got here? We got an outbreak of iritis? We can probably fix that."

"Contact trouble," Ann said. She shut one eye and swiveled around, looking for the ladies' room.

"Mine are fine," I said, and when the toast was on the table I picked a piece off the stack. The toast was as thick as a paperback, crisp at the edge, collapsed in the center.

Charlene pointed Ann toward the front office, then stood in back of me looking out the window, her hands crimping on my shoulders. When the door shut behind us, Charlene said, "Now, you be good to her, hear?"

"Yes'm," I said. "I'm trying."

"No . . . I'm serious," Charlene said, giving me a squeeze. "She's bananas about you. Any fool can see that."

I craned my neck, looking up at her.

She nodded at me. "Sure is," she said. Then she popped my forehead with a finger in a way that was friendly but hurt like hell. "Just be nice. Give her what she deserves."

▼

We went to dinner at a drive-in that was once a Dairy Queen, now a local outfit called Princess Snack. There were hand-painted drawings of snacks all over this place. And princesses. A young girl in red satin took our order and brought the food. We sat in the car and ate. Neither of us had much to say. I watched the cook and the cashier and the girl carhop mill around inside the building. They were mechanical, the way they kept repeating the same movements, the same gestures. Watching them, I got angry about Ann leaving.

I said, "I hate it when you're polite."

She raised her eyebrows. "Did I miss something?" she said.

"You were real nice to Ketchum, and I hated it."

"I see," she said, drawing it out, while she refolded the tissue on her hamburger. "It's going this way, is it?"

I looked out the window.

"My guess is that Ketchum's not the problem," she said.

"Right," I said. "I don't know why you like all these other people better than me. Why you have to leave."

146

"I explained that," she said.

"Yeah, I know," I said. "But we get along, don't we? We have a good time. It's not so bad."

"Days are good," she said. "Nights aren't."

"They might get better," I said. "Who knows?"

She sighed, and we both watched employees for a while. The cook must have been a basketball fan. He kept doing skyhooks when he was flipping the patties.

Finally, Ann said, "Why don't we just have a nice time, huh?"

I started to say something about how it was hard to have a nice time with her departure looming, but as I was talking I was gesturing with my hamburger and I lost the meat. It slipped out of the bun and fell down around the foot pedals. I had to scrounge for it, and it broke in two when I found it. I got it off the carpet and out onto the tray, and when I turned around Ann was sitting there grinning at her lap.

"What?" I said.

"Nothing," she said.

I smiled at her and pointed at her hamburger. "You finished with that?"

She handed it to me. "You still want it?"

I squinted at her when she said that. A line of pink light reflected from the restaurant sign cut across her forehead, over the bridge of her nose, down her cheek. We sat still for a minute. Then I took a bite of the hamburger she'd given me and I grinned. "Why, sure," I said. "On the something-is-better-than-nothing principle."

She reached over and messed with my shirt collar, then sat back and looked out the car windshield. "That's sort of one of my favorites," she said. "The other one I like pretty much is better-late-than-never."

"Yep," I said. "I'm crazy about that one."

▼

Later, when I couldn't sleep, I got a glass of tap water and stood at the front window of my bungalow looking at the lit-up grounds. I'd only been there a minute when I saw Charlene Vesco creeping across the grass.

I opened the venetian blinds. Charlene went up on the porch of Ann's bungalow and tested the screen, then stood there moving foot to foot, scanning the property, her back to the door. She patted her hair a couple of times, getting it into place. I checked my watch. It was almost four. When I looked outside again Charlene was gone. Nothing moved for a while, and then Ann's door opened and there was Ann, barely visible through the screen. She had on shorts and some kind of big shirt, and she was wearing her glasses. She hated her glasses. Her arms were crossed over her chest at first, but then she opened them, holding the edge of the door with one hand, rubbing her thigh with the other. She was just looking around. In a minute she pushed the screen and came out onto her porch. She sat on the steps. I watched for a long time. There were shadows all over the place, and there was moonlight. I filled up my glass and pulled a chair to the window, propping my heels on the sill. I stared at the tree trunks, and the flat, nearly iridescent lays of grass. There was something set and fearsome about the scene, like a little tableau at the start of a Hitchcock movie: mist drifting through, water sparkling, lights high up in the pines — and Ann, in the clearing, on her steps. Two cars rolled by almost silently, almost in tandem, on the narrow road in front of the property. My window shined. I studied the scene outside my window. I tried to see the future.

STUDENTS OF HISTORY

▲   ▼   ▲

CHROMA

ALICIA'S TAKING her weekend with her boyfriend, George. It's part of our new deal — she spends every other weekend with him, plus odd nights in between. The rest of the time she's with me. When we started this I thought it'd drive me crazy. One time I actually slugged her. I was sure she was leaving me, but as it turned out she didn't want to leave at all. She wanted to stay. She said meeting George was fate, an accident, that she didn't plan it. I guess I accepted that. Then I started liking the days alone every two weeks. It's quieter, the house is cleaner — things don't get messed up. I don't have to schedule around her. It's as if we have joint custody, George and I.

I'm spending Saturday with a neighbor named Juliet. She's in her twenties, a graduate student recently sold on health — free weights, the gym, night classes in anatomy. She owns the house next door with her girlfriend, Heather, who's thirty-five, tall and angular, and runs boutiques.

Heather's on a shopping trip, which is how Juliet and I happen to be together. It's raining. We're in an old section of town — lots of storefronts turned into eight-table restaurants — looking for a place to get a late breakfast. We hustle from one to the next, deciding each is wrong on decor, grease, or eaters. Finally, we go to this fried-chicken shop on Berry Lane called Bill's. It's been there thirty years, so all the things wrong with it are deeply wrong, which seems to make it OK. There's a lot of big old rope in the restaurant. Besides, Juliet's been there before.

Juliet thinks I'm depressed. She tells me this and asks several times what it is that's bothering me. I make up the usual stuff, trying to avoid the question, afraid that if I start to tell her, I'll end up saying a lot of junk now that won't be true this afternoon. She gets a chicken-fried steak, and I go for the chicken, and we eat watching the plastic tablecloth.

"We aren't very good friends," she says.

"Sure we are," I say. "C'mon."

"OK," she says. "OK. Tell you what. When we go back to the house I want to make love to you."

I'm cutting meat off a drumstick right at this point. I've had most of the skin and now I'm looking for what's left. I say, "Oh?"

"I think it's necessary and important," she says.

I get my fork into a piece of meat and whisk it around in the gravy that has slipped out of my mashed potatoes.

"Fair's fair," she says.

That's the last I hear of it until we get home. I park in my driveway, and she comes around the car and takes my hand, marching me across the grass toward her house.

All the houses around here are one-story brick jobs, paneled dens, sliding-glass doors looking out to backyards. She puts me on the sofa, which in her place faces the sliding door and the red patio where they barbecue. I notice they don't have a Weber, it's something else, one of the flatter, squarer kinds. Maybe it's from Sears or something. The trees out there are bent and dripping.

I say, "I don't know. We're friends, but we don't have to do this." I have the idea I'm taking the top line on the thing.

Juliet's moving around between me and the window, not really doing a show, but sort of doing a show. "Sex is my guts. It really makes me sting."

"Uh-huh," I say. I get off the couch.

She laughs, the muscles in her neck rippling prettily. She's got a lot of muscles. "I'm sorry. That was dumb. I was just trying to be, you know, seductive." She suddenly droops, going limp on the couch. "So I guess we ought to forget it, huh?"

I come up behind her and rub her hair in this way that's much more awkward than I intend, then I stop that and get down behind the sofa so that our heads are about at the same level. Only our eyes are above the sofa back. I say, "It's real sweet," and put the emphasis on "real," and now I'm doing her hair in a much better way. It's working. "It's a lovely idea, it's very flattering, but..."

"My friend Allie?" Juliet says. "She told me about this one time she made love in front of a bank in Paris at two in the morning with this girl she met on one of those boats they have? There was a French dumpster in the street there, and they got in — she said it was crazy. She said she couldn't walk right after. She says when it feels that good you know it's gotta be true."

I look at her real slow, giving her what I imagine is my older-and-wiser look.

"She married the dumpster?" Juliet does a smile that's kind of sad around the edges. "Maybe I'll just put on a record — you think that'll help?"

She does wobble-knees on her way to the stereo and plays something by Nat King Cole, and it's on tape, not a record. The music gives me gooseflesh. I haven't heard Nat King Cole since the seventh grade, and I feel like crying about it. I get up and stand behind Juliet, wrap my arms around her and hold her, listening to this awful music, thinking it's crushing the way she loves, that she's such a child.

153

She says, "Is this OK?"

I say, "Sure," and let her take me back to the couch.

Juliet's nice — we hug some more, kiss a little, mostly sit and stare at the points where our bodies touch. We don't talk. I feel close to her, like I want to protect her from everything.

▼

At four I'm out driving around in the family car, trying to figure out what kind of take-out food I want to take out for my dinner. At a stoplight somebody jiggles a rubber fish out the window of a bus next to me. It's a pale green fish, about ten inches long — shark, or whale. I've seen lots of them, beach toys. I'm a little behind the bus, in the next lane, bent over the steering wheel, trying to see who's doing this fish. I think it's a kid, then realize it's Heather, and she's signaling me, so I nose in behind the bus and wait while it discharges people. Then I unsnap the door lock and move up so she can get in.

"Howdy," she says, sliding in alongside me.

"Hi," I say. I reach out and touch her hand, waiting while a carpet truck goes by, then steer into the center lane and say, "Got yourself a belt-fish."

"What's a belt-fish?" She holds the fish up in front of her and carefully looks it over.

"That," I say. "You put the tail under your belt and then walk around just like normal. A guy I know is the father of the belt-fish."

She shakes her head and drops the fish into a shopping bag. "I don't know what you're talking about. This is a present for Juliet, who is fish crazy." She crinkles the bags getting settled. "I was downtown. I used to go down there on the bus to the Majestic Theatre, where I saw *A Fistful of Dollars*, and some Bond movies, the first couple. Today I went to a mall in an office building and bought shirts. Have you looked at shirts? They're nuts. These people think we're fools."

I give her a squint. "Which people?"

"The ones with the shirts. I got four shirts and a bathrobe for three hundred eighty dollars." She reaches over her shoulder for the safety harness. "So how's the perfect Alicia?"

"OK," I say.

She makes a sorry-I-asked face and nods knowingly. "Oh. Her weekend. That would be...George?"

I point at her.

Heather doesn't believe spouses should tell each other too much. We've had this argument before. I say it's easier to handle what you know about than what you imagine, and she says it's better to keep your mouth shut and your eyes closed.

She grins. "You guys still playing Donkey Kong, huh?"

I wait a minute for that to make sense and, when it doesn't, say, "I don't know what that means, Heather."

She shrugs. "Me either. I just said it. I guess it means that it'll never work. You let this go on much longer, and she's going to think you don't love her anymore."

"She knows I love her."

"Well, she may know it but not think it."

I lift an eyebrow at her and do some blinky stuff with my eyes. "Logic needs work," I say.

"It's possible," she says. "Tell you what. You and Juliet quit coveting and I'll let her deviate his septum for you — is it a deal?"

"I thought that was my secret."

"You don't believe in secrets," Heather says, flapping her hands like a pair of toe-heavy socks on a line in a wind. "But hey! You guys over there do what you want. It doesn't bother us. We can be savage. We wouldn't be *we* very long..."

"She wants something interesting in her life. There's no big harm in it. You can't blame her."

Heather says, "I'm not blaming her, I'm blaming you."

I swerve to miss a broken-up microwave somebody has dumped in the street. When I get going straight again I smile a patient smile.

"I don't know. Whatever works, right? This is the eighties." She makes a flustered, dismissive move with her hand. "Let's forget it. I don't even know what I'm talking about." She's doing flat karate chops in front of her. "I'm having my ongoing struggle with the language," she says.

"Ah, language," I say.

"You touch the doughnut girl, I'll do your teeth in piano wire," Heather says, grabbing her front teeth for emphasis.

Alicia is staking potted plants when we drive up. I don't know why she's home, except that sometimes, on her weekends, she comes back for a couple of hours to get different clothes, or just to say hello. She waves with something that looks like a car antenna. Heather shakes the fish at her.

Alicia says, "Nice fish."

"We call him 'Morodor,'" Heather says.

Alicia taps Heather's arm with the antenna. "Well, who's going to get my cactus? It's by the kitchen door, and it weighs three hundred pounds."

"We don't speak power-lifting," Heather says.

"She got new shirts," I say. "Very expensive. I found her on the bus."

Alicia looks next door, toward Heather's driveway, at the Volvo parked there. "Something wrong with this car?"

"Nope," Heather says, spreading her purchases on the hood of our car. Alicia and I nod at each shirt. I stop Heather on a black one with a thin silver diagonal stripe, a shirt she says cost a hundred and forty dollars.

"That's mine," I say.

Heather shakes her head, slipping stuff back into bags. "If it's new it's wrong — that's my feeling. You see the pockets on these guys? I don't know. It's a big risk."

Alicia says, "They'll be great. Carry books in there."

"Books?" Heather falls back, holding packages up as if to protect her eyes from a bright light.

Alicia says, "I'm making eight-thousand-jewel rice for dinner, and you're invited."

"You're here for dinner?" I say to Alicia.

"Yeah. Sure." She shoves me a couple of times. "What's it to ya?"

When Heather leaves I bring the cactus around, hurting my back in the process. I sit with Alicia while she plays with this plant, trimming parts off, giving it a bath, fertilizing it, putting sticks in the dirt trying to get it to stand up straight.

I'm on the concrete with my head dropped back against the brick window ledge. I say, "She asked about George."

Alicia thinks a minute, but doesn't speak.

I narrow my eyes at her. "That had the look of something there."

"If I thought something, I only thought it for a second and I don't remember what it was, so leave me alone."

"Yes, ma'am. Moon rises when you hove into view."

She does a little bow. "Thank you. Why don't we hove on in for a nap? You can hold me. What do you say?"

I put an arm around her and pull her toward the door.

▼

Heather and Juliet arrive at eight on the nose, Heather in jeans and a brown blouse, Juliet in chrome-yellow shorts and one of the new shirts, the black one with the diagonal stripe. It falls open at the slightest deviation from perfect posture.

Alicia brings them into the living room, where I'm fixing the feet on the coffee table. "He's into handy," Alicia says. "Here, he's being handy under the coffee table."

Heather does a polite smile and picks up an audio magazine off the table, easing into the couch.

"Can I turn this on?" Juliet says, stopping in front of the television. "See how the Braves are doing?"

"Sure," I say.

"Keep it low, OK?" Heather says. "We're guests."

Juliet says, "Gee, Mom. If you're sure Mr. Anderson won't mind."

"I'm sure," Heather says.

George calls in the middle of dinner. Alicia answers the living-room phone, then moves to the bedroom and has me hang on for her. I listen to him breathe a minute, then hear the click of the other phone, and Alicia says, "I've got it."

I go back to the table. Heather and Juliet are looking hard at their plates. Juliet has pushed her food out to the edges of her plate, so it looks like a wreath.

"Just eat it," Heather says to her. "Let's don't attack the poor man with food-play."

"Hey," I say. "Who's poor here? I'm licking wounds as fast as she can inflict them."

Juliet gives me a look I like a lot, a sweet look out of the tops of her eyes. We stare at each other for a minute and it's like some force is shooting back and forth between us, like vases are rattling on their tables.

It makes Heather nervous. She stares at Juliet until she gets her attention. "Settle down," she finally says. "Let's don't OD on the compassion thing."

▼

After they leave I watch Alicia fix up the kitchen and, when that's done, make a sandwich and sit on the cabinet eating it. I take a Diet Coke out of the refrigerator and sit with her, watching her eat, telling her about Juliet. She listens, eyeing me carefully as if to see what my face might give away that I won't quite be able to say. When I finish, she takes a long pause, staring at the part of the sandwich that remains. She has picked off the crust and pinched the rest into some kind of animal shape.

"I don't like it," she says.

"What?" I say.

"All of it. Any of it. You're supposed to sit here and love me and me alone while I go out and do the rope-a-dope all over the place. Isn't that the deal?"

I look at her.

"So what's this about? I mean, we got melancholy in the mug here." She points the sandwich fragment at my face.

"Mug?" I say.

"Whatever." She downs the sandwich and slides off the cabinet, smacking her hands together. "I guess it's fine if you like tragic longing. Are you going to be OK if I go out?"

"I'm fine," I say.

"You look terrible. Maybe I ought to stay? You look like you're going to hang yourself, or slit your throat, or something. Call your girl."

"I'm OK," I say. We're standing in the middle of the kitchen and we sort of self-consciously lean toward each other, then start hugging, shy at first, then tight. It's nice to feel her against me again, how warm she is, how strong she is. We rock side to side like that for a minute, and then pull apart.

I say, "Well, I guess I won't hang myself."

"Cute," she says.

I head for the bathroom. Alicia follows me and watches me brush my teeth. "I think I like her," I say, stopping in the middle of brushing, holding the toothbrush in my mouth.

"You'd like her more if she was on you like bug repellent." She gives me one of those woman looks, the kind that usually comes complete with poised eyeliner brush.

I say, "I'll take some roaches next time."

She's twisting her head back and forth to check her teeth in the mirror. "Take rats," she says.

There's a tiny double beep on a car horn from the driveway. George. He isn't allowed in the house. When he comes for Alicia he pulls up in his Porsche and taps the horn. I've never heard such a discreet beep as George's.

She says, "I feel funny about this. Why am I always leaving? Am I ever staying home anymore?"

I give her a look that means it's the wrong time and the wrong question, and then walk her to the door. I go out on the porch so George gets a good look when I kiss her. "Don't be late," I say.

I'm inside, in front of the television, before they have a chance to pull away. The TV sound is annoying, and then, when I cut the sound, the things on the screen seem strangely distant, like from another world. That's OK for a minute, but then I feel sad, so I hit the remote button and sit there on the couch, stretched out, looking around the room. Nothing's out of place. It's dark and spotless. I sit there thinking about Juliet, seeing her in disarray, twisted up on the sofa, or relaxed in her bed, or on the floor next to the exercise bike. She's incredibly lovely and sexy in my imagination. Then I think about how fast things fly through your head when you're thinking, about how you see only key parts of stuff. I look at the cover of an issue of *Artforum* that's been on the coffee table for the last two months. It's this painting of an upside-down kangaroo I like pretty much. The only light in the room is from outside, a mercury-vapor streetlamp that leaves the shadow of the Levolors stretched along one wall, broken by a gladiola on the pedestal where we always put outgoing mail. The shadow has a flicker to it. I get a fresh drink and sit there watching this shadow and feeling like somebody in an Obsession ad, sitting there. I put my feet up on the far arm of the couch and drape my hand over my eyes, staring at this shadow — it's gorgeous. I unbutton my shirt and pull it open. I wish Juliet were with me, on the floor, leaning against the couch, so I could touch the back of her skull, comb her hair with my fingers, watch her cigarette smoke, blue against the perfect gray of the room. I think about tracking my knuckles on her cheek, resting my hand on the freckled skin of her shoulder. I imagine our conversation cut with pauses, her voice always hanging in the dry silence of the room, like something lost.

The next thing that happens is I hear the doorbell and don't know what's going on. I think it's tomorrow. I get to the kitchen and look at the clock, see it's eleven-thirty, and wonder why it's so dark at that time of morning. Then I figure out I fell asleep on the couch, and go answer the door.

It's Heather. I say, "Hi. Come in."

"You're a real pony," she says. "With Juliet. I hear she offered the full show this morning." She brushes past me into the house, hitting every light switch she can find. "How long have we been friends?"

I squint at the street. "Pony?" I shut the door and follow her into the living room. It's too bright in there. "Years," I say.

She sits in one of the straight chairs. Her clothes are stuff I've seen in magazines, but that she never wears — balloon pants that get clownish about the calf, a shirt similarly enlarged, skinny purple shoes. "I ought to use an ice pick on her gums," she says, drilling a finger back and forth under her nose.

I say, "It's OK, Heather. We're friends. Nothing happened. It was a sweet gesture. Nobody took it seriously." I look at my hands, backs first, then palms. My neck feels thick. I sit on the forward edge of the couch and crack my knuckles.

"Juliet," she says.

"Yes," I say. "That's why it was sweet."

She watches me do four or five fingers, then starts to fidget with her hands, doing what I'm doing. "I can't do that. It's supposed to be so easy, but I can't even do it."

"Sure you can," I say. I crack my forefinger by looping my thumb over the first joint and pressing hard. "Try it."

She does what I'm doing. There are no pops, so I take her hand and try to do the knuckles myself, but I can't. I say, "No knuckles."

She pulls the hand away and stands up, heads toward the kitchen. "I don't want us in your mess. I can't handle organized infidelity."

I say, "She was being kind, Heather. C'mon. What mess are we in, anyway?"

"Sicko," she says. "The wife's out with a college kid, doing God knows what, and you're around hitting on the neighborhood girls. Feeling modern."

"I feel lousy," I say. "As a matter of fact."

Alicia's back before midnight. I'm listening to cassettes I've made of a tune off a solo guitar record, comparing three different kinds of chrome tape. They sound the same to me, but I keep listening, trying to find the differences. Alicia says I should come talk to her while she bathes. I finish with the tapes and shut off the recorders, giving her a minute to get settled, then go knock on the bathroom door.

"Hello?" she says.

In the bathroom I sit cross-legged on the bath mat, facing her. She's lying in the tub, hair up, eyes shut. She's having a bubble bath, but her shoulders are out of the water, wet and shining. I look at her for a long time before I say, "I didn't sleep with Juliet."

"I know," she says. She doesn't open her eyes.

"It was OK, though. We touched a lot. I had a great time. She had a terrific time. It changed our entire lives."

"Good work," Alicia says, sitting up in her bath. Her shoulders curve forward into hollows at her collarbone. Her breasts are spotted with bubbles. She starts soaping the sponge, and the bubbles sizzle.

I nod. "I was feeling mighty crazy."

"I believe that," she says.

"It wasn't too bad," I say.

I stare at her, thinking how gorgeous she is—cheekbones, the shape of her face, her eyes, the skin. I like her skin because it's rougher than most women's, kind of Texas-prairie-looking, toward swarthy. I look at the tiny scar, three-sixteenths of an inch, right of center over her lip, and I remember her telling me how she got it—going over a chain-link fence to a boyfriend's at age eleven. She has three other scars on her face, all imperceptible unless you know where to look, and each with a story. A baseball bat, a fall from her father's shoulder, a car wreck.

I say, "You look great. You look high-toned, like you ought to be at some bop club."

That makes her nervous. She starts messing with her hair, dropping nests of bubble bath.

I sigh. "So Heather comes over and says we're in trouble, and she doesn't want trouble like ours, and how come I have to mess with Juliet."

"I was wondering that myself," she says. She's waving the sponge back and forth between us. "Are we in trouble?"

I shrug. "I don't know. You tell me."

She cups some bubbles and looks at them up close. She pokes them with a finger on her free hand. "My guess is we don't have to be if we don't want to be," she says. She shakes her head. "I mean, we're made of steel, right? We're the ones."

"Right," I say.

"We make the rules, we write the songs."

"Right."

"Are you OK?"

"I'm good," I say.

She rinses her legs, then turns to me and holds up both hands as if she really wants to straighten something out. Now. In some big, final way. "Look," she says. "I don't want you to think I'm not a serious person, OK?" She looks at me, waiting.

"What?" I say.

She says, "I mean—could you use some cheese ball right about now? I am *dying* for cheese ball. I've been thinking about it all night long. I'll even make it."

I sit there looking at her, my chin cupped in my hand. I'm wondering about how to react to that, about how I feel about it, about her, trying to figure that out. After a while I reach out and put my hands on the edge of the tub—they're like bird feet, thumbs on my side, fingers on hers—and I pull myself up to my knees so I can kiss her.

She laughs. She's so beautiful.

COOKER

I TELL LILY I'm tired of complaining about things, about my job, about the people I work with, about the way things are at home with her, about the kids and the way the kids don't seem to be coming along, about the country, the things the politicians say on television, on *Nightline* and on *Crossfire* and the other news programs, tired of complaining about everybody lying all the time, or skirting the truth, staying just close enough to get by, tired of having people at the office selectively remember things, or twist things ever so slightly in argument so that they appear to be reasonable, sensible, and thoughtful, tired of making excuses for my subordinates and supervisors alike, tired of rolling and tumbling and being in a more or less constant state of harangue about one thing and another.

Lily, who is sitting on the railing of our deck petting the stray cat that has taken up with us, nods as I talk, and when I stop to think of the next thing I'm tired of complaining about, says to me, "I'm tired, too, Roger."

Our children — Christine, who is eight, and Charles, who is eleven — are in the yard arguing about the hose. Charles has the nozzle tweaked up to maximum thrust, and he's spattering water all around Christine, making her dance to get out of the way.

"Charles," I say, waving at him to tell him to get the hose away from Christine. "Quit screwing around, OK?"

"Aw, Dad. I'm not hurting her. I'm just playing with her. We're just playing."

"We are not," Christine says. "I'm not, anyway. I don't want to play this way." She twists herself into a collection of crossed limbs, a posture that says "pout" in a big way.

"Why don't you water those bushes over there?" Lily says, indicating the bushes that line our back fence. "They look as if they could use the water."

I say, "The thing is, I hate all these people. There's almost nobody I don't hate. Sometimes, I see something on TV and I just go into a rage, you know?"

"What things?" she says. "See what things?"

"Somebody says a self-serving thing, I don't know, some guy'll say something about preserving the best interests of something or other, doing the best job he can and all that, upholding standards, and you can look at this guy and tell that what he's thinking is how can he make this sound good, how can he sell this thing he's saying whatever it is."

"You're talking about the preachers, right?"

"They're all preachers now. They're all holier-than-thou, self-righteous killers. I mean, everybody's a flack these days — they'll say anything just as long as they can keep on making their killings. I see this all the time at work. A guy'll come in and make a big argument for his own promotion, and when he's done I don't even recognize the world he's talking about. Remember that intern we had last fall, kid from Colorado? Then we hired him, right? You know why? Because he made friends with Lumming and what's-his-name, the other guy in production."

"Mossy—isn't that it? Mosely?"

"Something. But when the personnel committee met to talk about this job, Lumming and Mossy didn't say a word about being friendly with this kid. They said he was the greatest thing since sliced bread. It was a clear and simple lie. No question."

"You're complaining about the office," Lily says. "I thought the point of this talk was that you wanted to stop complaining."

"I do, but this stuff is driving me nuts. I don't want to be in a world where this stuff goes on."

"Go to Heaven," Lily says.

"Thanks. That's real interestingly cynical."

"Why not do a little discipline? Ease up." She spins herself off the railing and thumps as her feet hit the deck. "Besides, what would you do if you didn't complain? You wouldn't have anything to talk about."

"You're a charmer," I say. "You're a swell guy. An ace wife and companion."

"Mother of your children," she says, rolling the Weber into place.

"You cooking out here tonight?"

"You are," she says. "Therapy."

I don't mind that. In fact, I'm pleased that she's found something for me to do, something to occupy me, take my mind off the office and the things people are doing wrong. I used to be a lot more easy-going than I am now, and Lily, of course, recognizes that. Watching her mess with the grill, I wonder if she doesn't miss that more than anything else. "What am I cooking?" I ask. I should know the answer to this. I helped bring the groceries in from the car, helped her put them away. I have no idea what groceries they were.

"Lamb chops," she says.

This makes me feel better. Lamb chops, and suddenly the world is new, a place of mystery and possibility. Lily and my mother are the only two women on the planet who believe a lamb chop is a reasonable and appropriate thing to cook for dinner. That she wants them barbecued means I get to look up the recipe in the twenty-four-page, no-nonsense Weber Kettle cookbook. I say, "We've got lamb chops?"

"Yep." She's redistributing the coals in the Weber, evening them. She squats beside the cooker and wiggles the bottom vent back and forth to release the ashes into the ash catcher, then dumps the ashes over the side of the deck. "I am serving corn and the lima beans, if you're interested."

"I love the lima beans," I say.

"So get cracking."

I go into the storage closet that opens onto the deck, getting the barbecue tools. As I come out of there, I think: I have no desire to touch Lily. I don't know why, but that's what I think. She's not unattractive — in fact, she's quite lovely — but I don't want to touch her. It's not a desperate thing. I'm not thinking how awful it would be. But at the same time it's a clear thing. There isn't any question. She probably doesn't want to touch me, either. I wouldn't blame her. It's been a while since I've been in any kind of shape. I don't even like to touch me. I try to remember the last time we touched — apart from the usual, casual touches that happen without thinking. It's been weeks, maybe months. Not twelve months, but two, maybe.

I arrange my tools — barbecue tweezers and fork, hickory chips, Gulf lighter fluid — on the redwood table, and I think what brought this stuff about Lily to mind was a TV show I watched last night after midnight on CNN: a Los Angeles sex therapist answers all your questions. What struck me were the assumptions this woman made. She managed, without literally specifying, to predicate everything she said on a version of the ideal relationship, which was a joke to me: one man and one woman having happy sex together forever. This was the implicit ideal. Now, we all know that's just plain wrong. It'll never happen. And yet here was this woman taking callers' questions, answering with the kind of dull-witted assurance and authority that characterizes these people: Here are the solutions, follow these three easy steps, put your little foot there. I got angry watching this program. Somebody called in from Fairfax, Virginia, and said sex wasn't interesting, and asked why this woman didn't get real.

I watched for an hour. This woman wore a lot of eye makeup. Not as much as Cleopatra, but plenty, more than enough. She was good-looking — a dark-skin, dark-hair type, with a handful of freckles — but there was something of the born-again about her, that kind of earnest matter-of-factness that makes you want to run the other way. Almost everybody's born-again these days; if you're not born-again you're out to lunch, you're in a minority, you lose. Anyway, this woman had an easy rapport with the announcer, who was a newsman, and they traded asides, little jokes between callers' questions — he apologized a lot about his hopeless manhood.

▼

I don't make too much of a mess with the cooking, though I'm pretty angry when I bring the chops in and drip lamb juice on the carpet in the living room. But before I have time to get worse, Lily's got the plate of chops out of my hands and is telling me to remember three weeks ago, when I threw barbecue at the kitchen window.

"That was pork," I say. "And I don't know why you feel you have to remind me about it all the time anyway. I cleaned it up, didn't I?"

"Yes, Roger." She's circling the table, dropping lamb chops on the plates. "It took you two hours, too."

"But it was real cool, Dad," Charles says, making a throwing move. "Splat!"

I say, "No, my little porcupine, it wasn't."

"I agree," Christine says. "It was childish." She's repeating what she heard her mother say immediately after I tossed the pork chops.

"How old is she?" I ask Lily. I kiss the top of Christine's head and then take my chair. "If you're real good," I say to Christine, "we can get a dog later, OK?" She knows, I think, that this is a joke.

"I think maybe you're trying too hard again, Dad," Charles says. He's taken to adding "Dad" to every sentence. It's annoying.

"Yeah, Dad," Lily says. "Take it easy, would you?" She pinches Charles's ear and turns him to face his dinner.

Charles squirms, trying to get away from her. "Jesus, Mom," he says.

"None of that, kid," I say. I wave my fork at him for emphasis, point it at him, wiggle it.

"Who wants a stupid dog, anyway?" Christine says. She's using an overhand grip on her spoon, shoving the food on her plate around to make sure that nothing touches anything else. She's always eaten this way, ever since she was four. She'll eat all of one vegetable, then all of the next, and so on. I've tried to stop it, but Lily says it's OK, so I haven't made much progress. She says Christine will grow out of it. I say I know that, but what will she grow into? Lily says I'm a hard-liner.

"You want a dog," I say to Christine. "What are you talking about? All you've said for the last three weeks is how much you want a dog."

"That was before," she says.

"Before what?" Charles says. He turns to me as if we are co-conspirators. "She wants one, Dad. I know she does. She's lying."

"Don't call your sister a liar," Lily says. "Roger, tell him."

"Your mother's right, Charles. Don't call Christy a liar, OK? Not nice." I'm just about finished with my first lamb chop. The mint-flavored apple jelly is glistening on my plate. I feel pretty good.

"It's true," Charles says. "What do you want me to do? Do you want me to lie, too?"

Christine is playing with her food, twirling her chop in the clear space she's left for it on her plate. "I wanted a dog," she says, "but now I don't. Can't anybody understand that?"

"I can't," Charles says.

"Eat your dinner, Charles," Lily says. "You can understand *that*, can't you?"

I know I shouldn't tease the kids the way I do — like telling them we can get a dog. It's a standing joke in our house. They know we're not getting a dog. And they know why: Daddy's bad about dogs, about pets in general. Daddy looks at a dog and what he sees is a travel club for ticks and fleas. Try explaining that to a kid. Lily and I used to have big fights about it, but I won. I outlasted her. I'm not proud of it, but it's OK. I don't mind winning one every now and then. She still thinks I'll come around after a while, but she's wrong about that. I've told the kids they can have fish, but they don't want fish.

So there's a history going on in the family about this dog stuff, and I tease them about it all the time. It might sound cruel, but it seems to me they ought to understand. You can't always get what you want and all that. It's important they know what's going on, that once they know no dog's forthcoming, then the dog is fair game. Lily says I'm crazy on this one, that kids don't work the way we do. She says I'm building a horrible distrust. She says it's not smart, that when I'm old and pathetic they'll trick me — tell me they're coming to see me and then not show, or take me out for a drive and slam me into a home or something.

"OK," I say. "I'm sorry I brought up the dog. The dog remark was a bad idea. No dog. Christine?"

"What?" She's petulant. "I know," she says.

"I shouldn't have said a thing about the dog, OK? I don't know why I did. I'm upset."

"Daddy's upset about the office, sweetheart," Lily says.

"I'm sorry," Christine says.

"He shouldn't take it out on us," Charles says. He turns to me, gives me a real adult look. "You shouldn't, Dad."

I don't think I like the way Charles is turning out. For a time, his early moves toward adulthood — the grave looks and the knowing nods — were charming, even touching. After all, he's a boy, a kid, and it's nice to see him practicing. But it gets old.

"I know that, Charles," I say. "Thank you."

"Well," he says, "I'm just trying to help."

Lily pats his arm. I don't know why mothers always pat their children's arms. It's disgusting. "Yes, Charles," she says. "But Daddy's tired. Let's just be quiet and eat, what do you say? Daddy's had a hard day."

"Another one?"

"That's enough, Charles," she says.

And it is enough. After that, we eat in silence. I watch Christine, who eats her corn first, kernel by kernel, then the beans. She doesn't even touch her lamb chop. When I finish eating, I take my plate to the kitchen, scrape the used food into the brown paper bag we keep under the sink — only now it's out on the kitchen floor in front of the cabinet — and put my plate under the faucet. I turn on the water for a few seconds to rinse, then go back through the dining area, stop behind Lily for a minute, and cross the room toward the back door. "I'm going to straighten up out here," I say. "I may water for a while."

"You're going to water?" Charles says.

"Finish eating," Lily says. "I think your father might want some individual time."

"What's individual time?" Christine says.

"Don't be dumb," Charles says to her.

▼

What I'm thinking about, out there on the deck, is that I'm not living the way I ought to be living, not the way I thought I would be. It's all obvious stuff — women, mostly. I'm not Mr. Imagination on the deal. A woman stands for a connection and another way of living, something like that. So I'm thinking about the woman on *West 57th*, the TV show, and the dewy young girls in the movies — though you don't see them as much as you used to — and thinking of the poor approximations that throng the malls. I'm not thinking anything *about* these women, I'm only thinking *of* them.

I put the charcoal lighter back in the storage closet, finger the hickory chips, think for a minute about sitting down in there. This closet is about six feet square, lined with empty cardboard boxes that our electronics came in. We've kept computer boxes, stereo boxes, TV and VCR boxes, speaker boxes, tape-recorder boxes. Then I decide to do it, to sit down just the way I want to, and I go back to the deck and get one of the white wire chairs and put it in the storage room and sit down, my feet up on the second shelf of the bookcase that I bought from Storehouse so the junk we keep in the storage closet will be more orderly: charcoal, lighter, and chips on the bottom shelf, plant food and insecticides on the second, plant tools on the third, also on the third electric tools (saw, drill, sander), and accessories on the top. It isn't too bad in there. From where I sit I can see out across the deck to the small lump of forest that borders one side of our lot. She always puts plants out there in the summer, and I look at those — pencil cactus, other euphorbias.

Lily comes out and walks right past the door of the storage closet out to the edge of the deck, looking around for me. "Roger?" she calls. "Roger, where are you?"

"Back here."

She turns and looks at me in the closet. "What are you doing in there, Roger?"

I say, "Thinking about my sins," which is a thing my mother always used to say when I was a kid. She didn't have any sins to think about, of course.

"Why don't you come out of there? Sit out here with me, OK?"

I say, "Fine," and pick up my chair and carry it back out to the spot on the deck where I got it.

She closes the storage door behind me. "Now," she says, sitting down on the deck railing. "You've got this nice family, these two kids and everything, this good job, and things are going great, right?"

"Things are OK."

"Right. And you're complaining all the time about every-thing."

"Right."

"And you don't want to complain."

"Right."

"So you're like Peter Finch," she says. "In that movie, whatever it was. The one where he went out the window and said he was mad as hell, remember?"

"Sure," I say. "What's the point?"

"Where'd it get him?" Lily says. "He's dead as a doornail. I mean, that's not *why* he's dead, but he is dead. I think there's a les-son in that."

I nod and say, "That lesson would be . . . "

"Take it easy, Greasy," Lily says.

"But everything's wrong now. People'll say anything. Everybody's transparent and nobody minds — like you, for exam-ple. Here, now. What you want is for me not to be upset. That's all. You don't care what I'm upset about, you just want me over it."

"Well?"

"In a better world we'd deal with the disease, not the symptom."

"In a better world we wouldn't have the disease," she says.

"Good point."

"Thank you."

Charles comes out of the house carrying a sleeping bag, a yel-low ice chest, some magazines, and the spread off his bed. "I'm camping out tonight, OK?" he says as he passes us.

I start to say no, but then Lily catches my eye and gives her head a little sideways shake. This means that she has already signed off on things.

"Watch out for spiders," I say.

"There aren't any spiders," Lily says, shaking her head. She smiles at Charles and holds out her arm to him, and he comes over for a kiss, trailing his equipment.

I nod. "That's right. No spiders. I just said that."

"Your daddy's having a hard time," Lily says.

Charles is hanging around in an annoying way, lingering. It's as if he doesn't really want to camp out in the backyard after all.

"I don't care about them anyway," he says. "I play with spiders at school." He waits a second, then says, "Dad, I'm making a tent. Is it OK if I use the boards behind the garage?"

I say sure.

▼

It's dark, and we've got a pretty good tent in the yard. I'm in there with Charles. He's reading a car magazine and listening to a Bon Jovi tape on the portable we got him for his last birthday. I've already asked him to turn it down twice, and the second time he went inside for his earphones. It must be midnight. I'm lying on my back under the tent, my feet sticking out the back end of it, my head on one of the three pillows he brought out. The floor of our place here is cardboard, but we've got a rug over that, a four-by-seven thing that Lily and I got at Pier 1 about fifteen years ago. I got it out of the garage, where it's been a couple of years.

The bugs aren't too bad. Both of us rubbed down with Off, so there's this thin, slightly turpentine smell in the air.

I get along well enough with Charles. We're not like some *Father Knows Best* thing, but we do all right. He has his world and I have mine. Looking at him there in the tent, his head hopping with music, his eyes on the magazine, I have an idea what he's about, what it's like for him. I mean, he sees the stuff I see on TV and he believes it, or maybe he believes nothing, or maybe he recognizes that none of it makes any difference to him anyway. I guess that's it. And if that's it, he's right. Let 'em lie. We've got the yard, the bedspread tent, there are crickets around here, and pretty soon a cat will stick its head in the opening at the front of the tent, look us over, maybe even come in and curl up. What goes on out there is entertainment. I'm not saying it won't touch him, but the scale is so big that really it won't. We'll do another Grenada — what a pathetic, ignorant joke — but he'll be in school, or doing desk work for some army rocker, or waiting for his second child. He's just like me — he's out of it. He can get in if he wants to — he can be a TV guy, a reporter, a senator, a staff person. It's America. He can be anything, do anything. I'm stumped.

"What're you doing, Dad?" Charles says.

I keep looking at the top of the tent. "Thinking about you."

"Oh." He waits a minute, then he says, "Well? Is it a mystery or what?"

"It's no mystery," I say, rolling over on my side so I can look at him. He's got the earphones down around his neck. "What're you reading?"

"Bigfoot." He flashes the magazine at me. It's called *Bigfoot*. "The truck, you know?"

"Monster truck," I say.

"Right. It's a whole magazine about Bigfoot — how they got started, what happened, you know..."

"You interested in trucks?" I say. What I'm thinking is, I don't like the way this sounds, this conversation. It sounds like conversations on television, fathers and sons in tortured moments. "Never mind," I say.

"Not really," he says, answering me anyway.

"I don't know why I'm out here, Charles," I say. "Am I bothering you?"

"Not really. I mean, it's strange, but it's not too bad."

"I'm just a little off track today, know what I mean? I think I'm down on my fellowman — talking weenies everywhere, talking cheaters and liars. I mean, normally it doesn't bother me, I just play through. You do what you can. Pick up the junk and paste it back together whatever way you can."

"Dad? Are you drunk?"

"Nope," I say. "I haven't been drunk for ten years, Charles. There's nothing to drink about." I sit up, crossing my legs, facing him. "I never wanted to have a son — any child, for that matter. You and Christine are Lily's doing, what she wanted. I didn't mind, you see. It's not like I hate kids or anything, it's just that having kids wasn't the great driver for me. You're a problem, you know? Kids are. I don't want to treat you like a pet, but you're small — and, of necessity, kind of dumb. I don't mean dumb, but there's stuff you don't know, see what I mean?"

"Sure," he says.

"It's not stuff I can tell you."

"Dad," he says, "are you sure you're OK? You want me to get Mom?" He's up, bent over, already on his way out.

"Well... sure. Get Mom."

I lie down again when he's gone. I feel fine, I feel OK. In a minute Lily's crawling into the tent. "Roger?" she says. "What's going on? Do you feel all right?"

Charles comes in long enough to get his magazine and his tape recorder. "I think I'll stay inside tonight," he says.

"I talked to him," I say to Lily.

"Uh-huh." She's got an arm across my chest, and she's patting me.

"So long, Sport," I say to Charles as he backs out of the tent.

"'Night, Dad," he says.

I'm left there in the tent with my wife. I say, "I'm acting up, I guess."

"A little."

"But that's acceptable, right? Now and then?"

"It's fine," she says.

"It's by way of a complaint, huh? So we're back where we started from."

176

"Yep."

"It's not a vague complaint in my head," I say. "It's just that it covers everything. There are too many things to list. You start listing things that are wrong, and you either make them smaller and sort of less wrong, or you go on forever. You got forever?"

"Sure." She waits a few seconds after she says that. I can feel her waiting. Then she says, "Things are just not right out there."

"You got it."

She gets up on her knees and twists around so she can lie down on her back alongside me. She takes my right hand in her left. "See there? We're not completely gone. We're OK. We've just got to take it one thing at a time. We've got to go binary on the deal."

LAW OF AVERAGES

AT THE RECEPTION after the meeting where my daughter, Karen, got an award for "Most Mathematical" third grader, I went for the punch, even though the punch table was surrounded on three sides by earnest-looking parents — clean, bright faces, ready smiles, the knowing and glowing types. I got around behind the table and stepped over a brick planter, but I tripped and hit the woman who was serving. Punch went flying. Most of it hit the floor, but there was some on me, some on her. She patted at her clothes and introduced herself. "I'm Mary Quine. I teach here — fifth grade, civics." Both of us were looking around at the crowd. There were a hundred people there, among the tan folding chairs. "I hate these things, don't you?"

"I don't come very often," I said.

"Take a look at this beanpole over here," she said.

"Uh-huh," I said. I liked it that she called a man a beanpole. I waved to Karen to tell her where I'd be, then handed a guy who'd come for punch a couple of napkins. That became my job, the napkins. I handed them out while Mary ladled. We spent an hour doing that, talking about divorces — mine was more recent. When the reception thinned, I collected Karen and the three of us walked out together.

Mary started to fluff Karen's hair when I introduced them, but thought better of it and stopped mid-gesture. "You don't look like a Karen," she said. "You look like a Grace, or a Lily."

"What's a Grace look like?" Karen said.

We stopped between two lines of cars in the parking lot, and I put my arm around Karen and said, "I think she's more of a Roxy. She's got a Roxy look about her."

"What are you guys talking about?" Karen said.

"Nothing," I said. Ordinarily, Karen would have come with her mother, but her mother had chicken pox, so I got an extra night.

"And sometimes," Karen said, "he calls me Karen." She was towing me toward the car. "Can we go?"

On the way home I pumped her for what she knew about Mary Quine. Karen was uncooperative. She didn't know a thing. She said, "You want me to ask about her?"

I said no.

"I could go around to all my friends and tell them my dad is interested in Miss Quine and ask them what she's like."

"No, thanks," I said. "Let's change the subject. I'm sorry I brought it up."

We stopped at the light by Popeye's, and Karen said, "Do you like her a lot? I guess she's probably going to be your girlfriend now. You guys'll get married and everything. If that's what's happening, I'm telling Mama."

"Go easy on me, Rox," I said. "I'm a casualty."

"Oh, Daddy," she said, slapping at my leg. "What's that mean? Why do you always say things I don't understand?"

I pulled her over next to me in the seat, sat with my arm around her tiny shoulders as if we were teenagers, years ago. She leaned her head against my chest.

"That's the way it goes," I said. "When you get old like me, you get to be a mystery. It'll happen to you quick enough."

"I don't want to be a mystery," Karen said. "I never want to be a mystery."

▼

I dropped Karen at home and drove over to the Conestoga Party Club, a remade, windowless ShowBiz Pizza. I never did think ShowBiz would work. I was there once, for one of Karen's birthdays. Everything was done with aluminum tokens shaped like quarters. These things were as thick as quarters, and they cost a quarter. They were just like quarters, only they were these tokens. I guess they figured if you bought ten bucks' worth of tokens, you weren't going to cash in the leftovers. They probably had market research to prove that.

When ShowBiz evacuated, the Conestoga people refurbished the cinder-block building into a bar-restaurant combo, but instead of installing windows, which would have been costly, they hired a Junior League realist to do a floor-to-ceiling mural of the great outdoors — white-tailed deer, silvery fish leaping out of ponds, geese swimming across the cobalt-blue sky, jackrabbits eyeing the customers. I guess the artist wanted to make a statement: the animals in the painting were all packing guns — rifles, pistols, submachine guns. It was a real animal revolution in there.

When Mary arrived, we took a booth next to a wall on which a couple of bandito squirrels, cartridge belts slung across their bare bellies, stood up on their haunches, chewing pecans. We unwrapped our silverware. The napkins were small and thin as tissue. It was awkward at first. We studied the menus and placed our orders with a middle-aged woman in blue stretch, a woman who looked kind of scientific, as if she'd been in the beaker too long. Then Mary and I locked eyes across the tabletop.

For a second I was worried there was nothing to say. I was thinking about picking up women, something I'd done maybe twice in my life — thinking what do you say when there's no reason to be together? Then I decided we'd picked each other up, but that wasn't better — that just made us consenting adults.

Mary was eyeing the mural. "This reminds me of a TV show I saw," she said. "Twenty guys in this trench in a field, all lined up, with shotguns. Some of them had big black paddles, and when the ducks got near enough the guys started waving their paddles, as if they were wings, I guess. The ducks were beautiful — dark against lemon-color streaks. Then the jerks on the ground started flapping, and their friends started blowing birds out of the sky, and what I thought was, you know, that's wrong."

"I've had that feeling," I said.

"I mean, it's just like this," she said, pointing at the mural. "I wanted the ducks to have guns. Make it a fair fight. Ducks coming in plastering these fat guys, you know?" She made a jet fighter with her hand, diving it at the table and doing machine-gun noises. "I'd love to see that. A real bloodbath, while these yokels scramble out of the trench, heading for safety, falling over each other, splattering in the mud with the tops of their heads blown to smithereens." She made an explosion sound and popped herself high on the forehead with a flat palm.

"They'd try to shoot back," I said.

"Maybe one," she said. "The rest would be running. We'd cut 'em down. We'd drill 'em."

I noticed that she was looking in my eyes. I hate it when people look in my eyes. I mean, when they stare right at them, when I can see that what they're doing is looking right in there. Because it means they want something. It means they're way off the beam.

I said, "You're real nice, and I like you more with each passing day."

"What?"

"Joke," I said. "Kind of an icebreaker."

She got embarrassed, looked at the table. It was one of those tables with real planks encased in once-liquid plastic. "I'm sorry," she said. "I guess I missed it. I guess I did too much on the ducks. I don't know what's wrong with me." Then she looked up, showing new resolve. "So, you want to just zip through dinner and go back to my apartment and be careful? No . . . that's wrong. I also saw this show about the Peace of Mind club. It's a safety club. You know, for sex. You're not a member, are you? I hate it." She traced an outline around a squirrel in the painting. "This is wrong, too, isn't it? Aggressive? I don't care about sex, really."

"Well," I said. "I don't know." She sat up, straightened her place setting. "OK. Great. Can we just start again?" She tapped the wall. "Good squirrel," she said. "I don't know what we're doing. Let's talk about you or something, OK? I always get myself in a mess when I talk."

I said, "OK. Me."

"I am *so* sorry," she said. She was going into the tabletop again. "I always do this. I get out here, and I don't know what to do. I don't fit."

I said, "You're fine. Really. Where don't you fit?"

"School," she said.

"What's wrong with school?"

"I don't like it." She turned to look toward the cash register, drumming her fingers. "I used to love school, but now — I don't know why you'd want to hear this, do you?"

"Sure," I said. "I'm interested."

"We've got teachers you wouldn't let near your kid," she said. "Lots of them. But in our evaluations we all grade out superior. It's a joke. I mean, to hear us tell it we're all one in a million." She shrugged, shook her head. "I'm going to stop," she said. "I promise."

"It's OK," I said.

"So today I had a fight with the guy in the room next to mine. He had the TV on all day. I asked him to quit it."

"TV?" I said. "You have TVs?"

"What're you, a guy who's been asleep for a hundred and twenty-five years or something? You never heard of that? They're supposed to be for PBS stuff, but we use 'em to shut the kids up, because we're so good."

I watched her. When the food came she quit talking and started eating. She held her knife wrong, like a pencil.

▼

We took both cars to her apartment at Château Belvedere, an eighty-unit cedar-shake project buried in tall pines back off the highway feeder. It was near two when we pulled into the parking lot and walked up the hill to her block of apartments. I watched the wet sidewalk as we walked, listened to the wind chimes — lots of people out there had wind chimes. Two guys and a girl were in the laundry building drinking beer and sitting on tables. Mary's apartment was upstairs, a two-bedroom with fur-brown shag and a low, mottled plasterboard ceiling. There was a crummy light fixture in the center of the ceiling in each room. She went to get drinks out of the icebox, and I sat down in front of the television.

I thought it was going pretty well. I hadn't been out much since the divorce. When I had been, mostly what I wanted to do was go home. Sometimes I thought I didn't want to "get over" my divorce. I knew I was supposed to, but I wasn't sure I wanted to. There's something seductive about it, something safe and easy — like you've done your duty and you don't have to do what you're supposed to do anymore, you can go home and watch TV and do some scraggly cooking and not feel bad about it. You're not missing anything. I'd been so close to my wife that now when I was around somebody else I felt like I wasn't where I was supposed to be.

Mary came back with beer for herself, Coke for me. She sat at the end of the couch, her legs crossed under her, skirt punched down between her knees. I didn't look at her. I was staring at the channel changer that was on the coffee table. I was thinking I might pick it up.

"Why don't you tell me about your wife?" Mary said.

"Who?"

"That's great," she said.

"Sorry."

"Don't worry about it."

"Fine. I won't." I looked from her to the blank TV, then back. I was thinking about what I could say about my wife, and looking at the coffee table trying to figure out if it was an acceptable coffee table or if it was junk, and then I decided to go ahead and tell her. "The good stuff that happened, every nice memory I've got, came from her. I don't know why, but it's all hers."

Mary didn't say anything.

"I probably should have said that some other way."

She went back to her bottle. "It's OK," she said. "It's interesting."

"No," I said, shaking my head. "It's not. It's not good. It's like I feel like I'm going to be small and mean for the rest of my life."

"Well, I guess it's better to be small and mean than too sensitive," she said. "You know, we're all earnest, right? We don't have to be unctuous."

I thought about "unctuous," about what a good word it was. "I don't seem like a child anymore. I can't live like a child, feel that way. I could only do that with her."

Mary nodded, waited a minute as if she were thinking, then said, "I've got a fire engine."

I looked to see whether that was friendly or hostile. She wasn't smiling, so I figured friendly. I traced a knuckle on one of her hands. "What color?"

It was a nice night after that. We made love and it wasn't a disaster, and then we went for a walk through the project. It was cool out there, damp, there were quiet stars in the sky. We stuck to the sidewalks and didn't say much; but after we'd gone through the place once, we were holding hands. I was comfortable. I hadn't been in an apartment project for a while, and I had forgotten the odd comforts of them — being close to people in your economic bracket with whom you have almost nothing else in common, the community feeling even though you never talk to these people and only rarely see them. I had forgotten what it felt like to look down a five-hundred-yard line of apartments, cars parked in front, yellow streetlamps dousing the asphalt with little slicks of light; forgotten the pleasure of somebody pulling up across the street at two-thirty in the morning, some couple coming in from a party or a club, their too-bright, too-loud voices suddenly hushed when they see you. As we walked, heavy trucks soared by on the highway I could just make out through the trees. This wasn't a fancy project, but under the cover of night it was gently transformed into a place of small mysteries — elegant shadows cast by young trees on badly painted wood siding, the reassuring clicks and whines of air-conditioning compressors snapping on and cutting off, the almost inaudible thump of somebody's giant woofer. I could make out the music, I could picture the people, a young couple, turning up the wick any way they could.

Somebody screamed somewhere. It sounded to me as if it had come out of the woods, but Mary thought it had come from the other direction, from one of the apartments toward the front of the project, toward the highway. We stopped and stood perfectly still, listening.

In a minute she whispered, "The beast..."

We started walking again. The grass alongside the walk glittered as we passed. Things were getting kind of smoky. Mary and I went from hand in hand to arm in arm. She leaned her head against my shoulder. We stopped in front of a chip-filled garden to watch a gray cat box with a twig, flip it up into the air, and then catch it and roll over on its side and do Ray Leonard with its back feet. Even the fireplug out there was pretty good-looking — pale yellow with a lime-green top. We walked a little more and ended up sitting on somebody's doorstep, facing the central courtyard of the project, watching the shining blue water in the pool through a chain-link fence. After a time Mary asked me if I was ready for sleep. I said I was, and as we walked back toward her apartment I pointed out somebody's pretty, violet-lit bug zapper.

▼

Mary was apologetic about breakfast. "I didn't mean to force you into anything," she said, pointing at the dishes on the table. "Eating and stuff."

She'd made breakfast while I was showering, and she was self-conscious about it, about what it suggested or what it might suggest.

I said, "It was delicious," but I realized that sounded wrong, too formal. "I didn't mean that. I mean, I meant it was delicious, but I didn't mean the other part — you know what I'm talking about?"

"The repellent part?" she said.

That's when I started thinking I really liked her. I thought maybe we fit together. The real way, like people you can't imagine passionate, or passionate together, or who look as if they were passionate once and were done with it. I'd always wondered how those people got together in the first place.

Mary was clearing away the breakfast dishes. I watched the way she stacked. I liked it; she took out the utensils from between the dishes. I imagined her driving Karen to school, and then later, in the evening, the three of us in the car, picking up Popeye's. I looked around the apartment, and it looked a lot better in the daytime. There was plenty of sun in there — white Formica and light-colored wood, plants in the windows. The TV was on, tuned to one of the morning shows, the sound low. Even the carpet looked OK.

I figured if we were together we'd be like ugly people, or old people. We weren't either of those — I don't mean we were young and beautiful, but we were only half old, and we weren't so much uglier than everybody else that you'd run and scream if you saw us. If I had to say, I'd say regular. Mary had brown hair that was kind of wiry and specked with white, a slightly troubled nose, good skin, eyes that brought the beach to mind, and a fair body for thirty-five. Maybe I was a little on the short side — under six feet, although well over the average height for American males — and I guess I didn't help myself much with the khakis and the short-sleeved shirts, but my face was all right. People sometimes said I was "ruggedly attractive," if that's possible for somebody of my height. I had all my hair, even if it wasn't trained. Brown hair. Washed nightly. I wasn't the best judge of what I looked like, but I was attentive, and I'd spent some time studying other men — in the movies, in the magazines, on the street. I figured I had a kind of look. Maybe we both did.

WAR WITH JAPAN

THIS WEEKEND I'm moving into the garage apartment behind our house. It's pretty much my decision. Lily says she thinks it's a good idea. "We've been having a kind of trouble for the last few weeks, George," she says. "Maybe this'll straighten things out."

The trouble is I'm "starting up," I'm getting agitated again, about the office, the news commentators, the squeaky politicians who go on TV and get self-righteous and super-moral—I get fed up listening to these people. They just want to get elected, or get better ratings, or get the approval of the focus group—I don't know why we sit still for this junk. And it's worse the last couple of years—I mean, it makes you want to get up on the Texas tower. That's the kind of thing I say that makes Lily mad. That's when she starts talking about the garage. "You're painting with the big brush again, Ralph," she says. She calls me Ralph when she thinks I'm way off base. "You're using the paint that's shot from guns."

We've had the "move out to the garage" joke ever since we got the house, but neither one of us has ever gone. We kid about it all the time—sometimes she's supposed to move out, and sometimes I am. It's a running thing. But today her voice says she means it. That's when I know I'm gone.

It's a two-car garage with the apartment above. We redid the apartment when Lily was planning a home office—got the tight little carpet, industrial gray, the cheap plastic blinds that look like Levolors, Wal-Mart's good white paint. When the office idea was over, we used our old stuff to fix the place up like a guest cottage.

Lily doesn't want to help me move, so she decides to go to the store. "What do you want for dinner?" she asks me.

I've already started sorting clothes. "Vegetables. I'm going on an all-vegetable thing."

"I don't know what they have that's fresh."

"I don't care from fresh. Corn, limas, black-eyed peas, rice — that's what I want. Bird's Eye. Modernize my system."

"Fine," she says, heading for the door. "I'll get a steak in case you change your mind."

"I'm not changing my mind."

"I know that," Lily says.

Our twelve-year-old, Charles, is out front working on the sidewalk with the Weed Eater. He's another part of the problem—I keep telling him stuff Lily doesn't think he needs to know. She says I'm doing just what my father did.

"You're more like your father every day," she says.

"It could be worse. I could be one of these lost-to-the-pan guys who wash their cars in driveways every afternoon, who look like kids ready for church when you see them out with their wives."

"You're always ready for church." She shakes her head and looks at the ceiling as if offering a prayer. "Hormones."

I tell her I'm tired in a new way, and she says she's waiting me out. I tell her something's snapped, and she says that's marriage.

▼

I hate everything now. Obvious stuff, like TV, and stuff that's not so obvious, like the screwdrivers they have at K&B drugstore. Don't get me wrong, I think they've done a hell of a job with that store — it's like a Sears that makes sense — but I don't see why if they're going to sell screwdrivers they don't at least sell respectable ones. Not excellent ones, see — all I'm asking for is a fair screwdriver, something a cut above a *Time* subscription gift.

Lily is back for her shopping list. The list has at least six misspellings on it. I hate that. I usually come around and check for misspellings, correcting them as I go, which she doesn't like, I know. She doesn't say anything anymore. She's fine on the brand names; it's the generics she can't handle. She hasn't spelled "raisin" correctly in the fifteen years I've known her.

We used to argue about my correcting her — not only spelling but grammar, syntax, pronunciations, the titles she gets mixed up, actors' names, product names, pronoun reference. There are lots of things Lily never got the hang of, so I used to be forever correcting, which was no fun for me, either, only I couldn't stop. She was the one who figured she could make intentional mistakes and throw me off track, and that worked, so we kept that in. The shopping list is about all I fix anymore.

I'm in the den watching her back out of the driveway, thinking she's going to clip the tree this time for sure. I'm wondering, too, if I can get Charles to help me move. I think I'll take the opportunity to explain why I'm switching out to the garage, and then I think maybe I won't, because it won't come out clear. I don't know why I want to explain stuff to him — I guess I want to win him, but I don't know why that seems necessary. Besides, the only thing Charles approves of is Spaceman 3. That and bullet bikes, which he calls crotch rockets when he wants to get my goat. I let him get it, I play along, doing some self-serving, self-righteous, hateful, low-road Pat Buchanan stuff, like on TV.

For about a minute after Lily's out the driveway, I watch Charles working the Weed Eater along the edges of the sidewalk. I stand at the window and watch, and then when I think enough time has passed so he won't think it's a put-up thing, I go out there after him. It's hot outside, a dull heat, and I remember when my father sent me outside on late summer days to do work I didn't think needed doing. My father was a drover when it came to getting work out of us kids. I hated it back then, but it makes sense now — work habits. I go to the office, and then I come home and work until it's time to go to sleep, and I do that probably because that's what he did, that's what he had us do when we were kids. He did carrot-and-stick stuff, too. Anyway, we worked, while other kids rode around in borrowed convertibles. They peaked out in high school, where they excelled in sports as well as academics.

I try to imagine that Charles looks like me thirty years ago, but I can't see it; I was a towheaded guy in hand-me-downs, with that late-fifties look — insulated, the way the world was then. Charles looks like a small Magnum, P.I., or somebody they're thinking about for the next Bond film; he handles the Weed Eater as if he's taking fingerprints off it. I'm guessing this can be called cultural progress — the *new day* as played out in homes and houses across the land. I go around him, giving him a wide berth, and then plant myself in his way so he can't avoid me. I wiggle my arm at the machine, telling him to turn it off.

"What's wrong?" he says, looking up the sidewalk at the portion of the edge he's already done. Now he's got the machine head down in the dirt, and he's leaning on the handle like a young Jack Nicklaus. "I guess I screwed this up, huh?"

I'm not old enough to have a son like this. Only weeks ago I was going to the bar to play bass with the Assassins' Band. And the majors were interested; they sent people down.

"No," I say to Charles. "It looks fine. It looks real good."

He eyes the sidewalk and then me, as if to ask how come I'm stopping him if it looks OK. He has things to do. He doesn't have time to stand around chatting.

I say, "Let's take a walk."

It's pretty clear he doesn't think that's the best idea he's ever heard. Something about the way he moves his shoulders, curls them over, crablike. "It's a little hot, Dad," he says.

"Never mind that. I want to explain something. Something I've been thinking about."

He's still there with the Weed Eater poised, so I take it from him and drop it in the grass alongside the sidewalk. Then I put an arm around his shoulders and turn him toward the garage. There's a path around the side of the garage. I want to have this talk in the backyard.

"In the first place, Charles, what you ought to do when I come up and say I want to have a talk with you is say OK. I mean, the way you look here is *Why doesn't he leave me alone?*"

He says, "Sorry, Dad."

I think I've got him on the defensive, so I carry on. "Never mind. What I want to tell you is that there are all these things wrong now, and they didn't used to be wrong. I'm figuring you're going to notice that they're wrong and start wondering *why*, so I thought I'd get a step up, you know? Doing my duty."

He looks uncertain, so I say, "Let me give you an example. I was sitting inside here, thinking about a war with the Japanese. Now, Charles, we're not about to have any war with the Japanese, you understand that, right?"

"We're friends with the Japanese," Charles says. "They give us all our stuff, don't they? They make the bullet bikes and everything."

"Right," I say. "But they're a different kind of people, and you get wars a lot that way. But bear with me, that's not the point, anyway." Charles is having trouble sticking with me, I can see that. He's more interested in his feet, in the careful placement of them as we walk, than in what I'm saying. For a second I remember something about what it's like to be twelve, but it goes by so fast that when the memory is gone I'm not certain I really remembered at all. That throws me, and I have to make a specific decision to carry on, to keep talking. "See, if we were to go to war with the Japanese — let's say we were going to do that, and let's say the Japanese were winning and came over here and took over part of this country the way the Germans did in Europe in the Second World War, or like we did in Vietnam, or Grenada—you know what I'm talking about?"

"Yes, Dad," he says. "You mean, like, liberating the country, right? Like saving it from itself?"

I stare at my son and realize that I don't know where he got that remark. I don't know what he knows, what he means, what's rote, and what's not.

I say, "So, I was thinking if they were here I'd help them." I wait a minute to see how he's taking that, but he doesn't react. "You're not supposed to—you know that?"

"Sure. They'd be the enemy."

"I mean, Charles, I wouldn't help them kill us or anything, but I'd cooperate. And the reason is that although there was a time when this was a wonderful country, and we did everything right —or that's what everybody thought, everybody who lived here, anyway—that was a while ago, and now it's clear that this country is as bad as the next."

"They still say we're the greatest. I hear that all the time."

"Me too." I'm having this feeling that I want to touch Charles, to hold him, press his body against mine—just father-son stuff, but it's stronger than usual.

"What I think is that we're not as bad as Iran," Charles says. "I've seen those people on television, and they're a lot worse. They're always smacking themselves over the head with chains and stuff. That seems kinda dumb."

"Bad for the hair."

"What?"

"It's a hair joke. It's shorthand. You know about shorthand, don't you?"

"I guess so," he says, but I can see that I've lost him. He looks at his pants and flicks away a slice of grass caught on one perfectly creased trouser leg.

The backyard looks like some kind of dump. I can see fifty things that need to be done, but I tell myself this talk is more important. On the other side of the collapsed chain-link fence that separates our yard from Bud Patrick's yard there's Bud himself, doing what he likes to call his weekly "malingering." This week he's malingering with his satellite dish — he's got the leg that sticks up toward the center of the dish sprung loose, and he's working on the feed horn.

I motion that Charles should sit on the edge of the patio, and I perch on a sawhorse that's standing there. "The Japanese are like us, Charles. They're like what we used to be — I mean, they actually believe what we used to say we believed. They work hard. They get a job and they try to do it right. I'm not saying every Japanese person in Japan is that way. In fact, I read something about Japanese workers wanting to be more like ours. Still, some of them, maybe most of them, have figured out there's a percentage in doing good work. We haven't figured that out yet."

"Sure, but we're a lot more democratic than they are," Charles says. "They have these little tiny houses and they are not very democratic."

I've got one eye on Charles and the other on Bud Patrick, and I'm wondering if the backyard was such a good idea. Bud's a friendly guy. I say, "What, Charles?"

"Well, we vote and everything. You can do anything here. Guys argue right out in the open, like on TV."

Bud's seen us, and he's heading for the fence. I give him a wave, hoping that'll keep him on his side.

Charles says, "At dinner, you know, when we switch between that show on the news thing, you know the one? And the one on the other channel? I listen to those guys sometimes. They argue, don't they?"

"Not really."

"Well, the first guy says his position, and that's usually a distortion of the other guy's position, according to what you always say, and then, if the other guy argues back, then the guy repeats his position."

"Yeah, but you see those people aren't talking, right? It's a first-strike thing. The idea is get your stuff on louder and quicker, and repeat it, so the viewer remembers yours and not the other guy's."

"I get it," Charles says, thinking about that as he stands up, brushes off. "I mean, is that right? You say that all the time, but I never really thought about it before." He points back the way we came around the house. "OK if I finish up out front?"

"Wait a minute," I say, grabbing his shoulder, wrapping an arm around him in a fatherly way, a way that seems fatherly, even though I know what I'm doing is restraining him.

Right at that point Bud says, hollering from his side of the fence, "So, what's up with you two? Am I interrupting?" He's starting to climb the little fence, and it sags under his weight. He's almost over the top, standing with one foot squeezed into a broken link and the other on the top bar of the fence — he's ready to vault into our yard.

"How's it going?" I say, waving toward his yard.

"I'm working on my dish," he says, hitching his khaki shorts, his knees knobby and white like a just-rinsed turkey. "You gotta get one of these things. They're great." Just then his phone rings and he tries to jump back off the fence, but his foot is caught and he buckles on it, falls, twisting his ankle and ending up on the ground on his side of the fence with a leg knotted in the loose chain mesh.

Charles is faster than me getting over there. "Are you all right?" he says, hopping the fence and squatting beside Bud, starting to peel the fence away from his leg.

"Don't touch the ankle," I say.

"He's not touching me," Bud says, flat on his back and doing a hand-pistol at Charles, keeping a stiff upper lip. "Your dad giving you trouble?"

"We were talking," Charles says.

There's an eight-inch scratch along the inside of Bud's left leg above and below the knee, and the scratch is doing lots of bleeding.

"You want me to get something for the cut?" I say, pointing at his leg. "Is it sprained or anything?"

"I'm fine," Bud says. "Put some peroxide on this baby and I'll be super."

I send Charles inside for peroxide and bandages, and then I sit down in the grass on my side of the fence opposite where Bud's stretched out. The grass is amazingly soft and cool. I could sleep there.

"You guys having a heart-to-heart?" he says, fingering the blood a bit. He shrugs. "I guess I've been watching. It's hard not to, you know."

"It's nothing," I say. "We're talking about the junk that's going on these days."

"Yeah? What junk?"

I've got trouble right here. This is not stuff I want to talk about with Bud Patrick. I say, "We're talking the usual—TV, newspapers, the mayor…kid stuff."

That doesn't slow him down at all. "Degeneration of family values," he says. "That's the issue that's got me worried."

"It's big for me, too," I say, checking the house to see if Charles is on the way. He's coming through the sliding patio door. Bud is still on his back, but I don't think there's anything very wrong with him.

"Still," he says. "We're doing better every day. A little bit better."

"Maybe so. I guess it seems that way."

"It's better," he says.

I watch Charles hand over the peroxide, a tube of Neosporin, some gauze pads. Charles looks solid for a kid his age. "I was reading this article about Russia," I say. "This is the new, open Russia, right? You know, *glasnost* and all that?"

"Sure," Bud says. He's sitting up, his leg sizzling with peroxide.

"So whoever wrote it says, 'It's an amazing thing, this new

openness. It even extends to the state. Even the government speaks some truth.'"

"That's right," he says.

Charles is watching Bud doctor his leg, which is much meaner-looking after the peroxide than it was before.

"You see what the guy's saying, right? That it's unusual for their government to speak truth, since it's a hotbed of deceit and moral decay. Ours, on the other hand, is the soul of integrity."

"Well?" Bud says. "Maybe it's exaggerated, but I don't know how far it is from the truth. I mean, the basic idea."

I look at Charles. Charles looks back at me.

"I saw this MTV thing," Charles says. "It was like . . . they're just like us, the people over there, I mean."

"I don't know, Chuck," Bud says. He's done with the peroxide, and now he's reading the Neosporin tube.

"Charles has some weed-eating to do out front," I say.

"Hey," Bud says, looking up. "Me and Chuck were getting ready to have a *talk*, you know?"

I say, "So the magazine quotes some Russian who says, 'We would like to get our workers to work as hard as your workers.' Now, you figure that's flattery, right? But the magazine plays it for truth, since, as the magazine has just said, they tell some truth over there nowadays. It's a little convenient, don't you think?"

Bud's shaking his head like a hundred self-satisfied guys I've seen on television. He says, "I don't know why you people always want to tear us down."

I'd like to pop his face for him right now, tear it down and drop it into somebody's night-deposit box. "Bud," I say, "it's only me here, and I'm not tearing anybody down. This magazine says these people don't work as hard as our people, and I say they probably do. The magazine wants to sell us something, Bud, it wants us to *feel* better, and it's getting us there by saying we work harder — you follow that? It's a pride con. Harder equals better; you feel all warm to be an American. And these days, feeling better is all-

important, Bud. If we've got some tragic losses along the way —
why, it's a small price for national pride. If some people get killed
— well, maybe *they deserve to die.* If we have to splatter and maim
so our dopey President thinks we're tough, so he can pass that
along to thousands of small-town papers and hundreds of local
nightly news shows, so people interested in breakfast eggs and
getting Jim Jr. through high school can say they, too, *feel better*
about our country — why, Bud, that's OK, 'cause we were born to
rule, right? We were born to minister. That's what *you people* say,
isn't it? And what does it matter if the body count includes law,
honesty, justice, fairness, decency, honor, and the rest? If we only
understood what was at stake, we, too, would be willing to forgo a
few of these niceties, right?"

Bud looks a little strange. He says, "Well, I wouldn't go that far."

"Hey, Dad," Charles says. "Take it easy on him, will you? Don't
bust him up." He pats my shoulder stiffly. "Are you OK?"

"Never better," I say, looking at him, feeling that I really like
him a lot, that I'm glad as hell he's my son.

"So, they work as hard as we do, right?" Charles says, trying to
get things going again.

Bud's on his feet, capping the peroxide bottle, shuffling gauze
pads — he's decided to forgo the Neosporin. "According to your
dad, they work harder," he says.

I laugh at him, and I don't feel bad for doing it. Somewhere in
my head I'm certain that this exchange, like all the others I've had
with Bud, will be forgotten soon enough.

"Charles," I say, holding on to my son. "The Russian guy was
being polite, and the magazine lied. The fact is that our workers sit
on their machines, smoke cigarettes, spit, scratch themselves,
punch out, and ask for more money. That's the American dream
these days. And I mean for all of us, from the auto unions to the
universities."

"Jesus, George," Bud says. "I think you're losing perspective
here."

What I'm thinking is that I do sound like my father, that Lily's right. Father complained about everything, bitterly, at length, and often at dinner, because there he could be assured an audience. At our house, if you wanted to eat you had to listen to the homily. According to Father, nobody wanted to do anything right. I thought he was crazy. What's the big deal? How right do you have to do things, and who's to say what's right in the first place? When he talked, all I could think of was the other points of view that people might have. His stuff was mostly about guys trying to save a buck by cutting corners, and I was always thinking, Well, maybe there's a good reason to cut a corner or two. Now I wonder what Charles is thinking.

Charles is flapping his shirt. He's got it by a button, and he's ratcheting the shirt in and out to cool off his chest.

Bud returns the medicines. "One thing's for sure," he says to Charles. He's using his snide-guy voice. "We're working hard today. I know your dad's just back from the Center for Constitutional High Jinks, but I feel compelled to say our people work plenty hard. They earn everything they get."

"Yeah," I say. "But earning isn't what it was. These days you take a pee right and get a thousand-dollar raise."

"I think you'd better get some sleep, George," Bud says to me. "You're completely off base now. Maybe you ought to barbecue something. Stick with juicier burgers and bigger buns."

"I hate those," Charles says, smiling. "Those fat wet guys people always make at home."

Charles is defending me. This is a first, I think. He's sitting here taking on the neighbor, defending the old man, doing a job. Bud doesn't quite get it.

"Say, Mr. Patrick, maybe *you* ought to cook out tonight," Charles says. "Do something for the whole neighborhood — your treat. How's that sound?"

"I'd like to," Bud says. He's limping away from the fence. "But I've gotta work tonight, gotta catch up."

I give him a glazed smile.

Charles says, just loud enough, "I always ask Mom to make mine thin, like Burger King. She does it right. She knows."

We have some silence between us, watching Bud hobble across his yard and into his house. Neither one of us says anything for a minute, and I'm sitting there staring at the backyard, which is unrestrained and poorly trimmed, and I've got my arm around Charles's shoulders. I'm thinking I want to tell him everything. I want to tell him I can't do it, I tried, I can't make it, and he'd better try. But I've probably run him down for the day, so I say instead, "Your mother makes a good hamburger. It's not a Whopper, but it's OK."

Charles laughs, gives me a defiant fist. Maybe this is the kind of thing I'm supposed to say, the kind of thing fathers and sons always say. Maybe I'm right for a change.

WITH RAY & JUDY

THERE WERE people all over the house — friends of Heidi's, people I'd never met or had met and forgotten. She was hosting a party, a reception for her boss, Ralph, who had been promoted, and she had called that afternoon to invite me. We were living apart — had been for two months, trying it out.

On the phone I said, "I want to come, OK? But these people — you know? They *believe* everything. They're so confident. They miss half of what you say, because they think they know everything you could say."

"I forgot about this," Heidi said. "Maybe you'd better go to a movie instead."

"I can't. I don't have my dark blue Volvo, my two children, both beautiful, and my lifetime subscription to *Mother Jones*."

"Well, that's a powerful argument." There was a quiet space on the phone, and then she said, "I just wanted to call, George. I'd like to see you. Come if you feel better."

I spent the afternoon worrying whether or not to go. We'd settled quickly into living apart — to the point of shedding some intimacy. When we saw each other now, it was sometimes like not quite best friends. Eventually I decided to go to the party, but when I got there I still wasn't in my best mood. I lost Heidi first thing. She met me at the door, gave me a good hug, and then was off showing Ralph around.

I walked through the house. Back to the bedroom, to the back bath, into the kitchen. I was thinking I didn't like Ralph and I didn't like his buds, not one of them. I wanted to sit down with Heidi. Rest. Besides, these people were always too correct — too clean, too well groomed, too earnest, caring, and genuine. I figured after a certain amount of announced earnestness nausea sets in. Not so the coworkers — they never ceased to be earnest and caring.

I was trying to get with the program, but I wasn't doing a great job of it. I kept telling myself how bitter I was. After a half hour poking what I thought was relatively good-natured fun at some of the guests, things got awkward enough so that it was easier to excuse myself than to carry on. I left my bunch poised around a glass-topped coffee table, admiring each other's shoes.

It was almost ten o'clock, and I was thinking I might sneak out and use the garage apartment, maybe sit in front of the TV out there, take my shoes off. It's the small stuff, the small stuff — I always said that. So I was on the patio, on my way to the garage, when I noticed a couple by the neighbors' fence. They were arm in arm and more, in a kind of ambulatory embrace, leaning against one another, pressing together, veering this way and that as their affection swelled and settled. They were walking and kissing at the same time, which meant shuttling sideways, then moving backward, then swapping ends and going sideways again, crab-walking, circling without separating, without stopping. I wanted to get out of the yellow light dropped by the patio bulb, so I stepped off the concrete and into the flower bed and shadows next to the kitchen door.

I almost bumped into Heidi. She said, "Well, howdy-do, howdy-do."

"Hi," I said, bobbing as I tried to make her out in the shadows. She was a couple of yards away. "What are you doing?"

"Shrinking," she said. "What about you? Taking notes on these two out here?"

I don't know why I said this, but I said, "I'm George Spencer, and I used to live here. This is my house, my flower bed."

"Oops," she said, stepping out of the bed and into the light. "I forgot you were into owner-oriented marriage. I'm your wife, Heidi, but everybody calls me Spider."

"What?"

"Many legs," she said.

I could see her, finally, and she was very lovely. I liked her a lot. I was happy she was out in the flower bed, happy to have found her.

"They don't really call me that," she said. "Nobody ever called me that. I always wanted them to, but they never did. Spider, or Frankie."

"I'll call you Spider."

"I don't want to be called Spider anymore. I'm over that."

"Whew," I said. "Time passes, doesn't it?"

▼

We went to the garage apartment. Going up the stairs, she kept saying, "I don't know about this." And I kept saying, "It's fine, it's fine." There was a screened porch running the length of the garage, facing the yard, and we sat there in director's chairs and watched the couple in the yard below. I brought beer from the tiny red refrigerator she'd repainted.

Heidi looked lanky, fortyish, well kept. She had twenty years of bad skin, and pale hair, and she slouched into the chair like a kid of fourteen. "I think I had lunch with them once," she said.

The couple stopped and stared in our direction, as if they'd heard us whispering. I waved, knowing they couldn't see.

I said, "I guess we're estranged, huh? Me and you? Half estranged, anyway."

"I wouldn't mind being estranged from Ralph," she said. "I think he has a head fracture, the way he talks. He's got congenital brain-fade."

"I haven't seen much of him."

"Tonight he's got his Mr. Curl hairstyle, the artistic glasses, the well-chosen shirt, the trendy shoes. The watch of the century." She leaned forward to look at the couple on the lawn. They'd sat down.

"I hate watches," I said. "And I don't like belts much, either."

"Wow!" she said, sitting back. "You sure are interesting."

From down below, a man's voice said, "Who's that up there? Is that you, Ralph?"

"Oh, dear God," Heidi said. "It's Ralph's friend. I thought that's who it was."

I said, leaning toward the screen, "George Spencer. I live here. Well, I don't really *live* here right now, but I used to. I own it — well, sort of own it."

"Make up your mind, hey?" the voice said. Then there was giggling. Then, "We haven't met. I know Heidi. My name's Ray Bivens."

Heidi whispered, "Bevo to his friends."

"Hi, Ray," I said, hushing Heidi, who was making faces right alongside me. "Glad to meet you. Don't let me interrupt you down there."

"We were just seeing what was what," Ray said. "This is Judy Carol." Then he laughed and said, "Well, I guess you can't see her, but that's who it is. Say hello, Judy."

The woman spoke up. "Hi." She had a tiny voice, doll-like — the voice that comes out after you pull the string.

"Hi, Judy," I said. "Nice to meet you."

"Nice to meet you, too."

Right then the patio door opened and somebody stuck her head out and said, "Who's out here doing all the yelling?"

"It's Ray and Judy," Ray said. "And George's upstairs here in the garage. Dreaming that dream."

"Anybody seen Heidi?" the woman asked.

"Not me," I said.

"I'd like to see Heidi," Ray said in a big stage whisper. Then he and Judy giggled.

▼

Ray and Judy came upstairs. I tried to discourage them, but they wanted to. They were surprised that Heidi was there.

"Just kidding," Ray said. "About that other, you know?"

"Forget it," Heidi said.

Ray and Judy wanted to talk about love. They were new at it, new with each other, and it was still exciting. Ray was the kind of guy who tells you things you don't want to know, intimate things about himself and his life, on the idea that public disclosure is required of every earnest man. He told us he was a libertine. "Not an organized libertine," he said. "But that's what I am. That's what I stand for. You saw me and Judy going around the backyard here, so you know what I mean. That's where we both are in our heads. Right, Judy?"

"You can say that again," Judy said.

Ray opened his mouth as if to repeat himself, then laughed. "It *is* a great life, isn't it? It's much better than anything I imagined, or anything I did before." He was making hand gestures, slicing at the air as if cutting away underbrush. "With my first marriage and my second — I didn't have a clue. You get married, have a baby, you have a car, have a job, and everything just gets away from you, lickety-split." Then he put an arm around Judy's shoulders, tugged her toward him. "Now everything's a lot better. You want something, you take it. That's how we go — bip, bip, bip."

Judy rolled her head back against his shoulder, looking up at him. "Bam, bam, bam," she said.

Both of them laughed.

Heidi said, "Well, what is a libertine, exactly? That's not an organized association or anything, is it? Is that a tax-exempt thing?"

Ray leaned forward, separating himself from Judy. He had his hands together, his elbows on his knees. He had a serious look on his face. "You know," he said, "I sometimes think I ought to be tax-exempt. I sometimes think I could get something going. But if you do that, then you got people saying you're wrong, blaming you. And you know, in a certain way, being a libertine is a relief from all that. I mean, I just don't think about it much anymore. I love Judy, here" — he patted her shoulder — "and we do what we want, when we want and where, and that's the whole ball of wax."

"Bam," I said.

"That's nice," Heidi said. "That's really nice. I wish that was the way it was for me. Most of the time nowadays, at night, I just sit there until something else happens — a new show or something, a telephone call."

Judy gave her a funny look. "Or a bath or something like that, right? I know what you mean."

"Yeah, a bath," Heidi said.

Judy waited for Ray to say something, and when he didn't, she said, "Where's that guy you were with? That Ralph guy?"

"I wasn't with him," Heidi said. "He's my boss. I think he's inside."

"Do you like him?" Judy said. "He's kind of an automatic guy, isn't he?"

"She must not like him much," Ray said. "Or she'd be inside." He tapped Judy's forehead as if to suggest her brain was not working. "Maybe you think she's just out here to cool down, to shake out her shorts?"

"Jesus," Judy said, screwing up her face at Ray, then taking a poke at him. "I apologize," she said. "He's always saying stuff he thinks makes him sound interesting. He's a real individual. He's a libertine, right?"

"I'm sorry," Ray said.

"It's hard in the suburbs," Heidi said, smiling at me. "Sometimes I want to be free and crazy, but that's almost impossible. You've got your dishwasher, your Maytag, your microwave— everything's working against you."

"I rent," Ray said. "When I want to be hot and crazy."

"Heaters," Judy said. "Hundreds of them."

▼

We took Ray's Ford Taurus to the yogurt shop for some cones. Heidi was worried about leaving the party, but Judy persuaded her.

There was a girl at the yogurt place in bicycling pants and a lime-colored halter top, and Ray couldn't take his eyes off her. I pretended to read a double-fold brochure about the nutritional value of yogurt, but I was looking, too. Judy slugged Ray a couple of times, three times, and they laughed together about it. Heidi finally went up to this girl and asked her what her name was.

"Marietta," the girl said. "Who are you guys? Are you at the university?"

We introduced ourselves all around, and then it turned out Marietta was walking, so Judy offered her a ride. The five of us got into the Taurus. Ray was telling Marietta how he and Judy were libertines. The three of them were in the front seat, Heidi and I were in back.

Heidi said, "We have decided that we think we ought to go bowling."

"Great!" Judy said.

I said, "Wait a minute. Why are you saying that, Heidi?"

"I just thought about it," she said. "Why? You think I should go back to the party?"

Marietta said, "Party? You guys have been at a party?" She had a banana split in a quart cup, and she was eating as if she hadn't eaten for weeks.

"Yeah, but it wasn't a good party," Heidi said.

"That's why we left," Ray said.

"I didn't think it was that bad," Judy said. She leaned over and whispered something in Marietta's ear, and the two of them started laughing.

Ray laughed, too, though it was somehow clear to me that he didn't know what Judy had said — that he was just pretending to know. "Yeah, I guess it could have been wall-to-wall chainsaw guys," he said.

We went across a couple of freeway overpasses, one right after the other, each with glistening razor wire twirled on top of the Cyclone fence that was supposed to prevent the kids from diving off or painting "Louie Loves Louise" and "Scar Tissue" all over the newly resurfaced concrete.

Something was wrong with Marietta's head. It was shaped wrong, like a spade or shovel, flat on top, and I was pointing this out to Heidi when Ray caught me in the rearview and gave me eye motions that meant "Cut it out."

"Do you really want to go bowling?" he said, still looking at me in the mirror.

"I don't," I said. I turned to Heidi. "We don't, do we?"

"We'll have to get some socks," Marietta said. "I'm not wearing anybody's leftover socks."

"Me neither," I said.

Ray said to her, "What are you, modern? Why don't you go live in New York, where it pays to be modern?"

"Doesn't pay as much as it used to," Marietta said. "I just moved back from there. I was in school."

"What school?" Heidi said.

"I forget. Art school, I think."

For a second I thought about life-with-Marietta as a replacement for life-with-Heidi, but I felt bad that I'd thought it. That happens. You think something and then feel rotten — it's beneath you, or disgusting. But there's nothing really wrong with thinking stuff you don't try to think but which zips through your brain anyway. That stuff's like dreams — you're not responsible.

Heidi gave me a small punch. "I'm kind of the Mike Tyson of romance," she said. "Banging away at them until they drop." Then she hit Ray on the back. "And I don't want to go bowling, Ray. Everybody goes bowling when they want to slum, when they want to get back. I hate that. Tennessee Ernie Ford and Ernie K-Doe and the fabulous Chantels — forget it. It's out."

"Bowling's out," I said to Ray.

"What?" He turned sideways in the seat, and he drove that way, facing Marietta and Judy, watching the road over his left shoulder. "No bowling? What are we going to do? Go to the tar pits?"

"What's with you, chum?" Marietta said. It sounded mean and fundamental, and it stopped all of us for a minute.

▼

We went to the Big Boy and ordered chicken-fried steak, which they insisted, wrongly, on calling country-fried. Ray wanted to order "Tiny English" peas, which he insisted he'd had there before. But as it turned out, they had no peas. That's when Judy told us Ray had a temper. "He throws things and screams," she said.

"Who doesn't?" Marietta said, snapping her fingers almost in Ray's face. "It seems like everybody's always mad about something."

Ray fidgeted with his water glass and looked at Judy, who was across the table. "I'm meditating," he said. "I saw this movie about the sixties on television, so now I'm trying it out. Everybody meditated back then."

Judy lifted her glass and wagged it at him. "Hand me some new ice, will you?"

He gave her a look, then took the glass across to the silver ice machine by the window.

"Short legs," she said. "Another couple of inches in the thigh and bang—Mr. Hermano Perfecto."

"Why, thank you. That's very kind of you," Ray said. He dipped the glass into the open ice chest. "Now, about Marietta—she's cute, isn't she? Young and cute."

"Endangered," Heidi said.

"Not at all," Judy said. "Ray? Come back over here and settle down. Come on."

Ray did a sweeping dance step, a waltz step, on the way back. "I'm harmless," he said to Marietta. "I'm a romantic."

"I thought you were a libertine," she said.

"Same thing," he said.

Judy was drawing water circles on the plastic tabletop. "Last night we go to dinner at this place, and this girl he used to know, a girl named Helene or something, slips up behind him and starts smooching his neck. Right in front of me."

Ray slipped her glass in front of her and said, "Go on, Judy."

"We'd just started dinner, and Helene slides up, shakes his hand, and then goes for his neck. I wanted to flatten her. But I sit there and smile, and, after a time, I wag my hand around in front of my face like I'm after a fly or something, thinking the girl will get the signal. Thinking *Raymond* will get the signal. Nobody does."

"I was trying," Ray said.

"You weren't doing a thing." She turned to me as if I alone understood what she was saying. "I'm sensing everybody's eyes on me, you know? In the restaurant. They're waiting for me." Judy took a bite of ice and turned around for a look at our empty Big Boy. "She's got on the leather jacket, you know, like from a few years ago—I mean, the girl's been watching a lot of Pontiac advertising. So she looks up from behind Ray's shoulder, looks right at me, and I can see this smile, these eyes, gleaming, like she's having a great time."

"This is spooky," Marietta said.

"She has these watery green eyes," Judy said. "Ray-gun eyes."

"So tell us what happened and get it over with," Heidi said.

"We had dinner with her," Ray said. "That's what happened. We sat there and watched her eat for an hour. That's it. Judy wouldn't eat a thing."

Judy sighed theatrically and put her head down on the table. "We had dinner with her," she said. "Way to go, Ray. Way to queer the deal."

"Well? We did."

Yes, I know we did. We heard all about her life. We know where she works now. We know there's nothing sinister about her — there's no mystery. We saw pictures of her boyfriend and his two kids, I swear to God."

"That's true," Ray said. "Ugly."

"She's a med tech," Judy said. "She works at the path lab. Do you know what she does? She sits in a room the size of a closet and puts stuff on microscope slides. Human tissue and stuff. I didn't believe her until she showed me her badge. You know, she has to wear a badge around, to show that she belongs."

Ray hit his fist softly on the table. "I always wondered about that. I mean, what kind of job is that? Plastic dishes lined up, one new menace after another. I mean, what's a girl like that do for excitement?"

Judy shook her head. "I guess she just remembers you."

▼

We ate fast. It was as if nobody wanted to eat, but we didn't know it until the food was on the table. It wasn't long before we were back in the car, headed for Heidi's.

I wondered if it was my fault we'd never made friends with the Ralphs of the world, the regulars, the ones who follow the rules and go home when they're supposed to, who stick with the spouses and families, go to church, believe everything's going to be all right. I said to Heidi, "I wonder how the party turned out."

She shrugged.

Marietta came climbing over the seat so she could sit in back with us. "You're acting too old," she said to me. Then, trying to get Heidi to agree, she said, "Heidi is not going to be sexually intrigued if you keep acting old."

"Oh, you never know," Heidi said. "He's not too bad." She dropped her head onto my shoulder.

"Good answer," Ray said, turning around to give Heidi his personal approval. "That makes me feel great to hear you say that. It's like I'm not really dead after all."

"He thinks he's dead," Judy said.

"He is," Heidi said. "I was talking about George. I wasn't talking about him at all. Not in any way."

MARGARET & BUD

LAST YEAR my brother Bud left his wife and adopted son and moved to California, because, he said, it was the perfect place for a guy like him. He said that on the phone after he was already there. I asked him what he meant, but he said he couldn't explain it, couldn't make it clear, that it was just one of those things. "You know it when it hits you," he said.

"So what about Margaret?" I said. "How are you two getting along?"

"Famously," he said.

He asked me if I would look in on her and Conrad to help out while he was out of pocket—that's what he called it. I asked how long he was going to be out of pocket, and he said he didn't know. Then, right after I hung up from Bud, Margaret called. Things were happening fast. She said she wanted me to move in over at their house. I said I didn't know if that was a good idea.

Bud was a couple years older than I, forty-six, and Margaret was forty-one. Before the breakup, when I went over for dinner or something, they acted like those people on TV on last year's grotesque-family shows, the kind where everything's supposed to be funny because it's so ugly. Still, I didn't mind it. Margaret and I liked each other, and I was living in a condo project, so their house was a step up for me, with or without Bud.

"Just on a temporary basis," she said. "While he's gone."

Bud didn't have anything to say about it one way or the other. Margaret and I had always had a pretty good time being brother- and sister-in-law, so I said OK and moved in. I wanted to get rid of my place, anyway. So for five months I lived with Margaret, and that was great, but then he came back.

They were out on the brick terrace having a highball — that's what they still called it. They had one drink every day at noon, to get the day started, and another drink at five o'clock, before dinner. Sometimes they cheated. I got out of the way a lot, watching them from a distance, watching arms and legs move, heads cock and twist, bodies lean toward and away from each other — after a while it was like watching stick figures.

They'd been having so much fun for the ten days he'd been back, I was beginning to wonder if he'd really intended to leave in the first place, if he hadn't been making up some gyp crisis so he could spend a couple months dicking around with his pals in California.

The night he got back I'd said, "So what's the deal? How come you're home so soon? I thought this was the big breakout."

"Take it easy," he said. "It didn't work the way it was supposed to."

That night he designed the new couch, a tufted thing with no arms or back — he called it a "lounge." It was the only thing he'd designed in his entire life. He designed it for about three hours that night, did drawing after drawing of it on a roll of shelf paper that had faint bluebells on it. Then we built the thing the next day. We all had to pitch in and help. When we got it done it was uncomfortable, but he said it was exactly what he'd always wanted.

The next big family project we had was Bud's drinking. Margaret said, "You're killing yourself and me both, and now that you're back I don't want to let that happen."

"I guess if I *was* drinking I'd be killing all three of us," he said.

"Four," I said. "Don't forget Conrad."

"You know what I mean," he said.

"He always forgets Conrad," Margaret said.

I had an idea what he meant, but the drinking wasn't the best thing to talk to him about — he hadn't been drunk since he came back. As a matter of fact, I missed how he used to get sloppy and bitter and explain everything in the world as if we were living in some brain-damaged-prisoner-of-war camp. He was funny. And then he'd just fall asleep and leave Margaret and me together so that we could talk. Now they went off with each other, every night, went to bed at the same time.

Margaret was worried about Conrad and his girlfriend, Lollie. She said they were spending too much time together for people their age. Conrad was thirteen, we figured — maybe fourteen. She was afraid he'd go too far with Lollie. We had talked about it while Bud was gone. She felt like Conrad's real mother, but Bud didn't feel like the father. Conrad was one of those kids the state's always discovering in abandoned shotgun shacks it's trying to demolish. After Conrad was discovered, he was put in a home with a special school, and then it turned out Margaret knew his teacher and they started talking about this new kid a bulldozer driver found living like a wild animal in this old cabin, and one thing led to another, and pretty soon Conrad (though he wasn't Conrad then) was coming over for a visit. Not long after that, Margaret had a lawyer doing adoption papers.

▼

I tried to stay away from Margaret as much as possible when I started living with her. I figured that made good sense — stay in my room, stay out of sight, go out with people. But the truth is it was a pleasure being with her, just the two of us, and sometimes Conrad; and when I should have started looking for a new apartment, I didn't really want to. I was working nights at the paper, so when I came in I'd watch TV until very late, news shows, the Soloflex ads, and I'd watch in the afternoons so I could catch Catherine Crier's lips. Sometimes I recorded those, they were so good — recorded them and played them back in slo-mo, frame advance. I'd be sitting there going in frame advance on Catherine's lips — they were two colors, three if you counted the line around them — and Margaret would come into the living room and laugh about it.

"Who does those *lips*?" she said once. "Is Way Bandy back from the dead?"

"Von Dutch Howard," I said. "The problem is, when they photograph her from the side she looks like a piglet."

"That's too bad," Margaret said.

When I watched in the mornings, there was always the cross-eyed newswoman, sitting there, living in denial. We had a new Toshiba color set that was thirty-five inches diagonally, the largest sealed picture tube available. Even Bud was excited about that when Margaret told him she and I had bought it, just after he left, but when he got back he barely even looked at it. Sometimes when I was watching TV I wasn't quite sure I *should* leave — I wondered what would happen if Bud decided to take off again. I'd just have to move back. Margaret didn't want to live alone, I knew that, not even with Conrad around to keep her company. She needed somebody like me, somebody who'd stay pretty close to home.

Bud had time off from work to get "straightened away" after his episode. Conrad was busy chasing after Lollie all the time. She came by one day wearing nothing but black tights, a lemon-colored tie-dyed T-shirt with "Buy One, Get One Free" printed across the chest, and some very big shoes. She was driving a motorcycle.

There was always planning going on. Margaret planned. Bud

did, too. I tried to stay out of their way. Sometimes it seemed as if he was performing for me, as if he wanted me to watch him live. That was how it looked — the way he talked and signaled Margaret, the way he touched her when I was looking. He did this thing with his hand, making a finger-gun whenever she antici- pated what he was thinking of or what he was about to say. I hated that. He was always shooting somebody with that finger. And whenever something hot was on TV he wriggled his stupid eyebrows.

A usual plan would be that Margaret wanted to go to the store to pick up her glasses and then get Bud's shirts at the laundry — that was a big midweek outing. Another was taking me to the doc- tor so I could get a checkup. They were also planning a pool trip. I told them I didn't like the pool, that I drew the line at the pool. It was one of those community pools surrounded with chain-link fence. It was built in the fifties, when just a few people lived in the area, but now people came from everywhere to use it — too many of them — doing things in the water.

Margaret put on her new bathing suit and went outside, trying it out, showing it off for Bud. It was aquamarine, with a V shape down the front — a "fifties-revival affair" she'd called it when she showed it to me. She had a white towel wrapped around her waist, so she looked dressed, but Bud was out there in an under- shirt. They were talking, getting along fine. They laughed as if they were telling each other jokes nonstop, and they grabbed at each other like kids. Sometimes when I saw them together, just the two of them, through a window or way off in another room, they seemed made for each other.

But at other times Margaret said that I was the good brother, the way I was always helping. Then she laughed and said she was jok- ing, but I could tell by her eyes that she wasn't joking as much as she pretended.

▾

I swiped Conrad's radio and listened in bed in the early morning hours. I'd close my eyes and try to see myself a kid again, sitting on the hood of a car or with a bunch of people at a drive-in. And when they played a song that I really felt, that I could get to hurt me, I wondered why I wasn't where I could hear it right — at the beach with somebody like Margaret, walking the crusty sand at night, foam rolling up on the shells, wind bouncing on her skin, or at some country club with her, sitting at a white metal table by *that* pool, drinking something silly from an awkward glass and noticing what pretty hair Margaret had, how it held the clean pool light.

I'd fall asleep listening to Conrad's radio and wake up the next day around noon. The sun would be high and round, the yard a burning green desert, another planet. Margaret always said the yard was important to her, but to me it was just a half acre of hot grass. I'd grab some breakfast and sit down with a book, even though I don't like books, most new ones. You sit there and slug away, trying to stay interested, trying not to start drawing little pictures in the margins — little guys hanging themselves, or dogs barking. Maybe if it's raining and I'm in the bedroom with the curtains closed but still hearing the rain, then an old book is OK, especially if it smells stale and has that thick, brittle paper.

▼

The doctor had a tiny office, cheesy furniture, bad lamps, plastic plants. His magazines looked as if he got them from a paper drive. He gave me a shot. He said, "How long's it been since you've had that tetanus booster?"

"Got me," I said. "About thirty years."

"Well, we'll give you one anyway," he said, patting my forearm. He had long hairs on the backs of his hands.

Afterward I took Margaret to have an ice-cream cone at the food court in the mall. She seemed to have a lot of fun watching the fountain. But then, when we got home, Bud wanted to have a talk with her, so I went out in the yard.

I just sat there in my khakis. I guess it wasn't all that hot once you got used to it. But time was stopped. I felt tired, too — Bud was starting back to work, Conrad was going to be grounded for something, there were no dogs around, the birds were too high up in the air to be interesting. I had to do something. I was thinking of making twigs my hobby. I found this twig stuck in the fence between Bud's yard and the Plossoms' yard and broke some of the bark off. I thought I'd sandpaper it until the knots were like hard bites under the skin, things you scratch over and over.

▼

It looked as if Bud was back for the duration, so I started thinking about putting my stuff together so I could get ready to move. It was possible he might take off again, but I guessed he wouldn't. I hated to leave Bud with Margaret, though. When Bud had moved out, she called me first thing. We'd always cared about each other, Margaret and I, so I wasn't surprised when it turned out the best thing was for me to move in with her.

Ten days after I'd settled into her spare bedroom — the one she'd used as an exercise room — the overnight-mail guy came with a package from Bud. I had to sign for it, because Margaret wasn't home. She opened it that night, and it was a letter from Bud and a video. She started reading the letter and then started crying, so I tried to comfort her, and then went to my room.

I stayed there for an hour, resting. When I heard the TV snap on, I opened my door to see what it was — the tape Bud sent, or some movie, or MTV, which Margaret watched all the time when he was gone. It sounded as if she wasn't watching anything, or was watching without the sound. I came out of the bedroom and down the hall — I wasn't sure this was a good idea — and leaned around the corner to the living room, curious, trying to get a glimpse of what was on the television. It was Bud. He was barely sitting there on the TV screen. Margaret was on the sofa looking at Bud on television. I watched from the hall for a minute. Bud wasn't talking, or even looking at the camera — he was working. He had papers and his briefcase up there on the desk beside him, and he was writing things on one of his famous yellow pads. It was clear there wasn't anyone running the camera — he'd just put it there, pointed it at himself. He had his head and shoulders in the picture, and a little more to get the desk in. Margaret sat there watching him.

He was whispering sometimes, things like "God *damn!*" and "Oh, I see. Thirty-one fifty-*eight*" — that kind of thing. After a while Margaret caught me watching and signaled me to come over and sit with her on the sofa, so I did. I sat next to her. She put her arm around me, pulled me close, and leaned her head on my shoulder. It was going dark outside, changing to a half-light that made everything in our room look filtered. I smelled her shampoo. We hadn't turned on any lamps yet.

We watched Bud on TV for two hours. Not once did Bud say a thing to the camera, although he did look up a couple of times. He smiled, or sort of smiled, doing this thing he does with his face when he wants to smile. I'd seen it since we were kids.

Later that night I caught Margaret watching the tape again, and I sat with her, and we looked at the whole thing all the way through a second time.

This became a regular event for a couple of months, a nightly thing we'd do together — sit on the sofa and hold on to each other and watch Bud work. Sometimes Conrad came around, but most times he didn't want to get involved, so it was something just between Margaret and me. We'd put the tape in during dinner, and we'd eat and watch Bud over there across the room, working on the big screen. Then we'd do the dishes, clean up the kitchen, and go into the dark living room and sit on the old couch. Sometimes we'd play around a little, sometimes we made love right there with his big face shining down on us, and sometimes we'd just stare at the screen together, enjoying his company.

TALKING WITH OTHERS

▲ ▼ ▲

RETREAT

THE ENGLISH department's first annual retreat was held at the Carlsbad Motel on the Gulf Coast of Alabama in late October. When Mac and Cam arrived they met Mac's brother Rudy and his assistant, Mimi, for dinner. It was the first time they'd seen Mimi, who was also Rudy's new girlfriend. Rudy had just taken over as chairman of the department and was having a bad time trying to be one of the guys. He wore a beaded buckskin jacket that didn't fit right, jeans, and motorcycle boots. He invited Cam and Mac for an early dinner Friday in the motel restaurant, the Schipperke.

After they'd ordered drinks Rudy said, "What is that?" He was tapping the name on the restaurant menu.

Mimi said, "Who cares what it is? I'm so excited about this retreat — I'm dying to see all these professors in action. The Personal Makeover people say when you get people out of the office you see what they're made of."

"I don't know about that," Rudy said.

"It's a dog," Cam said. "On the menu."

"People *need* a chance to open up," Mimi said. "Show them-selves. The PMI manual says they'll strip down for you, uncover their scars."

Mac pretended to wave for a cab. "Cab!" he said.

"They send you all this stuff," Rudy said. "They have great graphs, really killer graphs in their brochures."

"Killer," Mimi said. She was young and looked like she was about to sizzle.

The waiter brought drinks, and after they'd been delivered around the table, Rudy said, "I'm glad Cam could come." He reached for Cam's hand. "I heard you were thinking of not coming — why was that?"

"Mammogram," she said. "I was scheduled for this afternoon. I moved it."

"You going to eat these crab claws, Rudy?" Mac said, snapping four or five of the fried claws off Rudy's plate.

"PMI reps gross sixty to eighty thousand the first year," Mimi said. "I may moonlight for them."

"No kidding?" Mac said.

"Even if it's stupid, there are worse ways to spend a weekend," Rudy said. "You see Pokey Willis brought that graduate student of his?"

"See, that's exactly what I'm talking about," Mimi said, her face brightening as she pointed a crab claw at Rudy. "People need a chance to go public with their stuff."

▼

The Carlsbad Motel was six stories, as clean as beach places ever get, given the traffic. The staff was used to dealing with the small-bore conference trade, so Mac's job turned out easy — he did the setup, then stood around outside the meeting rooms taking care of people who couldn't find the public restrooms or the bar.

Friday, after dinner, he made sure the correct conference rooms were going to be available when they were supposed to be available, unpacked some handouts Rudy and Mimi had prepared, and went over the luau plan with the motel's Director of Conferences & Workshops. Then he set up the projection video system in the Matrix Room for the nine o'clock showing of a taped program Rudy had gotten off C-SPAN, a panel on the film *JFK*, which was back in the news for some reason. That was followed by a discussion period moderated by a regional assassination buff who had slides, and who went through the evidence again, including some of the new material released the previous year from Dallas police files, details about the detention of the "three tramps," and some CIA materials recently leaked to the press. He had a lot of slides of car crashes, too. Snapshots taken right after the crashes, with body parts strewn around, splashes of blood dripping down windshields, ripped-up faces.

It was hard to know, since Mac was in and out of the conference room, whether these deaths were related to the assassination or a separate interest of the speaker.

Finally there was the two A.M. Late Sky Seminar. An astronomy guy took everybody to the beach. They stood in a circle holding hands and staring up, while this guy told them what they were looking at. Cam stayed in the room, but Mac was out there, squeezed between Mimi and some hefty woman. Mimi's hair was wolf-like.

Most of Saturday was free — the faculty went into town, sat on the beach, or slept. There was a late-afternoon roundtable discussion of departmental priorities. Mac made sure there was coffee and the correct number of Style Three snack trays, but that was it. Saturday night was the luau.

▼

All afternoon a pig had been roasting in one of the two fishponds in the courtyard. The pond, which was twice the size of a Jacuzzi, had been filled in with dirt, then dug out again to make a pit to cook the pig. Mimi had xeroxed "Pig Hawaiian" handouts that explained the long Hawaiian tradition of cooking a pig this particular way, buried in dirt, covered in palm leaves and pineapples. She had encountered this style years before in her travels for the Geiger Foundation, the handout said. The pig was her baby.

The luau was scheduled for the courtyard, but as soon as people got their first drinks it started storming, and everybody had to trail inside. At first they all stood there staring out the huge glass. Mimi had gone overboard on the decorations — dime-size glitter disks, Christmas lights, tiny white paper flowers, sagging used-car-lot boas of twisted mirror-finish plastic. It was third-worldish when the rain hit.

The pig was hustled out of the courtyard strung between two six-foot Pier 1 bamboo poles carried on the shoulders of Ken and David Whitcomb, twin homosexuals who team-taught a class in rock video, baseball, and Madonna, and taken to the motel kitchen where it was cut up into oven-sized portions and rushed to completion.

Cam had dodged a lot of the weekend, so she had agreed to attend the luau, but when the rain hit she caught Mac in the lobby and said, "I'm going to the room. I'm bringing you bad luck."

He said, "I'll be there in a minute. Just as soon as I get these pig eaters squared up."

"I'll wait for you," she said.

Mac moved everybody to ballroom two, the Blue Conquistador Room, which he had arranged to have available against just such a contingency. When he got it set up, he went and sat out in the courtyard for a minute. The rain was spotty by then — unnaturally large spurts of water that looked like there was somebody on the roof shooting a hose.

He sat on the lip of the still-working pond and stared at fat goldfish circling in the alarming blue water. There were hidden lights in the pond, and when fish swam through them it was as if the fish themselves were strangely shaped bulbs. One fish was almost as big as one of Mac's new cross-training shoes. The shoes seemed much bigger and brighter than they'd seemed in the store — he'd been thinking about that all afternoon, wondering if he'd made another shoe mistake. He stared from fish to shoes, then back to fish. The fish was much smaller, he decided, about the size of a believe-it-or-not potato.

▼

When Mac got back to the room Cam said, "Thank God they roped it off." Cam was on the bed in her ribbed underpants and a kid's T-shirt. "I thought for a minute we'd be staring into the burning eyes of that thing as it was yanked out of the dirt. I thought we'd have to watch them burst."

"They take the eyes out," Mac said.

"In Hawaii they probably suck them out," she said. "Like they do out of chickens in France."

"They're too big," Mac said. He stood at the mirror pushing the tip of his nose to make it a pig nose.

"Your brother's new gal said it was the most beautiful pig she ever saw," Cam said.

"Let's go home," Mac said. "Or leave here, anyway. I'm ready."

"What, tonight?"

"Let's tell them we're going home and then move to another motel — what about that? Just you and me on a high floor. Romance. Wind. Pounding rain."

"Sounds good," Cam said.

They were sprawled together on the satiny comforter that spread over the bed like simulated icing on a microwave cake. "I hoped it would," he said.

"But we're probably not going anywhere," she said. "Are we?"

She'd spent Saturday rooting through a few stories from the

local newspaper, then she linked up her little Toshiba with Compuserve for a quick scan of the AP and UPI wires. She told Mac she found a piece about a woman who was out of work and beheaded her three children while they slept, then told her neighbors she was offering them as a sacrifice for the Darlington 500, a stock car race. The woman's name was Lolita Portugesa. She had gotten up at midnight in her trailer in a quiet fishing village north of Tampa, grabbed a Chicago Cutlery carving knife that had been a Christmas present from her ex-husband, Fernand, and slashed off the heads of her children Miniboy, 8, Squat, 6, and Junior, 3. All this was from the police report, Cam said. The woman then hacked at her own wrists in an unsuccessful suicide attempt. The Florida authorities said she would be given a psychiatric evaluation to determine if she was sane. A note Portugesa left in the kitchen for her ex-husband read, "I am leaving to you the heads of our children. This is what you have deserved."

There was a knock at the door as Cam finished telling him this story. "Jesus," she said, getting out of the bed and pulling on jeans. "What, now they catch us?"

Mac put his hand over his eyes as if to hide.

Mimi was at the door. "Rudy wonders if you will join him in the garden," she said. She was wearing a swimsuit, one-piece, way low in the front, with a long but open wraparound skirt and backless heels.

"What's the Big Rudy want?" Cam said.

"He wants to thank you," she said. "Both. He's proud of the way things are turning out."

Mac said, "I guess he's deaf, dumb, and blind?"

Cam frowned at him, and said, "It hasn't been so bad."

"You haven't been out of the room, how would you know?" Mac said.

Mimi said, "Everybody downstairs loved the pig."

"Well, I didn't *love* the pig," Cam said.

"So I guess you're not in the preponderance, huh? You guys

want to come down now?" Mimi said. "Or later? Like in a minute or two, when you have time to get straightened away?"

"You go," Cam said. "There's one other story I want to download. It's a guy who caught a fish with a human thumb in it. Six people disappeared in this lake recently, so they don't know whose thumb it is. It's a detective thing."

"Yeeech," Mimi said. "We have to talk, Cam."

"What other kind of thumb is there?" Mac said.

Cam tapped Mac's shoulder. "Go on. I'll find this, and then I'll change, get my makeup all straightened away, and then I'll be right down. Show Mimi your elevator moves."

"She likes me in elevators," Mac said.

"I do not," Cam said, ushering them out the door. "I just said it was possible."

The elevator was lined in seat-cover vinyl, dusty-rose colored, with a thick, padded handrail all around the interior to prevent kids from hurting themselves when they bashed their heads against it while rampaging up and down in the building — as the designers apparently knew they would. Mimi leaned against the rail on the far side of the car, her head turned to stare at the clicking numbers over the door. Mac studied her calf.

"I need to get away for a while," she said, not taking her eyes off the numbers. "Maybe I should go back early. Maybe tonight."

"Ah," Mac said. He smiled and nodded, but felt that it was too much, too phony. "We were talking about leaving, too. Everything's done, really."

"Yeah. Maybe we'll go together," she said. "Why not?" She hit the Emergency Stop button.

"What's this?" Mac said, pointing to the control panel. "What're you doing?"

"Let's rest a minute," she said. "OK? Let me just rest a minute here, Mac. I don't ever get to just rest, you know? Since Rudy took this job I'm all over the place, and I don't say a thing. I argue, smile and nod and wave and make my eyes twinkle and draw my lips back and do my nostrils — but I never rest. I'm not like most women."

"Mimi," he said.

"Have we ever talked, just you and me?"

"No," Mac said. "But we will, we'll talk all the time."

"I like you, Mac. From the moment I met you. I love Rudy, but that's not the same thing. I suppose you know what I'm talking about, don't you? One of those suddenly-out-of-whack things?"

"We did that, didn't we? Back when we were thirty?"

"Yeah, that was fun. Two years ago. Longer for you, huh? I miss it already."

Mac caught himself nodding again in a silly way. He stopped.

"I used to want children," Mimi said. "I always figured I'd be good at that. I always think of the kinds of things I'd say to them. I'd tell them not to let anybody kid them, that people will say anything, they'll say they love you, but they really don't. They try, but no matter what they're after, they're not after what you're after. Not usually."

"That's kind of depressing, Mimi. I don't think we're supposed to tell kids that kind of thing," Mac said. "It's OK to get depressed, and maybe it seems like it's that bad, sometimes, maybe it even is, but we're supposed to keep it to ourselves, I think." Mac had his arm around her. They were slumped against the back wall of the elevator. The call bell was ringing.

"That's why I don't have any. I keep pointing to Rudy, talking to him about little Rudys," she said. "But he isn't buying."

"Well, say good-bye to projectile vomiting."

She gave him a look, and there wasn't any laughing in it. "I'm pretty forlorn tonight," she said. "Sorry."

"Never mind. It was stupid," he said, gently finger-combing her hair.

"Once, I was at the store, and this guy who looked like Rudy came in," Mimi said. "He held a stun gun on this checker. I'm standing right there. I couldn't get over it — Rudy's double. After all the TV shows, the cop shows, the movies, the mystery books, here was this guy in Pass Christian. Anyway, so I talked him down. Just like TV. We had a talk about stun guns. I told him the way he was holding his he was going to take big electricity."

"When was this?"

"Couple months ago."

"He was holding it wrong?"

"How do I know?" she said. "A guy talked somebody down on *Cops*, so I tried it. I said he was going to burn his ass if he zapped her. He was thin, sick-thin like cancer, so I asked him if he'd been checked up recently. I pointed at this spot on his neck with my fingernail and asked him if anybody had looked at that. There wasn't anything there, a smudge, but I made it sound like there was something, trying to give him a little doubt. He said he thought he was holding the gun right. He'd read the instructions and shot it off on a dog that way. I asked what happened to the dog. He said it spit up and then bit him, and I just shook my head. 'There you go,' I told him."

She was threading her fingers in and out between the buttons on Mac's shirt.

"Rudy likes gun magazines. You don't, do you? He gets dozens of them, but he never reads them. *Soldier of Fortune*, stuff like that. He's always decoding the mercenary ads in the backs of those magazines. Like, when it says 'rotunda OK,' that means the guy does kidnapping. 'Wet work' used to be one. Stuff like that. And *Paintball* — have you seen that one? Rudy's dying to play paintball. The magazine's full of masks and paintball guns, crossbreeds of forties futurism and nineties street weaponry. Full-head dressings, choice of ball colors. I look, too, but I'm afraid of guns. Aren't you?"

Mac caught her hand, slowed it down, then held it for a minute. "Let's see, I shot a squirrel once, a long time ago. I felt bad afterwards — it was worse than after really ugly sex. Once I shot a bird out of a tree, one off a wire, and I killed a groundhog at my uncle's farm when I was ten. I think that's the complete catalog."

"I guess killing's not about manhood after all," Mimi said. "I'd be afraid to have a gun, though. How would you avoid it? How would you stop playing with it, pointing it out the window at passersby and stuff? Going over the line?"

"That'd be a problem," Mac said. He eyed the panel with the floor numbers on it. "Bell's ringing," Mac said.

"At least there'd be the risk," she said. "Don't we all go a little nuts and slam the hammer through the bathroom wall sometime? Crack up one of those hollow-core apartment doors? Wouldn't we use a gun then, if we had it? Or like when Rudy started to jump up and down on the mini-satellite dish because it wouldn't find G2-A? What we do in private is scary sometimes. Maybe that's a good reason not to have a gun."

Mac started to slide out from behind her but didn't make it. She had him pinned. She had a bittersweet aroma, a new scent, dark and slightly overdone in a nasty way.

"I figure we can do anything we want, Mac," she said. "Whenever we want to do it. Anytime. Anywhere. Just get right down and do what we want, and nobody ever knows the difference, nobody ever knows what goes on."

"Rudy's waiting, isn't he?" Mac said.

"I guess, but he's way down there and we're way up here."

"We're not that far," he said, sliding sideways on the rail, pressing out from behind her.

She backed away, holding up her hands the way TV wrestlers do when they want to persuade the ref they're making a clean break. "Hey, if that's what you want," Mimi said. "I was thinking you might want to open up some, like PMI says, you know, show yourself, but if that's not the way you feel, OK. It's up to you, I'm just following the keys here — that's what these things are for, right? These retreats? To let you guys catch up?"

"You are lovely, Mimi," he said. "Really."

Then she stalked him playfully around the edge of the little elevator, and when she caught him they held each other for a few long seconds, then separated. Mimi smiled at him, tracing his cheek with the backs of her nails. "I'm fine," she said. "I'm a lot better than I appear." She fingered the red Emergency Stop button for a minute, eyeing him, then shoved that button in, and hit the one that said Lobby.

▼

Rudy was on the edge of the goldfish pond staring into the lighted water at the big things circling in the thickened sea grass. "I love these," he said to Mac, pointing into the water. "If I had it to do over again, I'd be a fish, I swear to God. See how they move? Look at that, look at the white one there."

"Mimi said you wanted to talk?"

"Yes, sir." Rudy leaned to one side to look around him. "Where's your partner?"

"She's resting. Too much Hawaii, I think."

"Ah." Rudy shook his head and stared at the fish more. "I tell you, that Cam. She looks a little like Mimi, you know? She's just real nice and young. And so on."

"Thank you," Mac said. "I'll pass along your compliments."

"How'd you like the weekend? No problems?" Rudy asked. "You and Mimi get along OK? She's peculiar, like she seems one way at the college and completely different when she's not there."

Mac took a minute, then shook his head. "I don't know what you mean."

Rudy reached out to shake his brother's hand. "Doesn't matter. I just wondered. We're going over to the beach. You and Cam can leave if you want to. Tomorrow's nothing."

"Probably not," Mac said. "We'll probably stay."

"Up to you," Rudy said, noticing Mimi in the lobby. She was waving.

"I guess I *do* know what you mean," Mac said. "About Mimi.

233

She's so calm. We came down in the elevator. It was the only time we had to talk, you know — "

"Yeah," Rudy said, rocking his head back. He dropped a finger-tip into the water, and the potato-size fish swam up for a look.

Mimi came out the doors into the courtyard and strode toward them, her heels clicking on the paving stones.

"I gotta run," Mac said, getting up.

Mimi did a little circle right next to him and brushed a hand across his shoulder. "You ready?" she said to Rudy.

"About," Rudy said.

"Boy, I like it out here," she said. "I used to be out all the time, at clubs and parties, I used to see people, I used to do stuff. I remember what it's like, what night smells like when you're out here on your own. Sometimes I watch MTV, those dance shows where the kids jerk at each other every way they can, so hard, and it just carries me away, you know? I feel every move they make."

SPOTS

CHERYL WAS fourteen years younger than me and a hundred pounds lighter, my new girlfriend of a month. She'd bought a carving knife at Kmart, a serrated cut-anything deal like guys demo on TV, slicing aerosol cans and sawing finger-size bolts that hold flywheels on generators. She was playing with this knife, cutting things for fun — a book I liked, a shoe-polish bottle — and waving the blade at me to make a point, which was that I shouldn't have been messing with my brother's wife, Susan, the week before while my brother Knox was out in California on his annual visit. She was right, of course. The playing around didn't amount to much more than teasing, some little body wrestling, but I regretted it already, for the right reasons and the wrong ones. Cheryl regretted it, too. There wasn't anything I could do about it, though, and I was trying to get it behind us.

"You haven't told me everything," she said, training the knife tip on my chest. "Not the whole story. Knox told me his side, and his side makes you guys look slimy, especially you. At least Susan was upset about him going off to California."

"The whole deal is I said I'd always liked her and one thing led to another," I said. "That's all." I waved and reached for a banana that was turning black on the counter. "At least we had enough sense not to go to bed."

"Yeah, that's a big deal. Thanks. Besides, how do we even know that? Can you prove it? What if you two just agreed to say that and stick to it? How would we ever know any different? Why don't you just say how close you got, in detail, describe all this rolling and tumbling shit, and that'll be that. Just go ahead and tell me."

"I don't want to do that," I said. "I don't see that helping any-thing."

"Blah, blah," Cheryl said. "It's really great being your new friend. Really. If I'd known what you were like, I'd have stuck with the last bozo I was with, that fat one with all the hair down his back."

"C'mon. Susan and I go way back. We like each other," I said. "There's this natural affection. We just let it get away from us a little."

"Yeah, a couple hundred times. You tell me you have to stay over because she's nervous, and I just buy it. I'm over here watch-ing TV. Jesus." She shook her head and took another swing in my direction with the knife.

We were in the kitchen. It was tiny, things were tight. Cabinets were full of cookery, spices, electronic aids. Her stuff was all over, stuff she'd just brought, packed in, crammed onto the countertops.

"It wasn't anything," I said.

"Yeah? What, you hugged, kissed? That it? Never got your clothes off, right?" She swerved the knife at my shirt, then my pants, then did it again, not seeing that I was headed for the refrig-erator, and accidentally caught my cheek. I got a slice from my ear to my chin and forward.

I was surprised more than hurt, startled by blood scattering down my neck. The cut wasn't deep, I couldn't imagine it being deep, but it stung and bled like crazy. I grabbed a paper towel roll and used the whole thing to mop my face.

Cheryl screeched for a second, holding the knife out in front of her, then suddenly stopped, as if realizing she was in some kind of fright movie act. She said, "Are you all right?"

"I think so," I said. "It's not that bad, I don't think."

"I'm *really* sorry," she said, her body curling down on the word, as if to demonstrate how sorry she was.

"Not that bad," I said. "It wasn't that hard, was it?"

She got another roll of paper towels and reeled off big swaths she used to wipe my shoulder and shirt. I bent over the sink, dropping blood onto the metal.

When the phone rang I said, "Will you get it?"

"I don't want to answer," Cheryl said. "What if it's Susan? What if it's for you?"

I wedged her aside and reached the receiver mounted on the wall by the kitchen door. "What?" I said into the handset.

I listened for a second, then shut my eyes and handed the phone to Cheryl. "It's your mother. Tell her you sliced me up, and we've got to call the hospital."

I leaned over the sink again, watching the blood, which was slowing some, thread its way into the running water and slide fast into the drain. There were white specks in the drain, and I couldn't figure out what they were. I was trying to think what we'd eaten that would end up these tiny white bits in the kitchen sink, and, at the same time, I was soaking towels in faucet water, pressing them to my chin.

Cheryl was calm on the phone, chatting with her mom. All the time she kept wiping at my neck. She said, "I just cut Del accidentally with this knife and he's bleeding some, but we don't think it's that bad, at least we hope not." Her mother must have missed it, and Cheryl repeated it right away, louder. "I just accidentally cut his face with a knife. We were playing around, and I cut him. He's bleeding now. We probably have to go."

237

She listened another half minute, then hung up the phone. "You ready? We'll go to St. Christian's, OK? They have an emergency deal."

"Urgent Care," I said. "They're quicker." I had my head turned sideways, cut side up, trying to stem the bleeding.

"Yeah, but they're like vets," she said. She was leaning on the counter next to me, twisting her head around for a better look. "They're going to have to stitch the hell out of this."

"That's great news."

She said, "I didn't mean to do this, you know. I was just playing around. I wasn't playing around about Susan, but the knife stuff . . ."

"You didn't mind sticking me."

"Oh, come on. Like I really *want* to slice your face in a million pieces."

"OK," I said. "You didn't mean to hit me."

"Later I want to rip skins off rabbits and stuff. That's me. Carjack some Cherokees, OK? Spit at people, crash store windows, whatever. I want to be modern, sleep with my brother's wife, you know."

"Fine," I said. I was bleeding, but it was slowing down. "Can you hand me a towel?" When I pulled the paper towels off the cut, blood only bulged out, making a line down my face, dripping off. I pointed at the cut. "Would you get with it? Are we going to the doctor?"

"Fine," she said. "If you think it's necessary."

I was mopping with the towel she'd handed me, going into the next room looking for my shoes.

"I'm sorry," she said, following me. "I'm nervous, I think. Are we going? What're we doing?"

"Have you got keys?" I said.

She shook the keys.

"OK, let's go," I said. I was at the door.

Cheryl was driving, fast but not too fast, whipping her head back and forth checking cross streets. "I didn't really cut you," she said. "Maybe if I was Mexican, I'd have cut you. White trash, cut you. Middle class, no. Too many jobs, too many cars—I can't cut anybody. Unless I go crazy, and then I can cut shit out of whoever—there'll be an explanation. If I'm not crazy I can only screw around in the kitchen and nick you a little by accident." She stopped and tilted her head looking at me. "You know, this might look pretty good after a while. Before it heals up."

"It's going to look like a cat scratch," I said.

"Way too big. You're getting lots of compliments on this at the shop. They'll regard you with a new respect, maybe even fear. It's just what you want."

▼

At the emergency room a tiny doctor, an Asian, took a look at my face, then looked at Cheryl, then back at me and just shook his head. His black hair was shivering. He pointed to some plastic seats in an examination room. "I'll be back," he said. "Keep the towel on it."

Then he left. Cheryl sat at the opposite end of the room. It was cool in there, lots of aluminum and shiny steel.

"How's it feel?" Cheryl said.

"It doesn't feel," I said. I took the towel off, tossed it to her, then unspooled paper towels from the roll she'd brought, folded them, dampened them under the faucet.

"If you're thinking I did this on purpose you're crazy," Cheryl said. "I just wanted you to know that. I don't like this Susan stuff at her place, or in the fucking elevator, the two of you riding up and down like teenagers watching the sun go down, but I'm not crazy."

"I told you I don't think it was on purpose. I think you slipped."

"Right," she said. "But that was stupid for you guys to do that in the elevator."

"I was leaving," I said. "She didn't want me to leave."

"What's this, no-fault sex? How do I know that's where it stops? Wouldn't you rather have this really open relationship, tell each other everything—that way it'd be easy for the other guy, you know?"

"We have that," I said. "I told you everything."

"Sort of. I'm thinking seriously open. Who I think about when I masturbate. Everything. It'll be great. We'll tell the truth. We'll tell more truth than anybody ever told before."

"Fine," I said, pulling the towels across my face.

"And we won't have to pay too much attention, because everything will be up on the surface. We won't have any peculiar or difficult thoughts, either, you've got to promise that. It'll be like CNN."

"C'mon, Cheryl. Settle down, will you?"

"Let's go on Arsenio, anyway," she said.

"What?" The bleeding was slow, almost stopped. I smeared it with my finger, then blotted with the towels.

"He's black, he's modern, he's happening, he's huh-huh-huh." She made the grunting noise and did that business circling her arm.

"He's canceled," I said.

She slumped on the stool. "I know. He's going to be. He's bad meat. He's over—I know that. It's fast out there. What do I think, they're going to wait for me?"

"Jesus," I said. "Put a rag in it, OK?"

"What a romance this is," she said. "Here we are in the middle of the night at the hospital, and you're telling me that. What is that?"

"You're babbling," I said. "We're trying to get my face fixed, and you're raving about Susan and sex and I don't know what."

"Hey," she said. "It's not sex, I got plenty of that." She got up and leaned against the wall of the exam room, popping her shirt snaps, loosening her pants, and slipping her hand down under the zipper. "All you have to do is watch. Every man I ever met wanted to watch. Get over there, stand this way, stand that way—"

I shut the door and stood in front of the little glass porthole so nobody could see in. "Please, Cheryl. Christ. What's wrong with you?"

She was like, "Do this, do that, move this way, rub it, finger it, squat, bend over, twist that, squeeze it, hold 'em up, pull it this way, lick it, bite it, hold 'em apart, rotate, ride it way up, kiss it — every man I ever met. That's the kind of babbling *I* get. You're no different."

"I agree," I said. "Fine. Just get dressed. Snap the little snaps."

"I don't know what happened to the old days when people felt things for each other, touched each other, cared for each other — I had better sex in high school than I've had since."

"If that's what you think," I said. "Just button up for the here and now, OK?"

"What, am I scaring you like this? Hey, we can tape it and sell it to Cinemax. We'll be ahead of the curve," she said. She closed her pants and started on the shirt.

"What's with all this?" I said. "Have we been sticking a little too close to *The Week in Rock* or what?"

"Well," she said. "Being modern is making a difference. It's having our voices heard."

"You gotta have one of the nine recognized voices to get heard," I said. "And it's gotta be saying one of the nine recognized things. Outside of that you can forget it."

"There you go again," she said. "So what are the nine things?"

"Check your local listings," I said.

"See, when you say stuff like that you sound like Susan," she said, sitting again. "I mean, I can take a certain amount of cynicism, but after a while it's as phony as anything else. It's just depressing. Besides, I pick and choose the stuff I pay attention to. I don't buy it whole."

I opened the door and stuck my head out, then redampened the paper towels. "Thank God for that," I said.

We had been in the examination room for about ten minutes when a nurse came in, took the towel pack off, dabbed some

Mercurochrome on my face, pushed the towels back into place, and told me to go home.

"I thought he was coming back," I said.

"Who?" the nurse asked.

"The doctor," I said.

"We saw a Japanese doctor," Cheryl said to the nurse. "Short guy? Black hair?"

Right then the Japanese doctor came in. "What's going on?"

I said, "I don't know. The nurse was thinking I was ready."

He said, "No dice. We've got to do a few small stitches. We're very well trained in stitches, but we've still got to practice sometime, don't we?" He grinned at Cheryl.

The nurse went to get some things the doctor needed, and, meanwhile, he washed his hands in the metal sink, whistling something I couldn't figure out. He had me sit on a low white stool and cleaned the cut with cotton and alcohol, then shot my face in three places with tiny bursts of anesthetic from a yellow plastic syringe. When the nurse returned he took twelve black stitches at the front end of the cut along the curve of my chin.

▼

When it got to be four in the morning, and I still wasn't asleep, I decided to clean up the kitchen. I wiped the counters and the floor, rinsed the sink with soap, then alcohol, packed up all the garbage I could find in the house, and took it out to the Dumpster that was at the back of the property, across the parking area from the building.

The street that ran alongside the condo dead-ended into Highway 90. It was a quiet, tree-shaded, narrow street lined with a couple of old houses and a bunch of rental townhouses. There was a flash of heat lightning as I carried the garbage bags across the parking lot, and then the sky looked a calm, midnight blue. I flipped the two bags, one after the other, into the Dumpster, and I was standing there looking distractedly around when all the streetlights, and the porch lights on the buildings across the street, suddenly flashed off. There wasn't a noise, just the sudden with-drawal of the light—I could still see, of course, but the buildings were all faced in shadow, were almost silhouettes. It put me on edge, gave me a pleasant but slightly nervous feeling, as if some-thing might be happening. It was like one of those movie scenes where the intruder, before he goes in, cuts the power to the house where the woman is hiding. It was silly to think about it at all, but the anxiety was pleasant, so I stood for a minute there on the blacktop, arms crossed, scanning townhouses across the street for a clue, a movement, anything out of the ordinary. There was noth-ing. I waited another couple of minutes, then started on a walk toward the highway and the beach. The air was peculiar, the way it just hung, motionless, drifting off the water, and the only sound was the faint hiss of little breakers running over rock jetties. There weren't any cars on Highway 90, and only one streetlamp burned about a hundred and fifty yards down the road. I stood on the cor-ner in front of the condos and looked up at our place, the dark bed-room where Cheryl was sleeping, then walked out into the middle of the empty highway and crossed to the beach side where the sand was gritty under my shoes, then came back, looking all around, soaking up everything. With the lights out things seemed to have lost their power. It was like nothing was holding anything, the resistance was gone, that little pressure that's always against you, obliging you, keeping you in place. I thought about calling Susan on the telephone, about walking up the beach highway until I found a pay phone that was working and giving her a ring. That seemed like a good idea, and I started walking. I thought if my brother Knox answered, well, I'd ask him how he was, and then I'd ask to speak to Susan. Just straight out. Just like that.

TRAVEL & LEISURE

IT WAS NINE-THIRTY when we got into Pie Town, which was so small we drove all the way through and rolled out the other side before we realized what we'd done. Then we turned around. Lora had been right about the motels — there wasn't a Holiday Inn or anything like it. The town was about three-quarters of a mile long and straddled the highway, and it didn't look very prosperous. There was a blinking orange traffic light at the main street, and when we cut off the highway, we were instantly in the town square, where there was a giant pie sculpture set in the middle of a fountain. Water was flowing out of the simulated cuts in the pie sculpture's simulated crust.

"We'd better find a phone booth with a Yellow Pages," Lora said.

We looked around but couldn't find any phone booth, so we went back to the highway and drove all the way through town again. The buildings along each side were old, dusty, run-down, falling apart. There was a laundry, a closed gas station, a handful of adobe houses with open porches, a few older wooden houses. The one luxury the town had was large trees that towered over all the buildings, good for shade in the daytime and wind-catching at night.

On the second trip through town we found a little dive called the Cabana Motel at one end. Some of the rooms were lit up, and the office was at one end of the property with a badly damaged neon sign. There was a shell parking lot in front of a series of little buildings with bright white roofs that were spaced out along a tiny creek running diagonally through the property. These were the cabanas, we figured. Lester and I got out and went into the office where a guy who looked Native American asked if he could help us. We said we needed some rooms, and he said he had some rooms and how many did we want? Lester looked at me.

"Three," I said.

"Three," Lester said to the guy.

He had a free-form kidney-shaped desk with a pale green Formica top, and a lamp made from a hunk of driftwood on one end of the desk. It was a movable desk, like a portable bar, only bigger. There were a couple of dogs in the office, too: small, ratty, and mean-looking. At one end of the room was a glass-top case with handicrafts inside — bamboo flutes and ceramic bowls and beads of all kinds and some little bits of silver jewelry.

We got our rooms and went back to the car and then crunched across the shell and stepped across the little creek to the cabanas. We had 3, 4, and 5. A big woman in a print dress was in 2. She was sitting out on the steps into her room.

"How's it hanging?" she said to me as I unlocked the door to number 3.

"Pretty tired," I said.

"Just go in there and splash some water on your face," she said. "It'll perk you right up."

Lora came into the room behind me with her eyebrows raised. "What's the deal here?" she whispered.

"Some friendly woman," I said. "Shut the door, will you?"

Our room was barely big enough for a double bed and a couple of dinner-plate-size bedside tables. The bathroom had a plastic shower stall with a galvanized pipe hanging over the top of it where the showerhead should have been. I splashed some water on my face just like the fat woman suggested. It felt good. I used one of the two towels we had to dry off.

After we got settled, the four of us went to get something to eat at a gas station and all-night restaurant on the highway. Lora picked up a new travel guide for Arizona and New Mexico out of the rack, and we went back to the motel. Lester and Olive decided to sit outside for a while, take the air. Lora and I went inside and locked the door. There was an old television, but it got only one or two channels, and both of those were frosty. I tried the handheld Casio TV we were carrying, but there was nothing doing, so I rested in the bed while Lora was looking through her new travel book. After a while I got up and looked out the window and saw that Lester and Olive had moved to the little bridge over the creek. The moon had come out into the middle of the sky. It was nearly full. There were some wisps of cloud around it. The moon showered the parking lot, made it a pretty basin of light.

"I think it's on again," I said, climbing back into the bed. "Lester and your pal."

"I could have told you that," Lora said without looking up. "You know, we missed a lot coming this way. We could have gone up to Santa Fe and Taos and up there."

"We still could," I said.

"No. It's backwards," she said. "I'm thinking we shoot straight up to Gallup and then over to the Petrified Forest and the Painted Desert."

"Inching west," I said.

"Don't remind me," Lora said.

I got up and went to the bathroom, then stopped back by the window.

"What are they doing now?" Lora said.

"They're still on the bridge," I said.

Some night bugs were flying around over by the office. Crickets were howling. I saw Lester look up in the direction of our cabin, and then I saw him wave. I dropped the venetian blind I had been lifting with my forefinger.

"He caught me," I said.

"Serves you right," Lora said. "You know, there's a lot of interesting stuff in this book. New Mexico is full of stuff, so is Arizona, so is Utah. There are a lot of Indian ruins around here and up in the top of New Mexico and the bottom of Colorado. You should see these pictures—they're gorgeous." She turned the book she was looking at around so I could see a few pictures. They were gorgeous. "I didn't realize how much stuff there was out here to see," she said.

"It's just tourist junk," I said.

"Just because everybody looks at it doesn't change what it is."

"That's not very modern of you," I said.

"Unless they've Carlsbad Cavern'd it to death," Lora said. "And even then, you can see through what they've done to it if you try."

"First-order experience," I said.

"Do you think we ought to go out there and check on them?" she said.

"I think we ought to leave them alone," I said.

▼

I started looking at Lora's computer, paging up and down. "What's on here?" I said.

"I've got a story about a four-hundred-twenty-pound man on death row in Minnesota who can't be hanged because it would be cruel and unusual punishment to rip his head off his neck with a rope, which is what his lawyers say will happen if the state tries to hang him."

"So what are they going to do?" I said.

"I don't know. Hit him with a speeding car, maybe," she said. "It's the new, life-affirming mode of capital punishment. Integrates capital punishment into the culture in a fresh way."

"You know, Lora," I said. "Sometimes I think you're just a little too something for your age. You know what I mean?"

"I watched a lot of MTV," she said. "In the early years. I hung around with older men. I was 'bad to the bone.'"

Lora went to take a shower, and I shut off the computer, putting it into its sleep mode, and then went out for a walk around the grounds.

Lester and Olive were no longer on the bridge. The fat lady was shut inside her room. I couldn't tell by the lights whether the guy was in the office or not. It was pretty dim out there. I stood on the bridge for a minute, the little stream trickling underneath me. I crossed to the shell parking lot and walked out to the highway. There, I turned around and looked over the Cabana Motel. We were in the Cabana because there were no ordinary motels in town, but it made me feel happy to be staying there because the place was so odd. The office and the shell parking lot were in a little clearing surrounded by large trees. The cabins looked like puffy cinnamon buns with their icing-white roofs. The stream flickered slightly in the moonlight. I looked both ways and crossed the highway to an abandoned cinder-block building with a plate-glass window in the front wall and a bench beneath that. I looked in the window but couldn't see anything except for a couple of bicycles leaning up against the window on the inside, so I sat down on the bench facing the highway and the motel. Cars came by occasionally, usually at a fairly good clip. Some had people in them reading maps that were unfolded like giant birds in the front seats of the cars. More often I just saw the silhouettes of the drivers and passengers buzzing through Pie Town on their way to somewhere else. I wanted to imagine that I knew what these people felt, what it felt like to be them in their cars going where they were going.

But I didn't know. I didn't have the slightest idea. It was easy to imagine them grimly pursuing their goals through the night, but that was too easy and made me think that was probably not what they were doing. But they weren't happy families either, necessarily. Some were businessmen, salesmen on the road. Some could have been criminals. Some would be people from the community going home late after a dinner party at a friend's house. There were carloads of white people and carloads of black people and carloads of Indian people. There were new cars and old cars. There were trucks and vans. There were sports cars and clunky family sedans. There were many dusty pickups, a couple eighteen-wheelers, an RV or two, U-Hauls, boat trailers, motorcycles — all manner of wheeled creatures.

When I wasn't watching the passersby, I was studying the motel, studying our room, Lester's room, Olive's room. Lights were on in all three. At a certain moment, Lester came out of his room, went to our door and knocked, waited there until Lora opened the door, and then talked to her for a minute, kissed her good night, and returned to his room. Then the manager came out of his office and stood on the steps outside the door and stretched. He wandered around in the shell parking lot for a minute, looking up at the sky. Then he picked up a shell and sailed it across the lot into the trees on the other side. Then he saw me. I don't think he recognized me, don't think he knew who I was, but he turned around and headed back for the office.

There weren't any real blocks per se in Pie Town, there were just driveways and dirt roads heading off perpendicular to the highway, so it was a guess how many blocks it would have been from one end of town to the other — a half dozen, maybe. There was a shoulder on either side of the highway, and, after a while, I got off the bench and decided to walk. I headed back toward the eastern edge of town. It was about midnight, and there was nobody out. There were a few dogs around, but they seemed friendly. Small black dogs wagging their tails, some beat-up brown dogs. There was a wonderful old gas station that was shut down, but it must have been the standard model for 1955, or something. There were a couple of wood-siding houses, weather-beaten, sort of ramshackle, each with a light or two in its windows. There were old barbed-wire fences and rusting cars in small fields, and the trees with their leaves flapping with each breeze. A couple of houses on the other side of the highway had cows behind them. I saw one pale gray horse. I got to the far edge of town, crossed the highway, walked back on that shoulder. I felt happy out in the middle of New Mexico, walking along the side of the highway. Even though I didn't go very far, it was wonderfully refreshing. When I got back to the motel, I didn't want to go inside, so I went straight past it, passing the café that was closed, a grocery store and a gas station that were closed, a feed store and a couple of little adobe houses back off the road. I stopped at the edge of town and sat down on a folding chair that was on a platform that I thought must be the bus stop, and I watched the road, the hills, the sky, the stars shining. After a while I was scanning the whole sky, going left to right, raising my gaze each time I went across looking for I don't know what.

▼

The motel was a little less inviting in daylight. Still, with the shadows cast by the tall trees, and the stream running like a children's toy across the property and the dusty shell parking lot, it was a place I was glad I had spent the night. We got our stuff together and got out to the car a little after ten. Lora went to the office to get our receipt and gave me her set of keys, so I started the car to get the air-conditioning going. An old guy with khakis and suspenders, a T-shirt and a baseball cap went by, walking a duck on a leash.

"Morning," he said to me.

I waved at him.

"That you, Andy?" he said, raising his hand over his eyes to shade them so he could see me better. He had stopped right in front of me at the edge of the highway.

"Nope, not Andy," I said. "Must be somebody else."

"You sure favor him," the old man said. He gave a yank on his duck and looked at me even more carefully, leaning forward slightly. "You ain't the Gainor boy?"

I shook my head, held up both of my hands, raised my eyebrows.

"Huh," the old man said. "That beats it. I'm just an old man out walking his bird, I guess. You from around here?"

"No," I said. "We're from Mississippi."

"Oh," he said, doing a big understanding nod. "Well, no wonder."

"Uh-huh," I said.

"Well, that explains it," he said, and then he corrected the way his hat was sitting on his head and gave the leash a little tug. "Take it easy there, Spot," he said. "We'll be going directly." He turned back to me. "You stay here last night? I mean in the motel here?"

"Yes, sir," I said.

"I've never even been in that motel," he said. "All the years it's been here, not once. We had some bad trouble in that motel one year. That was a long time ago. That would be in room 4. You weren't in room 4, were you?"

"No, sir," I said.

"That's good," he said. "Because room 4 got a hell of a working over. We had some boys in from out of town, and some trouble developed between them, and, well, it was an awful mess."

"When was this?" I said.

"Oh, fifteen, sixteen years ago," he said. "Way before your time. We haven't had any trouble there in years. In fact, a young friend of my daughter's lives over there in number 2, that would be Misty. That Misty lives over there. She's a big girl, but nice."

"I think I spoke to Misty last night," I said.

"I wouldn't doubt it," he said. "I wouldn't put it past her. She likes to sit out there and talk to whoever comes by. She used to keep a lot of turtles in there, but they all died one winter. Nobody knew why. I think they must have gotten some kind of turtle poisoning."

The duck started making some kind of sound, half quack, half gag. The old guy tugged on its leash, which snapped the duck's neck back and almost knocked it off its feet.

"You don't have a snack for Spot, do you?" the old man said.

Lora was coming toward us across the parking lot.

"I've got some peanuts in the car," I said. "Will he eat peanuts?"

"Oh, sure," the old guy said. "He'll eat anything. He'll eat shoe nails."

Lora leaned over to pet the duck, while I went to get the peanuts out of the car.

"Careful there," the old man said. "He'll give you a bite."

"You won't give me a bite, will you?" Lora said, talking to the duck, combing her fingers back over its head.

"I guess not," I said, handing her the peanuts.

She poured the peanuts into her palm and fed the duck. The old man kept snapping at the duck's leash as if he wasn't pleased at how well the duck was getting along with Lora.

"He tells me there was some trouble in cabin 4," I said to Lora. "Some years ago."

"Yeah, it was like a slaughterhouse," the old guy said. "Worst killing in the town's history."

"Is that where Lester was, or Olive?" Lora said.

"Olive, I think," I said.

"It was a bloodbath," the old guy said. "They say the killers took off the victims' heads, hands, and feet, and put them in a pile in the corner. They had to gut the place because of the stains and the smell. The people had paid by the week, so it was about a week before anyone found the bodies."

Lora stood up and cleaned her hands by slapping them together. "So how come they call this place Pie Town, anyway?" she said. "I asked the motel manager, but he didn't know."

"Aw, he's just a youngster," the old man said. "The story goes that many years ago some settlers were staked out here, and they got cross-wise with some Navajos. One day the Navajos had them surrounded and were about to kill them off, when one of the women brought out a couple of pies, which she offered to the Navajos as a peace offering. The Navajos liked those so much they asked for more and eventually spared the people and what was later to become Pie Town. I don't know whether that's true, now."

"Sounds true to me," I said.

"Why didn't they just kill the settlers and take the pies?" Lora said.

"Well, you see, if they'd killed the settlers, that would have been the end of the pies. But the way it was, the settlers kept making the pies and giving them to the Navajos, so it came to be known as Pie Town."

"Oh," Lora said.

"Yep. It was known far and wide," the old guy said.

"Well, we've got to pack it up," I said.

"Yeah, I've got to get along, too," he said.

Just about then Lester and Olive came out of cabin 5, carrying their luggage.

"Whoops," I said.

"Those your friends?" the old guy said.

"Yes," I said. "We're all traveling together."

"You know, you and he are about the same age, and this girl here and that girl over there are about the same age," he said.

"Yes, that's right," I said.

"Hmm," the old guy said.

I opened the trunk again, and Lester and Olive put their bags in. Olive crouched down to say hello to the duck, and Lester started off for the office.

"We've already got it," Lora said.

"Oh yeah?" he said.

A couple of big eighteen-wheelers rolled by faster than they should have, kicking up big whirls of dust and little rocks, shaking the ground.

"Let's move out before the dust starts growing on us," Lester said.

He got into the car behind the wheel, and the rest of us climbed in, too. We all said good-bye to the man and the duck. The old man started shuffling across the parking lot toward the office.

▼

We were on the road headed out of town when Lora saw something off to the right that looked like a flea market.

"Look," she said. "It says 'Live Rattlesnakes.' Come on, stop."

"Lora, you don't really want to stop, do you?" Lester said.

"Yeah, we've barely started," Olive said.

"C'mon, pull over. It'll just take a minute. I want to see these rattlesnakes," Lora said.

We pulled off the road into an auto junkyard in front of a battered tin barn. Three or four adults and a couple kids were gathered around a waist-high fence that was built up against the building. As soon as we opened the car doors, we could hear the sizzling of the rattlesnakes. The tourists who were already there had long plastic sticks they were poking down into the fenced area.

There were eight or ten rattlesnakes curled up in this dirt-floored pit about two feet deep inside the fence. There was water and some stuff that looked like cat food in there, and tree branches the snakes could slither on, but that was it. The rest was these people with sticks that had balloons tied to them. They were putting the balloons right in the snakes' faces, smacking the snakes on the nose, trying to get them to strike the balloons. The rattles were going full tilt, and every once in a while one of the snakes would get pissed off and crack the balloon that was being poked at it. Then everyone shrieked. Just inside the door a fat guy with a lot of facial hair and a cowboy hat was reading some magazine about knives and guns. He looked like he had a corner on the local bacteria market. You had to pay him twenty-five cents to get a balloon, then you had to blow it up yourself and put it on the end of one of the sticks. The snakes looked tired of this. The people doing the stuff with the balloons were regular-looking mothers and fathers, sons and daughters.

"This is not good," Lora said.

"No kidding," Lester said.

A burly guy whose son was slapping a smallish snake over the head with his balloon gave us a dirty look. "They're just snakes," he said.

"We're just bananas," Lester said.

I wondered if this was a good idea, talking to the burly guy like that. I figured he wouldn't get what Lester meant, he might think Lester was saying he was crazy, and that'd cause more problems. But that didn't happen. The guy shrugged and put a meatloaf-size hand on his son's shoulder, and turned back to the fun.

We watched for a few minutes and then got back into the car and pulled out onto the highway, headed north.

A little distance out of town Lora said, "Now, people might say we should've stuffed that entrepreneur and all his customers, especially the fathead guy, into the hole and let them snakes bite bite bite. Then set all them snakes free and flamed the place, burned it to the ground."

I tapped the side of my head. "Yeah, but Lester said what had to be said."

"Maybe it wasn't enough," Lora said.

"You were the one who wanted to stop," I said. "We didn't have to stop. They didn't make us. We drove right in there and got out and started looking."

"Yeah, well, that would've been going on whether we stopped or not."

"You gotta start somewhere," I said.

TINY APE

MURRAY RAN the car wash at the Sunoco station just off the Interstate, where the highway curled down to meet the mall, for Big Willie Fryer. Willie was a Scandinavian guy, maybe six-six, three hundred pounds, not exactly fat, but not Mr. Olympia either. Just plain big. When he handled things — oilcans, trash barrels, crates — everything looked light as a feather. Pencils shrunk in his hand. Murray mostly kept track of the trash-kids that scrubbed the wheels and applied the scent and wiped the cars down after they ran through the Hogan, which was what everybody called the wash tunnel, though nobody could tell Murray why. Big Willie told him it was the name of the previous system, a felt-and-spray setup he'd ordered out of New Orleans when his father had the station back in the sixties. The Hogan had been replaced with an upmarket nothing-touches-the-cars system in the mid-eighties, so nothing there had the name Hogan on it.

Murray was thirty-two, closing on -three, and was happy to

have the new managerial position, especially since he'd been
ready to sign on to wipe cars himself. He'd shown so much initia-
tive in the interview that he'd shot up through the rank to wash
manager and had an office he shared with Ted Kiowa, the
mechanic who ran Willie's garage section and who was not Native
American, thank you, and Lillian Range, who ran the gas section.
This idea of middle management knocked Big Willie out. He'd
read an article about the advantages of spreading out responsibili-
ties in small businesses in *Entrepreneur*, and had decided to apply
it across the board at his Sunoco.

Murray was in the wash business because he'd lost a couple of
jobs, much better jobs, white-collar jobs — one as an architect with
his own practice, another as a draftsman for Rollie Odom
Associates, the firm to which he'd sold his practice when he had
to turn everything liquid to pay for a three-month gambling binge
in which he'd managed to lose about sixty thousand dollars, most
of which he didn't have. So there went the house, the mortgage,
the car, the tiny savings, the computers, books, stereos, TVs —
everything Murray could get a dime out of. And, after all that,
Odom was kind enough to pay a little something for Murray's
office equipment and a couple of clients, and kinder still to give
Murray a temp job drawing changes into the standard house
plans that Odom used to fulfill his clients' dreams. But Odom
wasn't altogether in the charity business, so, quick enough,
Murray was looking, and quick after that he was in the car wash
business with Big Willie.

"You a gambler, that it?" Willie said when Murray walked in
with the help wanted sign Willie'd put out.

"Was," Murray said. "Learned my lesson."

"Everybody says," Willie said.

"I need the job," Murray said. "I'll work at it."

"Drying cars," Willie said.

Murray nodded.

Willie stared at him for a minute, then raised his hands in a gesture of resignation. "You can have it. I got some plans you might fit into. You some kind of salesman in a past life?"

"Architect," Murray said. "Mostly houses, some supervision."

"Start tomorrow," Willie said.

▼

Murray celebrated his first paycheck at the Lady Luck Casino, but he didn't celebrate very long, and about nine o'clock he was standing outside the Lady Luck watching the nine o'clock show of the fire-breathing dragon.

He leaned on the thick red pipe railing, and when a clean-enough-looking woman came and stood about ten feet away, he smiled and said, "Winner or loser?"

"Who's asking?" she said, without even turning to look at him.

He liked that, liked it that she spoke straight out into the wind in front of her, made no effort to be sure he heard, did not care what he looked like — wasn't even interested enough to glance.

"Loser asks," he said. "Three hundred and change. I was up, but . . . you know."

Now she looked. She had the usual straight black hair in a kind of bowl cut they got from the movies, the usual how-ugly-can-I-get body stocking in meal-brown, the usual heavily patterned miniskirt, the regular open-collar sleeveless T-shirt with another flowered shirt over that but under the black jacket. She had the usual boots, black, laced on brass eyes.

"You look like a loser," she said to Murray, who was in chinos and a pullover.

"Yeah, well, you look like Bruce Dern, so you want a drink or what?"

"I want a drink all I gotta do is crawl through the door over here," she said, wiggling an arm toward the casino.

"That's what I'm saying," he said. "We go together. Have a couple drinks, check the action. See what you bring me."

"That's my job in life," she said. "To bring you something."

"You know what I'm saying," Murray said.

"I'm catching the dragon," she said.

"I can wait." Murray lit a smoke and turned away from the dragon, looking back across the inlet between the Lady Luck and its six-story parking garage toward the Grand Casino Biloxi. It was Sunday. He thought he was going to get lucky, felt it settling in his bones. He slid a little left seeing if he could catch a scent off her like off the cocktail chicks in the casinos. Sometimes he'd sit at the quarter slots playing real slow and drinking fast just so he could brush the babes in push-ups and scarlet hose who did the serving.

Didn't they know better? He was at the quarter slots, for Christ's sake. Didn't they teach these high-bra girls anything?

He liked to call them over with his eyes, raise his brow a bit, or catch them looking his way and torque his head to one side just a little. That brought them straight away. He'd put a half on their little trays and ask for Coke and Jack, knowing he wouldn't get it in a million years, but it made him feel better to call it by name, to make them think he thought they were taking care of him special.

The big dragon music was coming up now. All that tinkling and gonging and Oriental nasal stuff, and the smoke was beginning to roll out from under the garage-size fake rock the casino built that housed the fire-breathing dragon. The families were all gathered around on the walkways, fathers itching to get back to the machines or the tables but pulled out to watch the hourly display by their wives, who were ready to leave.

Name's Patti," she said, "I work here, you know."

"What? The Lady Luck?"

"Yeah. I run drinks. I've seen you in there dicking with the tiny slots — you're not big money, are you?"

"Little money," he said. "But I'm a swell guy."

"What's that mean?" she asked.

"Means I've got a job, I don't smack women, I clean up after myself. You know, Cary Grant."

"My luck," she said, flicking her cigarette into the army-green water. "Listen, I gotta get in costume and do a half shift, eight to two. See me after, huh?"

"No shit?" Murray said. This was big news to him. He'd hit on hundreds of women around the casinos, maybe dozens, anyway, but never gotten a flicker. He was so bad it'd become a no-expectation game. He carried it on only out of habit. "Maybe I'll come back and play some slots or something," he said. "Try the crap tables. You really going out with me later?"

"You can take me to breakfast," she said. "Anywhere you want."

So she went inside the Lady Luck, and Murray went home and took a bath, changed into his clean black jeans and a high-fashion J. Crew T, sprinkled himself with deodorant and cologne, and drove back to the casino a little after one. He played some Double-Diamond machines and hit a four-hundred-dollar payout, then cashed out and wandered around dropping twenties into other machines that took them without looking back.

He was pushing a rumpled hundred into a ten-buck Red, White & Blue in the Slot Salon when Patti slipped by behind him and asked if he wanted a cocktail. She had on the short black skirt, the scarlet hose, the white blouse. She draped her hand over his shoulder.

"You bet," he said. "You near done?"

"That's the bad news," Patti said. "They want me to go all night. Two girls are down with the flu." She nodded at a fat guy sitting all over his stool in front of one of the five-dollar machines. He was shaking his arm at her. "Let me get this Dumpster's drink and then I'll take you on break with me, that be OK?"

"Perfect," he said. "Better and better."

"See you cleaned up," she said, dragging the hand across his arm as she moved toward the fat one. "Nice going."

They screwed for the first time on her break in a closet on the third floor of the casino, a section of the place that was under construction, where they were adding some new offices. She sat on a sawhorse, rolled the tights down to mid-thigh, and got her ankles up over his shoulders. He worked with his jeans on.

▼

Murray got her for breakfast at six in the morning. She met him in the parking garage, still in uniform. "Let's run by my place so I can change," she said. "Then Buck's, OK?" Buck's was a pancake house off Highway 90, the beach road.

"Maybe I can help you change," Murray said. "You can just stand there, and I'll do all the work."

"Put a bag in it, will you? I'm awake twenty hours. I'm running down. Tumbling you is the last thing I want to think about."

"Maybe it's the outfit," he said.

"Maybe you're a cheese head," she said. She reached out as if to pat his hand but just patted the air near his hand. He felt the breeze.

Her apartment was a second-floor unit in a set called Ocean View Apartments, and there was a view — you just had to struggle to get at it. The metal railings rang as they went up the concrete steps. She was in 214. The rooms were small and dark, paneled, with rent-a-junk furniture. Stupid magazines were around, bent back, rolled up. She was reading a lot about the O. J. Simpson case.

"Help yourself to the kitchen," Patti said, heading into the little hallway that led to her bedroom. "I'll be back in a nip."

The kitchen was wood-look vinyl on the cabinets and a dark brown refrigerator with a plant dribbling off the top and down alongside the hinges. She had good refrigerator magnets — a TV dinner, a roll of Tums, a tiny cherry pie, and a manger scene. "I like your magnets," Murray shouted back into the hall.

"What?" she said, coming out to the edge of the living room. She had jeans on and was holding a T-shirt in front of her.

"I'm a fridge-magnet guy," he said. "I mean, I always study them. I don't collect or anything — I hate people who collect things — but I pay attention. Yours are good."

She gave him an eye roll and said, "Thanks. I spent ages picking them out."

"It's just something I'm interested in," he said.

"Life on the edge," she said. She stepped back into the hall and threw the T-shirt over her head. "You ready?"

"Ever," he said.

She grabbed a green sim-alligator purse that was strung over the back of a Gnu chair in the living-dining-combo room, and went past him headed for the door. "C'mon, Dingy," she said. "And what's that smell you got on? Are you wearing some damn men's cologne or something? Jesus — you smell like a camellia."

"Thanks, honey," he said. "Hang on a half minute while I tend to business." He pointed back to the hall and went that direction at the same time, hunting the bathroom. It was close and lilac. He dropped the shirt and washed down fast with water from the tap, trying not to get it all over. Then he tapped dry with a floral towel and got her Suave out of the medicine cabinet. Then he put his shirt back on and flushed the toilet.

The light was still lazy when they left Patti's apartment, and the air was thick the way Gulf air gets on hot, still mornings. They toured Beach Boulevard headed west, toward Pass Christian, where Buck's sat on a miserable little spike of sand that ran out four hundred yards into the Mississippi Sound. The land wasn't there, really, or wouldn't have been unless the Mississippi Corps of Engineers, or whatever they were called in Mississippi, hadn't poured enough concrete around it to build a couple of replicas of the Great Pyramid. They did this in chicken-wire boxes about a foot square and three feet long, then dumped these giant concrete blocks helter-skelter all the way around Dogleg Point, which was the name the locals had given this particular piece of land because it was shaped like same. Buck's was out toward the end, far enough out so that the noise from the highway went way down, and car tires crunching in the oyster-shell lot were the only thing that disturbed the constant light clap of the water.

THE GREAT PYRAMIDS

IT HAD BEEN raining for three days. Wallace sat on the heavy brocade cover of his sister's bed, watching the weather on television, the word "muted" in green in the upper-right corner of the screen, waiting for his sister to come home, waiting for a call. He'd been working on a Web site for an insurance company, a job Kelly had arranged. They did freelance Web design, the two of them together. He and Kelly had always gotten along. She was only a couple of years older.

The rain sounded like a TV somebody had left on real loud after a station had gone off the air.

Wallace's mother and father had died over a year before — one after the other, two weeks apart. Everybody remarked that it always happened that way. Wallace didn't know if it did or not, only that it had happened to his mother and father. He had dropped out of college and was living at home when his parents died. Later, his sister asked him to come and live with her, to keep her company. She was hearing voices, she told him. When she tried to sleep, she heard people breathing close by. He found this completely touching. She'd always been successful, straight, the one who got everything done right and on time. Now she asked for his help, and in doing so showed him a side of herself that he'd never known.

Less than a month after his parents were dead, Kelly and Wallace moved into the house on Cork Street, a forties bungalow six blocks off the coast highway, wood siding, a pitched roof, and window air conditioners, and, inside, a lot of heavy old furniture left by the previous owners who had moved into an assisted-living facility in Biloxi.

Kelly bought the house, but she acted as if it was theirs, as much his as hers.

She was Catholic still, went to mass, prayed. Wallace figured she was lucky. He'd quit with the incense and stained-glass windows.

"You can do it that way if you want to," she said. "It's plenty fair."

He said he didn't doubt it.

▼

He was comfortable in the house, though it was dark — the walls were dusty pastels, the windows had blinds and heavy drapes. There were thick padded carpets, and the furniture was all over-size fake antiques — knobby bedposts, shoulder-high chests of drawers, gaudy red-polished wood. He liked living there, because it felt like he was living in his grandparents' house, which made him feel even less responsible than he was in his parents' house, which was one reason he'd gone to live at his parents' in the first place. He hadn't expected them to die.

The old couple that had moved out of the Cork Street house were making a new start, so they left everything behind. Kelly kept it all, and left her things in storage. She adopted the furniture

—and the linens, the towels, the flatware, the dishes—all of the equipment the old couple had left behind.

▼

Kelly called him from the casino. She worked part-time as a craps dealer, and was studying to deal blackjack.

"I'm coming to get you," she said. "We're going out. You stay in too much. You need to get out more."

"Fine," Wallace said. "I'll be here."

"I want to go eat," she said. "Do you want to eat?"

"Isn't it a little wet outside?"

"How about Chinese food?" she said.

Half an hour later she called again—this time from a gas station about a mile up the highway.

"It's pretty bad here, Wally," she said. "I had to pull off because the water is up to the top of the wheel-opening. Everybody's splashing around, and the guy running this place says there are snakes all over. I've seen a couple."

"You've seen snakes?" he said.

"Yeah. They look like tiny Loch Ness monsters," she said. "They float around in the water with their heads sticking out."

"Great news," he said.

"I'm going to wait a few minutes, then I'm going to try to come up and get you, OK?" she said.

"What if the car stalls?" he said.

"Then I won't get you," she said. "You'll notice. If I'm not there in half an hour, you come get me."

"Why don't I just come now? Bring the truck?" he said.

"That's OK. Would you mind?" she said.

"No," he said. "You sit tight. I'll be there momentarily." He hung up and thumbed the remote on the television, going through the channels, looking for a quick update. The closest he could come was a disheveled guy in shirtsleeves with his collar loosened and his tie pulled down, waving vaguely at a chroma-key map of the coast. Wallace tried to punch the button to unmute the sound, but he missed and had to punch a couple other buttons, and when he finally got the sound turned up, the station was in the middle of a bean commercial.

Wallace did a quick change of clothes, and then went out the side door and got into the big Ford truck that his father had had. They didn't use it very often, but it started right up. It was late afternoon, but it was almost dark as night outside. The street was shaded by giant oaks, and the sky, where it was visible, was veined in pinks and pale yellows. Thunder cracked and ratcheted and thudded around in that sky. Lightning zigzagged every which way, as if it were the electricity in some maniac doctor's laboratory. The rain came down in gallons and sheets and crystal lead-colored stripes, spattering off the truck windshield, hammering the roof and the hood. He backed out of the driveway and got up in the center of Cork Street riding high. He left his window down, and as he drove toward the highway he saw that all the yards in the neighborhood were glistening, all the grass was knee-deep in standing water. The drainage ditches along the road were over-flowing, and occasionally he saw a woman wearing a housedress on a porch with her dog looking out the screen door. Most of the houses had their lights on inside. Occasionally he could see people moving about or sitting in old overstuffed chairs, reading or watching television.

He was barely moving along Cork Street in the truck. He'd give it a little gas, then let off the gas and let the truck roll. He didn't want to stir up a lot of water and didn't want to get water on the brakes, thinking it would be safer just to take it slow. He had a towel in the truck, and he put it over his left arm leaning on the edge of the window that was open. All the racket of the thunderstorm was kind of muted. The light had a greenish cast to it. Not a bright green, but something dull. The light seemed almost like fatigue light — army green, lit from the inside, so it had a kind of luminance.

The wipers on the truck were clacking back and forth, but he still couldn't see much out front. A couple of blocks from his house a black dog came up on the driver's side of the truck and started walking with him, eyeing the front wheel as if trying to decide whether or not he needed to chase this truck or bite that tire.

"What are you doing, Bugs?" Wallace said to the dog. "Why are you walking along like that? It's raining. Aren't you wet?" The dog turned its head and kind of squinted at Wallace, then went back to looking at the front tire. Wallace gave the gas a little squirt, and the truck jumped ahead. The dog stopped in its tracks and then trotted up again to walk alongside. "We're going to have Chinese food. Would you like to come? Oh—I guess you don't feel so good about Chinese food, right?"

The dog lifted its head up and rolled its eyes back, looking at Wallace almost upside down.

"Sorry," Wallace said. "Why don't you go on home now. Go on." He waved his arm out the window at the dog, trying to get the dog to stop following him. In the next block he saw two kids in the front of a gray clapboard house. They were inside a box that a refrigerator had come in. It was a Frigidaire box on its side, open on the end toward the street, and the two kids were sitting inside. It looked like they were playing cards, but Wallace wasn't sure. His headlights reflected off the flying rain. He could see only six or seven yards in front of him, just a glittering hash of water that kept falling, blown sideways, ricocheting off the road. As he came out from under the oaks near the highway, things lightened up. The sky was gray-white. He could make out the muddled shapes of cars going by with their lights shining. Everybody was driving real slow, single file, trying to avoid the deepest parts of the flooded street. He snapped on his blinker and waited while a bur-gundy-colored Cadillac went by, followed by a modern car that he didn't know the name of, and then a delivery van. When they had passed, he edged out into the street, looking both ways elabo-rately. When he didn't see anything coming, he made the left turn and rode the crown of the highway toward the gas station where Kelly was waiting.

Down the highway, there were a few cars stalled in the median and a few cars pulled off on the concrete seawall, but traffic mostly moved smoothly. When he got to the gas station, he found Kelly standing under the overhang, chewing on a stick of red licorice. There were three or four other people huddled in the protection of the gas station. He pulled in, and Kelly got into the truck, leaned over, and planted a little kiss on the side of his mouth.

"Hello, my brother," she said.

He arched an eyebrow and swung the truck back into the rain. Kelly patted his thigh.

"Let's roll," she said.

"Where are we rolling to?" Wallace said.

"Out into the weather," she said.

He got back onto the beach highway. Everybody was driving real slow. Everybody was being real careful. All the cars kicked up little waves. The windshield wipers cracked back and forth across the glass, unable to keep it clear. At Fodor Road, Kelly said, "Turn here. This is the place."

"You could have given me some warning," he said, slipping into the center lane, hitting his signal.

The restaurant was called Shanghai Garden. It was a place they went once in a while. The food wasn't great, but it didn't have too many customers, and the people who ran it were pleasant and friendly. The building was a converted convenience store, the front windows blocked with heavy red burlap curtains. Inside, there was some carved-wood latticework, a few green leatherette booths, a wall of mirrors, and a buffet table that the restaurant never used. The rest of the interior was painted all dark green with red trim and gold highlights. Here and there were white lanterns with red tassels hanging from the ceiling, and on the wall was the usual assortment of dragons.

Wallace and Kelly took menus and seated themselves in a booth by the front window. The menus were stained. The tablecloth was dark green and stained, and the place mats were paper, printed with the usual stuff about the Chinese calendar.

"Are you a dog?" Kelly said. "I can't remember if you're a dog or a horse."

"Horse," he said.

"Look at that," she said. "We're perfectly suited for each other. See here?" She tapped the section on his place mat under the drawing of the horse. "I'm highly compatible with the horse."

"Are we eating?" he said.

At one end of the room there was a giant rear-screen projection television hooked to a VCR, showing some kind of Chinese talent show.

"So here's what happened to me," Kelly said. "I've decided we need to go see where Mom and Dad are buried. We need to go see them."

Wallace was studying the menu, studying it hard. He didn't look up. "No thanks," he said. "Been there, done that. What about this lo mein?"

"Wallace," Kelly said. She reached across the table and touched his hand. "We need to go out there. We need to go together."

"Let's don't and say we did," Wallace said. That was some crack his father had picked up from some radio show, something he said every time he didn't want to do something Wallace's mother had suggested.

"We have to," Kelly said. She sat back and flipped open her menu, laying it flat on the table.

They ordered hot-and-sour soup, pot stickers, house vegetables deluxe, and lemon chicken, something Wallace always ordered when he went to a Chinese restaurant. They sat in the dark restaurant, listening to the rain, waiting for the food.

After a few minutes she asked him, "Do you think it's strange, us living together?"

He grinned at her. "It could be stranger."

"I know that," she said.

"I don't know," he said. "Does it bother you? Do you want me to move out? I can move out if you want me to."

"No, I don't want you to move out," she said. "I like you there."

"That settles it then," Wallace said.

Neither one of them had had a date since Wallace had moved in. Wallace used to have a girlfriend, a woman named Mindy — a thin little stick of a person who studied fine art at a local college. But she had moved away to Miami to study painting, and Wallace hadn't heard from her in over a year. Kelly used to have a lot of boyfriends, at least that's what he thought he remembered from high school and when she started college, but since their parents died, she seemed to be content with him.

"So I talked to Eve," she said.

"Eve?" he said.

"The girl I used to live with in New Orleans. She's a social worker. And, well, here's what happened. She had this client who really loved Hillary Clinton, and when Hillary was going around the country promoting her book, she went to New Orleans to do a book-signing, and this woman wanted to go. My friend Eve agreed to take her. It was a deal where you bought a book in advance and then you stood in line and got to shake Hillary's hand. This woman, Eve's client, had some kind of brain damage, some kind of tumor on the brain or something, and had had part of her frontal lobe removed when she was a child, so she was a little bit off center. Anyway, they went to the bookstore, and there was this huge line outside the bookstore, and this woman started crying because she thought she wasn't going to get in to see Mrs. Clinton. The longer they waited, the more hysterical she got, until finally Eve said, 'OK, I think we're going to get to see Mrs. Clinton, but what you need to do now is focus on what you're going to say to her. I think you ought to think about one question that you can ask Mrs. Clinton when you meet her and shake her hand.'"

"So your friend said to this woman that she had to think of a question," Wallace said.

"Right," Kelly said. "That seemed to contain the woman. She was really focusing on that. It was a pretty long wait, and about forty-five minutes later the line finally got back to them and they got to Mrs. Clinton. This woman grabbed Mrs. Clinton's hand to shake it. She started telling Mrs. Clinton how wonderful she was and saying that she was so excited about seeing her. She said, 'Mrs. First Lady, I just have to get down on my knees and thank you for everything you've done for mental health in this country. You and Mr. President have done so much for mentally handicapped people in this country.' The woman was down on her knees, and my friend Eve was sure the Secret Service was about to swoop in and pick them both up. The woman was crying and holding on to Mrs. Clinton's hand with both of her hands, and going on and on about how wonderful Mrs. First Lady was. She just wouldn't stop. Eve was leaning over trying to comfort the woman and trying to get her to stand up. Mrs. Clinton was standing there shaking her hand, but no Secret Service people came. Eventually, after a couple of minutes of this, Eve got her to stand up, got her to release Mrs. Clinton's hand, and they moved on. They left the store, and the woman seemed perfectly happy and content, because she had gotten to do what she wanted. They got in the car and started to leave, and then the woman started crying again. My friend Eve turned to her and asked, 'Why are you crying? What's upsetting you now?' And the woman said, 'I forgot to ask my question.' Eve asked her what the question was, and the woman said, 'Well, I really wanted to ask why the navy makes people retire early.'"

Kelly said this in a childlike, plaintive way, and Wallace laughed a little, and then more, and then stopped laughing altogether and looked at his sister.

"I know," she said.

"Some things are so wonderful in this world," he said.

Kelly smoothed her place mat and rearranged her napkin, the

glass, her utensils. Then she started on the lazy Susan where the mustard and duck sauces were, where the soy sauce was, where the little chrome rack of Sweet & Low and sugar sat. When she got that straightened away, she started to work on Wallace's place setting. He pulled back the red burlap curtain and looked outside into the frizzy rain. Two police cars had pulled up and blocked the highway. There were flashing lights, and the policemen were out in bright yellow slickers directing traffic, detouring it off the beach highway. The glass rattled with thunder. Across the highway, the water and sky were indistinguishable. Mottled gray from the beach up into the clouds. No horizon. The water was relentless. The policemen were calf-deep in it. The cars detouring off the highway plowed the water. The streetlight was blinking green. The trees outside were bent over and limp. They looked like they were tired of the rain.

The food came, and they began to eat. Wallace started listening to the music being played in the restaurant — a peculiar Chinese techno-rave dance music, high speed, insistent beat. The song sounded like German pop music with a few Oriental instruments tossed in. He watched Kelly cool her soup in the large plastic version of the Chinese spoon. She seemed to him a woman whom any man would find attractive. She was so sweet, so gentle, so deeply invested in the parts of their lives, so genuinely interested. He wondered why he hadn't met anyone like her. He remembered a girl from high school — a smart girl who had a kind of simplicity and ease about her, a directness. She reminded him a little of his sister, but she was the last girl he could remember who had anything in common with Kelly. He tapped his mouth with his napkin and then slid out of his side of the booth and got into Kelly's side. She was startled and slid away from him.

"Shhh," he said, holding up a hand. He reached out and touched her hair, ran his fingers through it, the tips of his fingers through to her scalp.

"What are you doing?" she said. "Get back over there."

"I'm going in just a minute," Wallace said.

"Go on," she said and shooed him with her napkin. He pulled her to him, and she resisted at first, but then perhaps sensing that he wasn't going to give up, she gave in and allowed herself to be pulled to him. He kissed her softly on the cheek and then on her neck beneath her ear. He let his head rest on her shoulder a minute, then kissed her there, sat up, and edged out of the booth. He stood alongside the table for a minute, took a drink of his Diet Coke, and stared across the room at the big television.

From behind Kelly caught his hand, gave him a little tug toward his seat. "We don't have to go anywhere if you don't want to," she said. "It's just that I miss them. I still see them in my head sometimes. I can hear them talking. I can hear things Mother said to me. I can remember what her hand felt like when she touched me. I can remember the way her skin looked — almost translucent, filmy. I can remember the way she squinted. I just think it would be good if we went to see them."

"I'll go," Wallace said. "I'll go right now. I'll get the check and we can go."

"No, I want to finish this first," she said.

He sat down again, facing her. He had no appetite, but he put two or three things on his plate and busied himself moving them back and forth, moving them clockwise around his plate. "How come you're not using chopsticks?" he said to her.

"No need to," she said.

"It makes for a more complete experience," he said. "That's what you told me."

"I think somebody must have told me once," she said.

He pulled back the curtain again. Outside, there were more flashing, glittering, blinking lights. There were new policemen and a wrecker, and there was a truck that had somehow jack-knifed off the low seawall. There were even some of those burning torches that are supplied in all emergency road kits. He could hear the buzz of the blinking Shanghai Garden sign mounted on the outside of the glass near the booth where they sat. Kelly pulled back the curtain on her side and looked out.

"'You long to see the great pyramids of Egypt,'" Wallace said.

"What?"

"The last fortune cookie I got here," he said. "The last time we were here."

"Oh," she said. "You do. You really do."

BAG BOY

WE WERE IN Dallas because Jen's father was an assassination
buff. It was his hobby, something to do when there was nothing
else to do. He wasn't new to it, but he wasn't a freak about it,
either. Some people go overboard on everything, but that wasn't
Mike. He was just interested in the assassination, the research, the
testing, the theories — he perked up whenever anything about the
assassination came across his line of sight. Mike was fifty-three
and already retired from an Aetna Casualty job, so he had plenty
of time on his hands to study the books, the videos, the gray-mar-
ket paperwork he'd ordered from tombstone ads in magazines, the
geek view he downloaded from assassination BBSs and the
Internet, and the half-dozen assassination CD-ROMs he owned,
including one he'd shown me called *A Practical Guide to the
Autopsy,* and others on the Warren Report, conspiracies in general,
and great assassinations in history.

Mike had never been to Dallas. Jen and I hadn't been there,

either, and we weren't particularly interested, but Jen and I had been living together for two years and Mike and I hadn't been introduced except by phone, so one Sunday in the weekly call we decided to go see Dealey Plaza, just the three of us. The next day Jen added an old college friend of hers, Penny Mars, to the mix, because she thought Penny would be good company for Mike, who was long divorced and a confirmed bachelor and twice Penny's age. We were sensitive to age because I was twenty years older than Jen, nearer Mike's age than hers, and we thought there might be some talk about that. So Penny had her uses.

After the drive from Baton Rouge the four of us were going up in the carpet-and-glass elevator of the Dallas Ramada with a young guy who had "Rhumbo" stenciled on his name tag. He was handling the bags. He was disease-thin, gangly, burr-cut, tattooed, and properly earringed. A man of his time. For the job he wore a too-big maroon uniform with bad gold piping.

"Where'd you get the name tag?" Jen asked the bag guy.

"The name or the tag?" He was naturally unpleasant, impatient, lots of attitude. "Which?"

"Name," Jen said.

I couldn't figure out why she was bothering — maybe it was highway-blindness. She was wearing cutoffs and a washed-out T-shirt and looked younger than the twenty-seven she was. Penny looked younger than that. Mike and I looked rumpled and tired, like we were on the wrong side of middle age.

"I was in prison in Minnesota," the kid said. "B and E. They called me 'Rhumbo.'"

"Oh," Jen said.

The guy was too tall and he stooped to look at her as he explained things, pointing with one finger at the palm of the other hand, as if he needed that for emphasis. "See, some dead man there had this kid's book about an elephant named Rhumbo, it was the only thing he could read, and he figured I favored this elephant, so that's what he called me all the time. I was, like, his pet."

"Cool name," Jen said, giving a little nod and digging into her purse searching for something.

He gave her a look. His skin was blotchy and sore red, patches the size of fists ran around his neck, and his eyebrows were furry and queer-looking on his shaved head. He had some kind of vinegary smell coming off the costume. "You want the tag?" he asked. "I can tell these Ramada dorks I lost it, I can tell them anything. That's something you get inside—how to take what you need, just rip it out of somebody's hands if you have to. These dips, what're they going to do? They're not going to fire me. They need a guy like me around here at night." He unhooked the name tag from his jacket and held it out to Jen. She hung back a minute, then took the tag.

"What about the Rhumbo-Dumbo thing?" Penny said, dodging her head back and forth in a way that meant she meant the question in a friendly way. "That a problem or anything?"

The guy rolled his eyes big, leaning his head off to one side. I watched his reflection careen around the elevator glass.

"Look," he said, like he was explaining something to a ten-year-old. "The Rhumbo book is *fact*. Elephants sleep on their stomachs. An elephant's height is calculated by measuring twice around the largest part of its foot. Real stuff. Dumbo was just some Disney slop."

Jen snapped the tag over the pocket of her T-shirt. "Hi, my name's Rhumbo," she said, shaking hands with an imaginary elevator-rider, practicing her introduction. Then she poked some high-floor numbers on the elevator panel. "Rhumbo, up!" she said.

The bag boy led us to our rooms on the ninth floor. He went in and did a lot of curtain-swishing and bed-patting in each room, then stood there at attention waiting for his reward. Mike gave him a twenty, and the guy went away grinning. We were still in the hall talking when the guy reached the corner by the elevators, did an elephant-trunk wave, and then disappeared.

▼

In our room, Jen stripped to the waist, went straight into the bathroom, and came out wiping herself down with a damp washcloth. "I'm calling Penny and taking her for drinks," she said. "You want to come with?"

I was on my back on one of the beds. "I think I'm staying in," I said.

"You're getting along all right, aren't you? With Dad?"

"Sure. Everything's fine. He's not so bad—I don't know why we were worried. He doesn't seem to care how old I am."

"Well, he was prepared," Jen said. "He was talked to. You think he likes Penny?"

"I think he thinks Penny is a great big apple on a stick."

We'd been driving for so long that I was still swaying like we were out on the highway. It was nine and the city was lit up, and all I wanted to do was stay still and let things stop moving. The downtown buildings were all outlined with lights. One place had twin spires and these circular towers and looked like it came from Buildings R Us. Downtown wasn't that big. One building had green wiggly lights all over it, reflected in its glass. I couldn't tell whether the lights were strange or it was fabulous architecture.

The room was cheesy in that motel way—silly-looking dressers, veneered night tables, a nondescript table-and-chairs set by the window. If somebody you knew owned the stuff, it would be horrifying, but at the Ramada, it was comforting. You knew where you were. No mistakes.

Jen called Penny and arranged to go out for drinks, then knocked on the connecting door to her father's room. Mike opened up wearing a royal blue satin smoking jacket.

"Check it out," he said.

"Where'd you get that?" she said.

"Found it," he said. "On a hanger in here." He thumbed back toward his room.

"Looks mighty suave," I said, getting out of the bed. It didn't feel right being in bed with Mike in the room, like I shouldn't be that relaxed. When I sat on the edge of the bed I saw some kind of food crumbs on the floor right by the night table. "There're crumbs here," I said to Jen, pointing to the floor where the crumbs were.

She came over for a look, then swept her shoe back and forth a couple of times over the spot. "There. All gone," she said. She invited Mike to go out and have a drink with her and Penny, but he asked what I was going to do, and when I told him, he said he thought he'd just hang out with me, if that was OK.

She said, "Sure. Fine. You guys can give each other lectures or something."

"No lectures," Mike said, raising his eyebrows at me as if he hadn't a clue what she meant. I didn't either, so I shrugged.

"This traveling together isn't so bad, is it?" Jen said, sliding past him, headed for the door.

"No, it's great," Mike said. "I mean, it's OK for me. I'm doing fine." He sat down in one of the chairs by the window.

"You guys stay out of trouble," Jen said.

We both waved at her, the same kind of wave. It was odd happening the way it did. Mike had a Coke can he'd gotten somewhere, and he was flipping the tab making thumb piano sounds.

"So, Mike," I said, climbing into the second chair by the window. "You OK?"

"Pretty much," he said. "I guess I feel a little awkward. It's hard to be the father, us being the same age. I guess I never was a father to Jen all that much. With the first two I wasn't so tolerant, I didn't give them a lot of leeway, but by the time Jen came along I'd just given up, I mean, I knew whatever happened would be OK."

He was alternating between thumping the tab on the can and rubbing his thumb on the wood-grained Formica table between us, making a squeaking sound, like he was trying to rub some spot off the tabletop, some sticky spot that wasn't giving up without a fight.

"Uh-huh," I said.

"I'm sorry, Del," he said, putting the can down and rubbing his forehead instead of the table. "I didn't mean to bother you with that. It's just I've been thinking about things all day. You know — Jen, the other kids, the family. I haven't seen her in a long time."

"Yeah, I know. And it didn't bother me. I just didn't know what to say. I don't have any opinions about parenting, families, all that. Well, I mean I have ideas about *my* family, but not about the parent side of it, or any general sort of ideas about parents, just about my parents, you know, like from the point of view of the kid. Me, I mean."

"Sure," he said. "You live one way and I live another. All my life I'm a little tucked-in fella, sitting in my neat house, paying those bills right on time. Looking into problems and acting like I knew what I was looking at. I guess I had more order than I really needed."

"Actually, that sounds great to me," I said. "No kidding. Mine's been a mess, first to last."

He laughed. "Yeah, I gathered that from Jen. What I don't get is how come you're not worried. Fifty, aren't you? Close to it? You've got a good job, but it's not paying you a fortune, is it? And I'll bet the retirement program's not going to turn out the way the brochure described it. It takes a lot of nerve to be in your shoes."

I glanced at him, trying to see if this was criticism, an aggression, but it wasn't there in his face, so I said, "I guess I am kind of worried. I mean, I never was before, I was always too busy being this or that, disdaining this or that — you know how that goes. But now I'm a little nervous."

"Maybe I could help out," Mike said. "I mean, setting things up, some plans so you're sure you're OK when you retire."

"You think you could do that? That'd be very nice. I could use help."

"Sure," he said. He got up and leaned against the window, looking down to the freeway below us, first left, then right, scratching his cheek. He had a heavy beard, so there was a loud sandpapery sound. "You think we ought to go over to Dealey Plaza tonight?" he asked, tapping the glass.

"We can if you want to." I was watching a helicopter flying on the other side of downtown. It reminded me of some movie. I couldn't hear it, but it was moving lazily around the buildings over there, doing that spotlight thing.

"I was playing golf," Mike said. "When he was shot. Somebody came by in a cart and yelled at us, and we headed back for the Pro Shop where there was a TV. I watched there for a while, then went home and stayed there for days. Saw Ruby shooting Oswald — all of that. I liked the music at the funeral, the cortege, the boots backward in the stirrups — that's what got me, that riderless horse. Walter Cronkite talking about the riderless horse — he must've said those words hundreds of times. 'And now the riderless horse —' That got me. The drums, the music. The procession. All that walking. The backwards boots — damn. That was something. That was new as hell."

I got up and skirted the table, then picked up my wallet and keys from the dresser where I'd put them earlier. "So why don't we go over there now? Take a look."

"Should we eat first?" he said. "We can eat. You want to eat?"

The light coming up from the freeway caught his face in an odd way, and suddenly I saw him as a much younger man. This had happened to me before — in some odd second you see what somebody was like when he was twenty years younger. Most of the time it wasn't particularly attractive, but with Mike it was nice, it made me like him more than I already did.

"Chicken-fried steak, mashed potatoes, brown gravy," Mike said. "Let's hit a One's A Meal. Open-face roast beef with mashed potatoes. Either one."

"Hey now," I said, doing the guy on *The Larry Sanders Show*.

"I've got that mashed potatoes thing going." He grinned and caught my shoulder.

"I'm right there," I said, touched by our sudden camaraderie.

We started down the hall for the elevator, but Mike had to go back and get something in his room. I waited in the hall remembering a scene with Eddie Constantine in some early Godard movie I couldn't even remember the name of — *Alphaville*, it suddenly came to me. That's what the Ramada hallway looked like — desolate, frighteningly utilitarian.

"The art of the chicken-fried is a lost art," Mike said, coming out of his room and raising both hands as if to forestall any argument. "Now, I know that mostly what happens in life is that stuff gets lost, all kinds of stuff, and that food's the least of it, but you'd think they'd be able to hang onto chicken-fried steak, wouldn't you? The rest I don't care so much about. These days it's all rude people and their rude hair, anyway. That Elephant Boy in the elevator. You and me, Del, we're the old cars out there in the way." He soft-popped my shoulder with his fist. "But sometimes, don't you just want to bump the little creeps, you know? Just nudge them with the front end — bam! Sixty miles an hour, that kind of thing. I'll bet you know that feeling."

"Yes, sir," I said.

"See," Mike said. "Yet another reason to like you."

▼

Rhumbo was backwards on a plastic chair at Jen and Penny's table in the Twin Sisters, the Ramada's house bar. We stopped there to see if they wanted to eat.

"You taking a break?" I asked him.

"I was just asking how come these girls were with you guys," he said. "What, you can't find women your own age?" He switched to a too-intense expression. "Just kidding. Jen told me she's" — he hesitated, ready to point at one of us, not sure which one until Jen nodded toward Mike — "your daughter, right? And you," he said, wagging a finger at me, "are the boyfriend."

"Good work," I said, then turned to Jen. "We were thinking of eating something."

"I can tell you where I'd go," Rhumbo said, swinging his leg over the back of the chair, getting up. "I'd hit that IHOP. Right around the corner here. Get me a batch of German pancakes. Real good." Something wet shined on his teeth when he smiled. He smelled sour. His little maroon suit was wide open over a white T.

"I don't play that pancake game," Mike said. "We're looking for chicken-fried."

"California Cafe, off eleventh," the kid said. "Go there all the time."

"I wouldn't hate pancakes," Penny said. She was fooling with her long and auburn hair, finger-combing it.

"We're going to see Dealey Plaza afterward," I said to Jen.

"He wasn't in prison," Penny said, patting the bag boy's head. "That's just something he made up. He's in grad school here. His name's Roy."

"Hey," the kid said, holding his hands out. "Caught me. But I can't believe you're going over to Dealey. I've been here eight years and I've never been there."

"Hello, Roy," Mike said, shaking the kid's hand.

"How about Roy shows us the Cafe and then we all go to the plaza," Penny said.

"What about work?" I asked. "Don't you have to work, Roy?"

"Fuck 'em," he said. "I'm on my break."

The California Cafe was greasy and small, just right, and chicken-fried steak was there. No brown gravy, only white gravy. It was nearly midnight when we got to Dealey Plaza, which was just a couple of highway feeders, half a city block with nothing on it, and a concrete train overpass. All the streetlights were orange.

"What a joke," Roy said, looking around from the sidewalk across from the Texas Schoolbook Depository. "Oswald's up here, and the limo goes there, and blam! Even I could have made that shot. Do it in my sleep."

"Oh, settle down," Penny said. "You couldn't make the shot."

"On TV shows, Dealey Plaza does always seem bigger," Mike said.

"What is it — a hundred yards from there to there?" Roy said. "It's tiny. Why'd they make a big stew about this? Anybody could make it. Glenn Ford could make it. It's a groundhog deal."

"Six FBI marksmen," Mike said. "They tried it with pumpkins and missed. I mean, using pumpkins for Kennedy's head. Did it here and did it in a field in Iowa or Wisconsin."

He looked a little shell-shocked. I grabbed his arm, and we walked across the street to see the Texas Schoolbook Depository close up. Then we came back and walked the route Kennedy's car had taken, then climbed up the grassy knoll and went around behind the fence into the vacant lot where the other shots were supposed to have come from. We watched a train go by on the overpass. "This is where the three tramps were," Mike said. "Maybe they were getting into a boxcar over there" — he pointed toward the tracks — "but some reports say they were over behind the Depository building there, that back corner there. This lot was full of cars."

Jen, Penny, and Roy were sticking close to the terraced part of the plaza where there was a reflecting pool and a commemorative plaque explaining everything. There was a spotlighted American flag in the middle of it, looking like red and white vinyl flapping up there. "I'm going to go see what Jen's doing," I said. "You OK here?"

He nodded, and I went back around the fence and crossed the street, climbing the little rise to the terrace. Jen drifted away from Penny and Roy.

"How're you doing?" she asked.

"Fine," I said. "But what's the deal with Penny?"

"She thinks he's interesting."

"Roy? She must be starved to death," I said.

"He's right about how small this joint is," Jen said. "Where's Dad?"

"Over here," I said, looking back toward where I'd left Mike. "He's behind the fence, above the grassy knoll. He's being the second gunman. He seems kind of forlorn."

Across the street I could see Mike's head poking out above the wood fence that separated the grassy knoll from the parking lot. The train going by behind the parking lot was squeaking and squealing, rocking on the tracks.

"Places are always letdowns," Jen said. "I wish it was scary, at least. You know, an eerie feeling like going back in time, or time could switch around and you'd be caught there that day, running to the limo, but it'd be snaking off toward the underpass. You know what I mean? *X-Files.* That'd be cool."

The big flag was snapping overhead, the wind was driving it so hard. Mike came out and stood for a minute in the colonnade on the other side of the grassy knoll. Then he headed our way. When he got to us he looked like somebody who'd gotten real depressed.

"You feel all right?" I asked him.

"Fine," he said.

"The Depository isn't open," Jen said. "It's open days but not nights."

Penny and Roy came up behind us. "Everything OK?" Penny said.

"I don't want to go there anyway," Mike said.

"This is cheap shit," Roy said. "It's a toy, like a scale model where a toy president was killed. Toy people scattering. Toy shots. What a shank."

Jen was trying to bring Mike around. "We can come back tomorrow, and you can get right up there to the window where Oswald did the shooting," she said.

"Unless he was hanging upside down from one foot with a squirrel in his teeth it ain't worth it," Roy said.

"I think I'll go back to the Ramada for now," Mike said.

Jen looped her arm through his. "Aw, c'mon, Dad. Let's sit here and just soak it up. Maybe it gets better if you hang out a while."

"History's always so small when you see it in person," Mike said.

"Yeah, this is Buck-A-Day," Roy said. "Who cares, anyway? It's like about as important as John Wilkes Booth, or whatever."

A busload of tourists came in behind us, maybe twenty Hawaiians in Hawaiian shirts carrying cameras and wearing funny hats. The tour guide gathered them on the terrace alongside the reflecting pool in front of the Dealey Plaza plaque and started explaining stuff. Mike went for the street and hailed a cab that was going by.

"I'm going to the motel," Mike said. "Anybody want to go with?"

"We're ready," Penny said, yanking Roy with her.

"Are you OK, Dad?" Jen said. She looked at me as if I was supposed to stop him. I started toward the cab, but her father waved me off.

"Forget it. I'm fine. I'll get some rest."

Then the three of them climbed into the backseat of the Yellow and rode off. The car squatted as it accelerated.

▼

Jen and I went back to the grassy knoll and sat down, watching the traffic dip left to right into the underpass. There were plenty of sightseers, not a crowd, but fifty or so, circling and pointing out the highlights, the Schoolbook Depository, the spot below us where the President was shot, the knoll, the fence. There was a big road sign in front of us, and I couldn't figure out if it was the one the President's car disappeared behind in the Zapruder film or if it was some new sign. It seemed as if it was the same sign but it was in the wrong place, as if it had been secretly moved, as if they didn't want anybody to notice.

"This is a big deal, isn't it?" Jen said. "I'm supposed to get the weight of history here. Great events upon which our future turned."

"Jen?" I said.

"It's not really working," she said.

"Maybe you have to believe things would've been different if he wasn't shot. You know, like coherence and history and all that," I said. The train had been squealing nonstop for twenty minutes. "I like this train pretty much."

"You would," she said.

"I like the way it's shimmering, and that steely noise the wheels make, and the way the cars shift back and forth into each other, kind of lurching," I said. "It's like a car-crash audio slowed way down."

"I wasn't even born," she said. "I think that's why for me. It's textbooks— You're supposed to think about it, feel stuff, maybe that's it. You're supposed to, so you don't, blah, blah. Pretty quick you resent it."

"Yeah?"

"I really don't feel shit, except I'm kind of pissed because it disappointed my dad."

I put an arm around her, then leaned against her, dropping my nearly fifty-year-old head on her shoulder. "Still, you don't want Kennedy killed, there's that. He got his skull exploded right down here in front of us. Think of that. We're ringside."

"People get that everywhere," Jen said. "Plus, who cares? Why's the President getting it worse than somebody else? He's just one more goofball going down."

"He had big ideas," I said.

"He was just another guy with a sore dick," Jen said.

She got up, and I followed. We went behind the fence where Mike had been earlier and toured the parking lot, then I leaned up against the fence. It was kind of broken down at the corner. I wondered if it was the real fence. Then I wondered if I cared if it was the real fence. We walked through the colonnade Mike had been through and back up alongside the Texas Schoolbook Depository, went and looked at the entrance to the museum part, and came back to where we'd started.

"I think things were different back then," I said. "There was a whole different deal, I vaguely remember. The idea is things changed because he was shot — that wised us up, made us all callous."

"That's junior, Del," she said.

"Hey, it hadn't happened before. Nobody thought it *could* happen. It was like something in those fifties movies with Henry Fonda or somebody, you know, the black-and-white ones?"

"Oh, please. If there's a change it was you and your buds cheating each other, stretching truth, pushing at the edges of things, getting that little extra. Everybody got used to it. You all held hands and evolved into us."

"My generation."

"That's it," she said. "Do the crime, do the time." She waved toward the Depository, then the rest of the Dealey setup. "This whole show looks like it's lit with bug lamps. It's yellow. Isn't everything kind of yellowish, or is that my imagination?"

"It has a parchment-colored thing," I said.

"Part of the plan, I guess," she said. "It's shitty to charge for the Oswald window. That's like, Kill a President so your town can make six bucks a pop on the yahoos. How many you figure they get a year? They even charge for kids."

"Do not," I said.

"Yes, sir. It's on the sign."

"So," I said, brushing off my jeans. "Let me see — you want to go back to the Ramada and get in bed and see what's on TV?"

"Exactly right," she said, smacking my arm. "Maybe that *JFK* movie. That'd be cool. Or some real rainy movie like that Kurt Russell Florida thing where he's the blown-out reporter and that Hemingway woman is his girl — that's really great rain in there." She kissed my shoulder. "I tell you, you older guys are slow but you're OK. You get there."

"Thanks," I said. "Now all we've got to do is refocus Penny, get her back on track."

"I'm getting her some new heels," Jen said. "Saw them in a cat-alog — chrome toe, six-inch stilettos, the works. They moan when you walk."

"She'll use 'em on Roy," I said.

"Well, then I'll keep them just for us," she said. "How about lemon yellow?"

We walked back to where we'd parked the car, which was next to some architect's idea of a Kennedy memorial — thick slabs of concrete making a sort of room that stood up off the ground in an open half-block space. You were supposed to stand inside it and feel the gravity of events. Somebody had posted a clown-show sign on its side. We got in the car and headed for the hotel.

The streets of downtown Dallas were almost empty, so it looked like one of those end-of-the-world movies, where all the people have been killed, and we get long shots of the empty downtown streets, and there's a wind blowing coffee cups across the pave-ment and pieces of paper are flapping in the breeze. But nobody moves. It was nice, so we ran the windows down on Mike's car and floated through the streets for a while — going six or eight blocks in one direction and then turning, coming up the next street going the other direction, the wind whipping into the car, twisting our hair. It smelled that strange way empty cities smell at night, clean and metallic. Jen switched on the radio, and we turned it up and let it thump as we rode through the streets.

▼

Roy met us in the corridor outside our rooms. He looked worse for wear, like he was loaded. "So?" he said. "How're you guys? The big man turned right on in. You want to come down to Penny's and get trashed? We've got some shit."

"I don't think so," I said.

"Why not? What're you doing? Don't go getting all historical, OK?" he said, his hairless little face twisted into a smirk.

"Don't know much about history," I said.

We tried to get past him, but he followed us.

"Where's Penny?" Jen asked.

He grinned way too big. "She's freshening up. Just, you know — freshening up." Then he laughed a kind of snort-laugh.

"Great," Jen said.

"See, what I figure," he said, "I mean Kennedy and all that, is there's no difference — Starkweather, 'Nam, this cute Oklahoma trick — it's all settled. It's going down. That's what's out there. You gotta have the hard stuff or you got nothing. The government does it best. Blowing hands and feet off Iraqis on that road out of Kuwait or whatever — you see that? Real time-morphing. Big trade in corpse and body-part snaps. Big profits."

"Slow it up, pal, will you?" Jen said.

"And great TV, too," he said. "Sometimes I like that militia thing, that time-to-clean thing that we're doing now — flush the bad, act with maximum efficiency, scrape out evil's eye. Know what I'm saying? That appeals."

"You're a moron," I said, giving him some phony thumbs-up that I didn't quite have control of.

"Maybe history is calling," he said, grinning.

"Yeah, and maybe it's not," Jen said.

▼

In the room Mike's connecting door to our room was closed. Ours was still open. I started to shut it as quietly as I could, fearing the latch. "I guess I'll just leave this alone," I said to Jen. "He's probably asleep."

"He's got a model of the plaza," Jen said. "It's wonderful. Made it himself, took years. Perfect scale, perfect grass, lampposts, signs, cars, and the different people who were there that day, all reconstructed from video and photos." She was hooking her notebook computer up to the telephone.

"I want to see that when we get back," I said.

"I'm sure he'll show it to you," she said.

I flipped on the television and went through a few stations until I got to the Weather Channel and stopped there and watched a new hurricane named Camellia messing around with Hawaii. A lot of the video of Hawaii was quite beautiful, so I watched that for a while. Buildings were falling down. A Holiday Inn fell down, or part of it did — the sign and the portico over the drive-in entrance. The trees were all bending vigorously, and the whole picture looked wet. It was lovely and relaxing.

In a minute I heard Jen's modem screech as she made her connection. She turned around and caught the tail end of the Hawaii video and asked me what it was.

"Hawaii," I said. "They're having a hurricane."

"Cool," she said.

There was a light knock on the door. I eyed Jen, then got up to answer. It was Penny. She was done up in a short black dress and lots of makeup. I let her in.

"Look out in the hall and see if jerk-boy is still hanging around, will you?" Jen said.

"Oh, don't be that way," Penny said. "He harmless, he's OK. Besides, he's down in my room."

"Here's what he is," Jen said, clicking some computer keys. Then she read something off the screen. "'With skillful manipulation of the Japanese rope harnesses you first find the middle of the rope and make a sizable overhand knot so you have a loop big enough to fit your partner's head. Employ a rope of appropriate dimension and surface. Consider the path of the rope from the breasts, just above the vagina, taking care to border the labia with the length running then to her head and neck, and have her hold her hands behind her back — '"

"OK," Penny said. "I get it. But he's doing the best he can."

"Like us," I said.

"Exactly. He's trying to be somebody."

"Why couldn't he try to be Alf?" Jen said.

Penny smoothed her skirt, what there was of it. "He wants to impress us. He's just trying to make himself more interesting. Anyway, we're going out for beers."

"Everybody always wants to be so interesting," I said.

"Yeah," Jen said. "That's our generation."

"I thought I'd tell you so you wouldn't worry," Penny said. "I don't think we'll be out too long."

"OK. We won't worry," I said. "You look mighty, uh, breezy."

"Let me be, will you?" Penny said, looking at Jen. "What's with him?"

"He is just a rat," Jen said, walking Penny to the door. "Go. Have fun. Be lucky."

When Penny was out of the room Jen tossed herself onto my bed. "Oh, baby, you're so right it just gives me chills. I just want to watch some TV with you. Watch those news gooks, potatoes with olive eyes, talking as if it mattered. I wish we had that Saturday night one with the guy from the *Wall Street Journal*, Novak, and the woman with the prissy little mouth and the mole. Everybody sits up so straight on those shows."

"You're a true postmodernist," I said.

"No alternative," Jen said.

They were doing local stuff on the Weather Channel — chance of rain. Jen shut down the computer, unplugged the phone cord and stuck it back into the phone.

"I thought Penny hated men," I said.

Jen shook her head and rolled her eyes and did a little puppet jerk, as if she were being controlled on strings from above. I took this to mean I was being stupid.

I clicked through the channels, stopped again at CNN. There was something about Whitewater, new revelations, more unending true drivel.

"Now *that* is pissing in the wind," Jen said, looking over my shoulder.

"You guys are supposed to be less cynical than us," I said.

"That's another generation," Jen said. "The one before us, I think. They were less cynical than you. We're more. Our cynicism takes paint off warships, knocks planes out of the sky — this is a problem for you old guys when you get three or four generations out of touch."

The O. J. backdrop came up on the screen along with the theme song. Jen lunged for the remote.

▼

I was the last one down for breakfast. The motel restaurant was all light wood and light Formica and plastic flowers in fifty shades of green. It was almost empty. Mike and Penny and Roy were sitting together at a small table near a window that looked out toward the freeway. I saw Jen in the lobby as I came out of the elevator. She waved me into the restaurant. She was getting a newspaper. Mike had scrambled eggs and toast. Roy was slicing his fork through a tall stack of pancakes covered with pretty syrup. Penny was eating a piece of bacon off his plate. I said good morning.

"Morning," Mike said. "Long time no see."

"I slept," I said. "What time is it?"

"Eleven," he said.

Penny was patting Roy's arm. She picked up her fork and got a one-inch square of pancake off his plate. She had coffee and a roll in front of her, but she was more interested in Roy's pancakes.

"Dealey wasn't too great, I guess," I said.

"It's putz country," Roy said, waving his fork off toward town. "That's the real deal."

"It's deadly," Penny said. "That's what we decided."

"Maybe if we go over today that would help," I said. "You know — it was night, we were tired, we'd been driving."

"I don't think so," Mike said. "I've seen enough."

293

"It's fucking pathetic over there," Roy said. "So what are you anyway, some kind of investigator? You trying to figure how many gunmen there were and all that?"

"Yeah. That's it," Mike said, smiling at the kid.

I thought about some things Mike had told me, stuff about the videos, the autopsy photographs, the little girl running — was she really looking back up at the Depository, or had she been called? — about Badgeman, Umbrella Man, Dark-Complexioned Man, and the skin flap on Kennedy's head, the fence people, the tramps, the boxcar deal, the woman on the Louisiana highway, the bar deal with the CIA, the Moorman Polaroid. I figured he was smart to keep it in his head where he could work on it in peace, let it show him new angles, where the questions were still viable and the pleasure was getting close to something that always disappeared when you tried to look at it. He could do that forever.

Jen came back to the table with a *USA Today* and a Dallas paper. I ordered eggs like Mike's. Penny went on picking off Roy's plate. Jen scanned the Dallas paper. I tried to figure the quickest way to get the four of us back in Mike's big Lincoln.

LARROQUETTE

SHEILA LEANED against her chain-link fence, fingering the deco-rative scroll bolted onto the top of the gate. She was looking across the street at the Terlinks' garage. The Terlinks were having a Sunday afternoon barbecue. Sheila watched carefully. She hadn't waved. She didn't know the Terlinks — Johnson Terlink and his wife, Emma, their two children, Rita and Herman — had never spo-ken to them except in passing at the mailbox — Hello, how are you? Nothing more. But somebody else was with them. A fancy rental car nosed into the end of the drive, so she knew they had company. Sheila kicked at Bosco, the dog who kept winding around her legs, in and out, panting, occasionally making little yipping noises.

She liked the neighborhood. It was the best she could afford. The houses were wood-siding things, falling apart, once painted white with colorful trim. The yards were thick grass, tricycles, col-orful volleyballs, soccer balls, plastic doodads and whatnots. A kite twirled on the telephone wire behind the Terlinks' house. The kite had been there since Sheila moved in eighteen months before, after her divorce. Eighteen months, Sheila thought looking at the kite. I should have introduced myself before this.

Sheila worked nights at the hospital, rolling patients over, wedging pillows under them, cleaning bedpans, changing drips and catheter bags. She had six hours before work.

The tall guy on the Terlinks' driveway laughed loudly. He looked familiar, she thought. He looked like John Larroquette.

She went inside to get her son, Tod, who was eighteen, in his room watching MTV. Tod had a job at Don't Nobody Eat Pizza? He strapped a Don't Nobody Eat Pizza? sign on the top of the car and delivered all night long.

"Come out here and look at this, will you?" Sheila said. "I think we've got John Larroquette across the way."

"What's he doing there?" Tod said.

"Don't know. I'm not sure it's him. There's a guy who looks like him, somebody. Got a fancy rent car."

"So walk across the street," Tod said.

"I don't want to meet him," Sheila said. "I just want to know if it *is* him."

"I don't care if it is," Tod said.

"I know," Sheila said. "But I do. So come out, look across, see if you can ID him, OK? I don't ask too goddamn much."

"You ask everything," Tod said. He rolled off the bed. She followed him, and Bosco followed her. They were a little parade.

Tod leaned on the fence, squinted hard, said, "I don't know. I give up," and headed back inside.

"Tod," she said.

"I don't know. I can't see. What makes you think it's him, anyway? And why do you care? You never looked at John Larroquette, did you? Wasn't he on *Cheers*?"

"Oh, like you don't know," Sheila said. "*Night Court*. But now he's got his own show. He reminds me of your father."

"Everybody reminds you of my father," Tod said. "Batman

reminds you of my father." Tod wore plaid green Bermudas and a soiled T-shirt. He walked around a bush at the corner of the house. "You need a life, Mother. That's what."

"Look who's talking. Come back here." She pointed to the ground in front of her. Tod looked, his hair a tangle of eight-inch spikes. He stood on the back steps.

Bosco tore a limb off the bush and ran around with the limb in his mouth, daring Sheila to chase him. She feinted at the dog, and he dodged away.

"What's wrong with me?" Tod said. He held his T-shirt at the hem, staring down at himself.

"You're eighteen and living at home with your mother," Sheila said.

"So I'll move," he said. He opened the screen door.

"You're just like your father," Sheila said.

Tod shut his eyes and leaned his head back and rubbed his left hand through his hair several times, holding his head. "I'm not just like my father in any way," he said. "I've never been like my father. I don't know why a person would say that. I don't know why you would say that. You know I'm not like my father."

Sheila sat down on the ground, gathering her skirt between her legs.

"Don't sit on the ground, Mother," Tod said. "Come inside. I'll fix you something to eat — a toasted cheese sandwich. Would you like that?"

"Nope," Sheila said. "I want to know if that's John Larroquette."

"It's not," he said.

"I saw him on Leno. He's from Louisiana. He said he visits his cousin in Florida, his only cousin. They have barbecues. In the garage. That's what he told Jay."

"I'm guessing he visits Miami or something. Coral Gables. Not likely his cousin lives in Quantum." Tod came down the steps, into the yard, and reached out to help his mother up, but just at that minute Bosco hopped into her lap.

"I could talk to Mrs. Terlink about her dogs," Sheila said.

"What dogs?" Tod asked.

"She raises Chihuahuas," Sheila said. "That's what Ellen told me. Ellen next door?" She thumbed to her left where Ellen lived. "Said she raises Chihuahuas. She's got maybe twenty-five Chihuahuas over there."

Tod shook his head. "OK. Here's what I'll do. I'll go out like I'm getting the mail. If it's him, I'll come get you."

"Why would you be getting the mail on Sunday?" Sheila said.

"I wasn't home Saturday?" he said.

"You're always home," she said. "Everybody knows that."

"Oh. Right," Tod said. He finger-combed his hair over his head, one side to the other.

"Why don't you wash it?" Sheila said.

Inside, she sat on an old green stool by the stove. Tod made her a sandwich out of Rainbow bread and wrapper cheese. She took some wrapper cheese to feed Bosco, made him stand up on his hind legs and go around in circles, then dropped cheese strips from shoulder height to see if he could catch them. Most of the time the cheese went right by him.

She walked out through the dining room into the living room and stood at the front window, pulling back the curtain, peering across the street. "I think that's him," she said. "I'm almost certain that's him."

"It's not," Tod said. "Come eat your sandwich."

"Let's go out in the car. We can get really close."

"I thought you wanted a sandwich. I'm making a sandwich. Are you going to eat?"

In the living room, Sheila picked up three copies of *Family Circle* magazine that Ellen had lent her. She gathered up some of Bosco's toys — a pink ball with a pebbled surface, a plastic bone the size of her forearm, a book he liked to chew on. She tossed all three into a basket in the corner of the living room where Bosco's toys were kept. For some reason Bosco wouldn't go near the basket. When he wanted a toy, he would stand about a foot away from the basket and whimper, looking back over his shoulder at her. It would have been easy enough for him to tip the basket over, or reach in and bite whatever toy he wanted. But he would never do that. He just whimpered. Sometimes, if a toy went under a chair or the bench in the entry hall, Bosco would stand there and look, whimpering. He was afraid the furniture was going to jump him.

"Ready," Tod called. She went in the kitchen and ate her cheese sandwich. Tod ate a peanut butter sandwich and stood at the window by the sink, looking at Ellen's house. "There are snakes over there," he said. "Ellen came over last week and told me the yard guy found a snake in the back and chased it under a tree stump, so she had the animal control people come out. But they said they wouldn't touch it. That it was her responsibility. If the snake was out in the open, they'd take it. Otherwise, no dice."

"That's a big help," his mother said.

"She was warning me about Bosco, to keep him out of the yard," he said.

"He can take care of himself," Sheila said.

"Said it was a copperhead," Tod said. "I went and looked, but I couldn't see anything. She wanted me to put gasoline in this tree stump and burn it. I didn't want to do that."

"She's fond of you," Sheila said.

"Oh, please," Tod said.

"Ever since the police came," Sheila said.

"Yeah, big turn-on," Tod said.

Two months before, the police had come to the house to talk to Tod about a case they were working on. Some pizza delivery guy was raping women. They called the guy "the pizza rapist." They didn't think Tod was him, but they thought he might know the guy. Two uniformed policemen and two plainclothes policemen came in and sat in the living room with Tod and Sheila, and, in the middle of things, Ellen had arrived.

"Can I help?" she had asked.

"No, we're just talking to the police," Sheila told her.

"Oh?" Ellen said.

"They're here to talk to Tod," Sheila said.

"Is he in trouble?" Ellen asked.

"Nothing like that," Sheila told her. "They need his help in some case. It's like somebody he may know or something he may have seen. They want a witness."

"Oh," Ellen said.

She stood on the front porch craning her neck, trying to get a look into the living room at the cops and at Tod. Sheila tried to stay in her line of sight.

"Can you come back later?" Sheila asked her.

"Sure," Ellen said. "Later. If you're sure you're all right."

"We're fine," Sheila said to her.

Ellen was twenty-two and an assistant to the pharmacist at the K&B drugstore. She had a junior-college degree and was thinking about finishing a four-year degree at Antonelli College. She wore chrome-rimmed glasses, and Sheila did not think she was unattractive. She wouldn't be a bad match for Tod, was what Sheila thought. But Tod wasn't interested. He had his face fixed for one of the MTV girls, or any girl like an MTV girl. Somebody about sixteen. He had dated a lot of younger girls when he was in high school, but when he dropped out he stopped dating altogether. He hadn't had a date in a year.

▼

Sheila opened the front door. "I'm watering the beds out front." She had on a straw hat and sunglasses, and struggled adjusting them.

Tod rolled his head. "Leave the damn beds alone, will you?"

"Just let me water," she said.

"Water the grass," he said. "But don't be staring across the street."

"I'll be careful. I've got these glasses on. They can't tell where I'm staring anyway," she said.

"That will really confuse them. They're not going to have a clue."

"Well, drive me somewhere, then," she said.

"OK. Fine. Where?"

"I don't care. I just want to go in the car so we can go by the driveway and see if that's him. I'd like to meet him. I'd like to take him dancing."

"Mother —"

"I've earned it," she said. "You're young. Nobody wants to go dancing with you."

"Thanks, Ma," Tod said.

"You know he has a wife. She's very English. That's what he said. He said his wife was 'very English.' Too English. She was upset because they were at this barbecue with his cousin," Sheila said. "Just like these people across the way. He was in the garage just like they are. He said it was cooler in the garage, that's why they were in there. Then his English wife came up and whispered he was a redneck. That's what he said on Leno. He seemed like a real nice guy."

"I'm sure he is. Very well-to-do," Tod said.

"What does that have to do with? Aren't you putting your contacts in?"

"No, I can see with the glasses," he said.

"We might run into Ellen. We might go to the drugstore."

"We're not going to the drugstore. Do you need to go to the drugstore?"

"I need garbage bags," she said. They went out to the car, an Oldsmobile, green, from the eighties. Tod drove. "Now go slow," Sheila said as he backed out.

"I'm going as slow as I can. If I go slower, I'll be going too slow."

"You're going backwards," she said. "How can you go too slow?"

"Mother," he said. He crawled the Olds past the Terlinks' house, past the driveway, and she stared up there and waved at the Terlinks. They all waved back from the deep shadow of the garage.

Two or three houses down the street there was a brown horse standing in somebody's front yard, tied to a tree. It had a bridle, but that was all. Nobody was paying any attention to it. It was just standing there.

"What's with this?" Sheila said, pointing out her window.

"Horse," Tod said. "Somebody got a horse."

"Well, they should wash it. Look at that. It's going to be hot, its feet are caked. They ought to get somebody over here to wash it."

Out by the shopping center on Old Post Road there were two police cars with their blue lights flashing.

"Check the heat," Sheila said.

"That really dates you," Tod said. "Heat."

"Oh, God, I'm so sorry," Sheila said. "Forgive me, really. Can you ever?"

When they got close enough, they saw that somebody had driven a panel van into a ditch. Somebody else had gone in right after and landed on top of the van. That person was still sitting in his car, sort of slumped over to the side. The driver of the panel van was on a board alongside the van, deep in a ditch, surrounded by cops and ambulance people.

"It doesn't look good," Sheila said.

"I've seen that head getup on ER," Tod said. "See the way they've got the Styrofoam thing around his head there?"

"That's not Styrofoam," Sheila said.

"You want some yogurt?" he said. "I'm stopping at the yogurt joint."

"That really dates you — 'joint,'" she said. "Look at this guy in the Caddy. He's just perched up there. Why don't they get him out? He looks sad."

"You'd be sad, too. I mean, come on," Tod said.

"What if those cars explode?" she said.

Tod changed lanes to get on the side of the street where the yogurt shop was in the strip shopping center. He pulled up to the drive-in window and asked Sheila what she wanted. She said a waffle cone with fat-free chocolate. He got a cup of vanilla and an oatmeal cookie. When the yogurt came, they paid and then drove the car out to the edge of the parking lot and stopped, rolling the windows down. From where they were sitting, they could see the wreck down to their left, the police and the ambulance, the road in front of them, and two shopping centers across the street.

"I don't remind you of my father, do I?" Tod said, after a minute.

"Some ways. What's wrong, you don't like your father?"

"I don't want to be like him. He didn't do well."

"He did fine," she said. "Just ran out of steam."

Tod left the car running and the air-conditioning on even though they had the windows down. "I feel like doing laundry. Dishes, too. I'm doing dishes when we get home."

"Fine. Do dishes all night long," she said. "Your father never did a dish in his life."

"I like my hands in the water," he said. "The way water sounds running. I could do dishes for hours — water's warm and soapy, you know, you've got a good sponge and you get some soap in that and rub it on the plates and the plates get a little slippery and everything gets a little slippery so there's some danger to it."

"Yeah," Sheila said. "That's how I feel about it exactly."

"Don't ruin it," Tod said. "Sometimes when you're gone and I'm there, I wash dishes and clothes at the same time, so I have the washer running and sometimes the washer and the dryer, and then I'm washing dishes, too. God, that's great. I really like that. That does it for me."

"You remind me of your father," she said, shaking her head. She looked out her window at a yellow dog that had its nose stuffed in a Burger King sack. The dog lifted the sack up, throwing its head back so that it could get deeper into the bag. It was walking around on the striped concrete with this bag on its face.

"I hope that guy in the van doesn't die," Tod said.

"Me too," Sheila said. "What do you want for dinner?"

"We had sandwiches," Tod said. "I can't think about dinner yet."

"You want to barbecue?" Sheila said. "We could do that in the driveway, just like the Terlinks. Maybe we could go over there, or they could come over."

"We could have a party," Tod said. "Maybe I'll take up with the Terlink girl. We'll become lovers — tonight, after you leave for work."

"Isn't she a little young for you?" Sheila said.

"Oh, yeah," he said. "She's a babe. She's a babe and a half. She's a twister. Sometimes, I sneak over there and look into her window, crawl around and peep in, see her in her underwear walking around the house. She always wears lace underwear — pink, black, pale blue. She's a real beauty. Sex hound."

"Oh, stop," Sheila said.

"She's probably poking Larroquette," Tod said. "He's grinning that stupid grin of his, revitalizing his . . ."

"Never mind," Sheila said. "Quit."

They were quiet in the car, finishing the yogurt. The only thing she could hear was the smacking of their lips. When he was done, Tod squashed the bag the cookie had come in into the cup, broke the plastic spoon and put it in the cup too, then opened his door and set the cup on the concrete of the parking lot.

"Why do you want to do that?" Sheila said. "Here. Give that to me."

"I'm leaving it here," he said. "It's a gift. I don't have dirty diapers or chicken bones, so this is the best I can do."

"Oh, Jesus," she said. "Tod, open the door and pick that up."

"I'm not," he said. He backed the car in a half circle.

She reached over and struggled with the steering wheel, trying to force him to drive back and pick up the cup, but he turned the wheel the other direction and drove diagonally across the lot.

"I need to get a magazine," he said.

"I need to get home," she said. "We need to solve this problem once and for all."

"Dinner?" he said.

"No," she said. "I've got chicken at home. I stewed some chicken. You can have that. I'm having a salad. I've got to get this cheese off my legs." She grabbed her thighs and wagged them.

Tod drove more cautiously than he needed to. She was struck by it. He drove like his father. There wasn't a bit of difference. If she had shut her eyes, or if she had worn blinders to prevent her from seeing who was in the driver's seat, she could have imagined being with Dan. The ancient Oldsmobile was his car, part of the settlement, the conclusion of their marriage. The car and the house — that was her part of the bargain. She had always liked the car, and the house was comfortable. Sometimes, when she looked at *Better Homes and Gardens*, she wished it was fancier, but most of the time she didn't worry. She kept it clean. It had a nice old-house smell about it, and sometimes, in the summer, when the ceiling fans were going and the attic fan was on and a breeze was being pulled through the house through the open windows, she could close her eyes and imagine she was at her grandparents' house when she was a kid in the fifties. She could remember the way things smelled, the way the air moved. Her grandparents had a house in Bay St. Louis, Mississippi, overlooking the Sound, and it had a certain sweet mustiness she always remembered. That was how her house in Quantum smelled.

She hadn't wanted Dan to leave. She'd spent seventeen years with him, but now she didn't know why she had stayed that long. He'd had different jobs — night watchman, car salesman, menswear sales in a department store. He'd hold on to one for six months or a year, then go crazy after some young girl. Start drinking, staying out all night, shoving her around when he was home. He wasn't much to miss, and he had always ignored Tod. Still, it broke her heart when he left. It did occur to her from time to time that she would like to have another man around, a boyfriend, but Tod was OK for the day-to-day, routine stuff — watching TV movies and renting things from the video store. He was even fun, because he liked things that were strange to her. She worried she was hanging onto him too much, clinging to him, poisoning him. She worried that keeping him at home, making it easy for him to stay, was wrong. But she'd never really lived alone since college, and, even then, she had girlfriends, and she didn't think she wanted to start being alone at forty. She'd brought men to the house before, people she knew at the hospital or at church. There was always tension between the men and Tod. After a while she stopped bringing them. They were just going to sit on the sofa, smoke cigarettes, drink her beer, and watch her television and scratch themselves. Tod could do all that.

▼

When they got home, the Terlinks were gone. The fancy rental car was gone and the garage doors were closed. All the windows were covered with miniblinds. There were a few lights on behind them. It was dark when Sheila rolled the barbecue pit out of the garage onto the driveway. She took off its lid, removed the grill, went back into the garage, got some charcoal briquettes, and poured them into the bottom of the grill. She sprayed them with Gulf lighter fluid, then walked around, looking at her flower beds while she waited for the lighter fluid to seep into the briquettes. Tod went inside and came out to tell her there were steaks in the freezer and to ask her if she wanted him to defrost them in the microwave. She said she did.

"Are there vegetables?" she said. "Spinach?" He said he'd look. She opened the aluminum folding chair she'd found in the garage and sat in the driveway with a hose spraying water onto the flower bed between her property and Margie's. A five-dollar nozzle was on the end of the hose. Tod came out of the kitchen door with two packs of frozen vegetables.

"Corn or lima beans?" he asked.

"Both," she said. She released the trigger closing the nozzle and dropped the hose onto the driveway, while she lit the charcoal.

Then she put the grill on top and scrubbed it with a wire brush. She sat down again and started spraying. There was a little breeze, and the water from the spray shifted slightly out of its path. Sometimes the mist flew back on her. It felt nice and cool. Refreshing. She swung the nozzle and sprayed the Oldsmobile and then started on the bed on the house side of the driveway. She kept an eye on the Terlinks' garage. She wondered what had made her want it to be John Larroquette. She thought it odd you could want something so bad and never get it. You could spend your whole life wanting something and never even come close.

When she married her husband, Dan, she had been in love with a black man she had met in nursing school. He was beautiful and powerful and very smart. He knew that she loved him, or at least that she had a crush on him. Sometimes he took advantage of it, touching her in ways that he shouldn't have — feeling her waist, letting his hand rest just beneath her breast, testing the strap of her brassiere, casually brushing against her buttocks. It happened too often to be accidental, but that was as far as it went. Later, he became the weatherman for a TV station.

On her wedding night, after she and Dan had made love, she had watched this black man whom she was in love with do the weather forecast on the ten o'clock news. She thought he was so handsome.

▼

Tod came out with the steaks on a cookie sheet. He'd put a lot of Worcestershire sauce on them. "How long?" he said, holding the cookie sheet up on five fingers, as if he were a waiter.

"Coals ready any minute," Sheila said. "They're getting gray."

"I've got the vegetables," Tod said. "I did them in the microwave. You want to eat by the TV?"

"Sure," Sheila said. "What's on?"

"Everything," he said. "Probably movies."

"I never watched his show anyway," Sheila said.

"What?"

"Larroquette," she said. "He seemed nice when I saw him on TV. I liked him. He talked like somebody you could like. You know what I mean? He pinched his fingers together and said he was a redneck just about that far under the skin. It didn't seem to bother him. He laughed when he said it. That's such a wonderful thing for a man to do."

Tod looked at her for a few seconds, then brought the cookie sheet down and handed it to her. He pulled a cooking fork out of his back pocket and handed that to her as well. Then he took the hose out of her hand and spritzed the water up in the air so that it drizzled on them, just a little bit—just lightly.

"Sure," she said. "Go on. Rain some more. Rain harder."

CUT ON THE BIAS

▲　▼　▲

GALVESTON

RACHEL DOESN'T want to know what I'm doing. In fact, what I'm doing is about the last thing Rachel wants to know. We've been married five years, and for her it's been one tragedy after another, one disappointment after another, one distaste after another. We got married because we thought she was pregnant. We thought we loved each other. We thought the world was a place we could navigate together. But it wasn't that, it wasn't that from the start. It was just like it had been before we got married — messy, uncomfortable, crazy, stupid. I don't know whatever gave us the idea that it was going to be different.

The week after we got married her mother died, so we had to fly out to Utah for the funeral. We were there for four days, and I can barely remember what her father looked like. She has some brothers and sisters, I know, but I don't remember them much, either, except for khakis. They all wore khakis. It seemed that everybody in Utah wore khakis. I'd never seen so many khakis anywhere. I mean, there are khakis around when you're in your ordinary life — you see khaki, but not like this. Not on everybody, not without exception. I'll say this for them, though: in Utah they didn't press their khakis, which I figure is a pretty big step forward.

We camped out in the car on the way to Utah and on the way back. That was what was fun about the trip — sleeping in the car pulled over at a highway rest stop. We had a new car. The seats were kind of comfortable and went all the way back, so you could stretch out.

▼

Rachel calls me at the office. "I want a divorce," she says. "I don't want you to come home tonight or any other night. I don't want to ever have to see you again. I don't want to hear your voice. I don't want to smell you. That's it. It's over."

Then she hangs up, leaves me there on the line. I hardly know what to do. Is this Rachel-whimsy? A sudden feeling that we aren't suited for each other? Has she been drinking? She does that at home alone during the day. She'll drink Jack Daniel's until she's blotto. Makes her feel things — she thinks she has ideas about the world then. She thinks she sees the world in a new, clearer way. It's not an unusual drunk, kind of routine. It doesn't happen all the time, either, but it happens often enough to make me think that there's more to it than just the odd discomfort, the odd unhappiness with our lives.

▼

We have a bungalow on the corner of Decatur and Tenth. It's gray and was built in the forties, and redone in the seventies or early eighties. It seems like a pretty nice place to me. Sometimes in the summertime we leave the windows open and turn on the attic fan, and it draws breezes through the house, breezes that remind me of nights at the beach. We lie on the bed together with these fast winds blowing over us. The smell of the place is kind of old—old wood, old flooring, old fixtures—and I'm reminded of the times I spent on the sleeping porch at my grandmother's house in Galveston, Texas, in the fifties. I don't think I loved my grandmother enough. I don't think I loved her at all. She was short and fat and talked a lot and smelled funny. She was wrinkled, wrinkled. She was kind of a big fireplace, a bossy woman who made my father into the pushover he was. I could never feature her with my grandfather, who was a lanky, easygoing, handsome guy. Not the kind of guy you'd see with some short, fat, wrinkled woman, ordinarily. She might not have been wrinkled all her life. That's a possibility. They had a black woman who cooked for them—I don't remember her name—Estie or Blattie or something. One of those member-of-the-family deals that make the race relations in the South a little less disgusting in practice than those in the North. I mean, they liked this woman quite a lot, and the woman liked them. Sure, there were limits and preconditions and expectations, but even with all of those, the people seemed to care about each other.

▼

In Galveston in the fifties, there was more light than I have seen in any other place at any other time. Nothing seemed to be dark at all. Everything was baked white and bristling with reflections. Sand everywhere, bright awnings, green shutters, fast winds. It wasn't bad. I wouldn't mind being there now. I wouldn't mind ditching Rachel and moving back there and running a restaurant, maybe some place like John's, or someplace up on the seawall, or someplace downtown.

Before I met Rachel, I knew a woman whose father was from Galveston. The only other person I ever met whose father was from Galveston. He ran a lumberyard. She was a nice woman, quite smart. A little too well-to-do, maybe. I never slept with her.

On the trip to Utah, driving down the empty streets of small towns through the night, going out there, it was like we were riding toy streets and train sets and plastic towns, little towns that I had seen as a kid. The green of the grass was bright plastic green or the white of the bricks was viciously white or the roofs were bright red shingles. The streetlights in these towns seemed to be wasting themselves over these empty streets in the middle of the night. Stoplights stupidly going red, going green, going red. It was a silly business, but very beautiful. It was like we owned the whole place, like there wasn't anybody else around, and it was ours. Little cats would run across the street in the middle of the night, hopping almost. Sometimes we'd stop and have a look at them. They would be orange or black or gray tabbies. The early birds would be out — milk trucks, people in pickups, people coming home or going to doughnut shops. The air would be sort of not-quite-black, as if you could focus on it. The sky was true black with millions and millions and millions of tiny stars, and all the same size. It's not a business, the sky at night. When you got out on the highway again it would be pitch dark, and your running lights would be all that lit the way. The odd motel on the side of the road was supposed to make you feel something, but we were at the point where we didn't feel a thing. We saw the signs and thought they were pretty.

▼

You never think you're going to dislike someone you've been living with for years. You know so much about them, spend so much time with them working, trying to make things OK. The idea that you'll end up not liking them is strange, remote, like some ship you don't expect to come into your channel. Somebody you don't expect to see in the neighborhood. That's the way it is with Rachel and me. We go to bed at night now and can't quite imagine why we ever got together in the first place—what she saw in me, what I saw in her—it just doesn't make any sense. I don't quite hate her, but it might be worse than that, just not caring about her, just erasing her out of my life. She doesn't exist for me. She might as well be some woman in a Jeep Cherokee in a parking lot somewhere. She's not one of those best-looking women you ache for when you see them. But I don't ache so much anymore, anyway. There was a time, but that time came and went. Now I see like some camera.

A new woman is in a parking lot, and I can see that she's attractive, and, yes, I can see that her skin is lovely, and, yes, I can see that her hair falls beautifully around her face, her cheekbones are high, clear, defined. She has a few freckles across her nose, and she has lips that say they mean business. She has good, strong legs, thin, focused. She walks with determination, aware of her body, of herself, of the space she sculpts. You can see it in the way her arms move and the way her butt moves. I see all of this. I don't care. I watch her go into the store, and I don't care. There was a time I would have chased her around the store, stung and intoxicated, following her from aisle to aisle, from produce to crackers to napkins to frozen foods—all for another sweet deep drink of her.

But Rachel isn't that good-looking, that exciting, and even if I saw Rachel right now, I wouldn't follow her. We live in the same house, but she's just vertical furniture. She's a table or chair or closet door. I wonder if it's this way for other people, if they look at their husbands and wives this way. I wonder if this is how Rachel looks at me, wondering what the hell I'm doing here, thinking she doesn't want to see me tomorrow.

HARMONIC

YOU ARE ON-LINE, looking at the three-month chart of a favorite stock, when a car hits the tree in your yard. At first you are afraid it's your daughter, Trinity. It is two in the morning, and she's out as usual. You look outside; it isn't her. You are relieved, but the car is burning, flames are running up the tree. You rush out but can't get close. There are already sirens in the distance. Traffic stops, people come out of houses — everything happens quickly. You stand nervously in the front yard, keeping your distance from the car, talking to neighbors, all of you gawking. Your numbers grow. People sort of materialize, *Star Trek*–style. In a couple of minutes the cops come sliding in, their sirens shut down.

The street fills with hoses and lights, cops, fire trucks, firemen, radio static, shouted orders. Bystanders. The burning car is at the center of things. The firemen douse the flames, and the street fills with smoke that looks like train steam. A dozen guys in rubber coats and big boots, in yellow slickers, carrying axes and flashlights, stand in little groups, smoking. Other guys move around, talk, point lights at people and things — the mailbox, a tree stump, a car in a driveway, two kids on the lawn next door. Some cops scour the grass, their flashes weaving like inverted searchlights. They're looking for scraps, parts of the car. The car is wrapped around a two-foot-thick pine. The car and the tree smolder. The fire really is almost out.

Someone recognizes the car. It belongs to a neighbor, a young woman who has recently moved to Lakewood. You don't know her name, you know her only to wave to when she walks the loop around the little lake. She always wears red shorts and a navy blue T-shirt when she walks. In the crash she has on a soaked white dress. She has been shot through the windshield, no chance to survive. The car is half its original size, bent like a horseshoe around the tree. It's smoking, giving off occasional small jets of flame, all the glass busted out.

It's cold. Everyone's breath comes in silver streams, caught in the lights circling the yards of the houses. You go back and forth at the edge of the street, toward the car and then away, closer each time. You know people who have lost limbs and children in car crashes. Your friend Mary was broadsided by a delivery van doing sixty. She caught a chrome bumper in the ribs and was crushed. Her car went seventy feet through the air and landed in a display window.

The scene hisses. Reflective yellow strips catch flicking lights. Water standing in the cold, cold grass squishes underfoot. Engines lope, generators rattle on the trucks, circling lights click quietly on the roofs of police cars.

The driver is half out the windshield, face down against the metal, bent at the waist. Her white dress is twisted, stained, and her hair is black, wet, long, curled. You've seen it before, this kind of thing, bodies beside the road covered in sheets, but in front of the house, looking at the girl who has driven her car eighty miles an hour into a stately pine, who came up the long gradual rise from Case Avenue accelerating hard and went straight into the tree, that makes you want to cry. No one is ever safe.

▼

You have always been interested in how dead people look. This woman coming out of the windshield looks broken. You're scared because the game has suddenly changed, something huge has happened, something so strange another world opens up, like when you were a kid and your parents got into a fight and you had to go to your room and wait, just stay out of it, hide from it, because the world had cracked apart, come loose from its moorings, and the night had become a dangerous time when anything could happen.

You wonder: had she known the tree was coming, had she aimed at it, or did she just abandon control, knowing that sooner or later something would stop her? You imagine those last seconds — engine screaming, car leaping ahead. Had she left it to chance, or had she tried to make the curve? What did it look like to her, through the windshield, those last seconds as the tree swept toward her faster, larger, inevitable?

If only she'd made it to tomorrow. The world seems different picking up the kids at school, coming home from the grocery, stopping at Blockbuster — with cars and people under control the world moves in an orderly way.

▼

Your wife has gone to bed and left you at the computer peering at graphs of stocks. You are studying Harmonic Lightwave, something you bought at Ameritrade after Stewart persuaded that little fat guy to buy, after the spiritual centering class turned into a stock fantasy and "eight bucks" became a mantra. Like everyone else you opened an account before realizing you had no clue what to buy.

Your daughter, Trinity, is nineteen. You and your wife have different views on how Trinity should be treated now that she is in her second year of college. You believe more should be expected of her — more discipline, more participation in your life at the house — that she should be treated as an adult. Your wife says Trinity is still a kid. "The teens last longer these days," she says. "Until their late twenties." To ask Trinity to behave "responsibly" — she puts it in finger quotes — would just force her away from you both.

So Trinity goes where she wants and does as she pleases. There is no curfew, there are no rules, she has no responsibilities. She has the white Mazda you gave her on her seventeenth birthday, and keys and credit cards and a license to come and go as she sees fit. Usually she's home by four A.M. She and her friends go to the bars, to people's apartments, they crowd into booths at the Waffle House in the early morning hours, call each other all the time, leaving cryptic messages in code on those hard little colorful pagers they carry, or they used to carry — recently Trinity has upgraded to a new cell phone and given you instructions not to page her anymore.

Harmonic has had a bad day. It is down seven and an eighth on volume. You are thinking of putting in a sell order when you hear the skidding tires. Headlights swing past the window of the small dining room you have converted into an office. There is an explosion right outside. You think of a water heater exploding, but it is too large and too close. You think: shotgun. You think: car crash. You know instantly and just hope the others. There is a second explosion, smaller but still deafening, an eerie yellow light blooms outside the miniblinds. You feel some sudden indescribable fear.

You live in a small community on a tiny lake. Eighty houses, and yours was one of the first, though you've had it only two years. You bought from the original owner. You have a lovely lawn, elaborate beds and gardens, a deck that overlooks the lake. You often sit out in the evening, when the weather allows. The lake is so small you could hit a golf ball across it. You've never done that — you aren't a golfer — but friends have said as much. Your neighbors are people who never seem to leave their homes.

The house is still after the explosions. It is always quiet when Trinity is out, sometimes eerily so. Your wife is used to Trinity's noise — always banging up and down the stairs, raking the TV or stereo up, talking too loud on the phone. You can never quite hear what she is saying, but you can't escape her voice, either. Your wife finds the quiet unnerving. You savor it.

Finally you scissor open the miniblinds. The burning car is two hundred feet from the window. Your stomach feels large and hollow as you stare between the blinds at the fire, the creased metal, the tree, the smoke.

▼

You say to your wife, "I have found that we are not all that tolerant of others, generally. We nod, we smile, we are a little bit polite, but mostly we are eager to return to our homes, lock the doors, play with our dogs, watch our TVs, and live in that tiny circle of confusion where we have some influence."

▼

Standing in the yard with the cops, listening to the radios and the muffled voices of the men and the noise from newspeople who have arrived, watching their bright flashguns, there is a curious sobriety to the scene, a quiet framed by emergency, as if someone has suddenly turned on the lights in the middle of a wicked party. The air is thin and brittle. People move hesitantly and they are dressed foolishly. Who are they, and what are they doing? Why are they so suddenly restrained? Do they feel what you feel?

Cops wave away accumulating traffic, sort out their duties, marshal the bits and pieces of the wreck that have flown off across your yard.

You hear footfalls in the street, boots scuffing the gravel at the curb, rubber boots sloshing on the soft grass in the yard. Traffic is blocked for a good distance in either direction. A fender is pulled out of the ditch and leaned against the white wooden post of your mailbox. Three cops in leather jackets walk three abreast from one edge of the yard to the other, their lights flashing on the ground in front of them. A big guy in a slicker turns people around, sends them on their way, directs traffic into and out of the driveways. This cop wears a jacket that says POLICE in big reflective letters, and he looks as if he is heading in your direction. Listen to the soles of his shoes as they slide across the concrete toward you. Nod at him as he gets closer. Step back into the yard and listen to wind slip through the trees overhead.

The cop says, "You live here?" flicking his flashlight toward the porch. "Yes," you say. "Too bad," he says, and he turns, stands there with his back to you. You nod and stare at the glittering letters on his back. You listen to the cops talk—their short little remarks, their rough laughter. You try to make out what they are saying.

RED ARROW

I was at the Red Arrow car wash getting the Tercel cleaned up when I saw this woman who looked like she walked off a TV news set. I can't help it, I love the way TV newswomen look. It's my pornography. I'd seen the woman before, around Permian, the Gulf Coast town where I live, seen her in grocery stores, Blockbuster. She was mid-thirties, handsome, with pricey clothes, straight long hair, broad shoulders, a perfect stride. She came from money, or she'd had money so long she might as well have come from it, she had that look that said she had time every week to take care of every part of her body—hair, skin, nails, you name it. Whenever I saw this woman I pretended to be objective and thoughtful, thinking how stunning she was, but thinking it in an objective way, like I was assessing a painting or something. All garbage. I was crazy on her and I did not come from money.

I'd seen her in a laundry joint near my place. That caught me— her at the E-Z Wash. It was a big place that was usually crowded with students—all the young happy folk who fill the half-ass strip malls down here in Florida—but when I saw her, the place was empty. I was tucked in back by the two huge blue dryers set aside for industrial work, rugs and such, thinking that I maybe ought to just walk right up, introduce myself. She was so cool-looking that it made me shake, but I wasn't showing her that. I was sitting on a table reading a copy of *Vogue,* acting cool myself, dryers rumbling away beside me, washers swishing around. The light streamed through the open double doors at the front of the place. I tried to imagine myself with this woman who was young and pretty and sucking all the oxygen out of the place, but she was elsewhere with a capital E, and I had to admit my chances were not good. So I sat and soaked it all in—evening light, big ceilings, dusty paint flaking off the dirty white beneath it, huge filthy windows, rusty pipes, and the noise, the incessant sweet noise of the place. The black-haired woman like some shimmering vision. I stared at her. I wasn't subtle.

So when I pulled in behind her at Red Arrow I said out loud, "There she is again," and pointed out the front glass at her, standing alongside the car right in front of mine. Her suit was tailored silk, taupe, and it fit like it was built with her in it.

She waved. We were old friends by now.

I went up and introduced myself. "I'm beginning to believe in fate," I said. "My name is Bob, and, even though it may seem like it, I have not been trailing you."

"I'm Terry Banks," she said.

"I work at the university," I said. "History department."

"I see you everywhere, seems like," she said.

I laughed and pointed ahead of us in the line. "We going to be a while or what?"

The wash girl was one of those startlingly handsome kids you always see slumming in some store and can't figure out why they're working there, why they aren't out at the country club where they belong. Those girls are in my classes all the time—perfect skin, perfect hair, big eyes, wide mouths with two perfect rows of handsome teeth. Their mouths are all the same. This wash girl was stuffed into tiny black jeans and a cowboy shirt, and her hair was all kinds of graceful. She was writing on a tablet she held in her open palm, talking to a big guy in a brown suit with a wide tie splashed with too many stripes. He had bristly hair carefully combed, and drove a Lincoln sedan, an undertaker's car. He was smitten with her, you could see that. A big friendly man with a wad of greasy hair—a repeat customer in the making.

The Red Arrow woman patted the man's arm and pointed him toward the waiting room, then slapped a ticket under the windshield wiper of his Lincoln and waved for one of the black guys at the head of the wash tunnel, a tall kid, maybe fourteen, with milk chocolate dreadlocks, very short and tight, wearing a white jumpsuit, who rocked toward her, grinning, whipping his chamois backward and forward, held in two hands, twirling it as if it were a bandanna, his walk a lope, a shuffle, his head a parody of those toy dog-heads that once bobbed in the back windows of people's cars.

The attendant came up and introduced herself, holding out her hand. "Hi. I'm Nell," she said. "What can we do for you today?"

"Just a wash," Terry said.

"Both cars, one ticket?" she asked, writing something on her ticket, then motioning back and forth between Terry and me with her pen. "We got a special on. You kids together?"

"Not yet," Terry said.

I grinned at that, caught off guard. "We live in hope," I said.

"You want me to do them tires for you?" Nell said, popping Terry's sidewalls with the shiny metal toe of her cowboy boot.

"Do them?" Terry said.

"Armor All," Nell said. "Two dollars gets you the tires and the whole interior. Another dollar gets you the bumpers."

Terry stepped back a pace. "Sure," she said. "Let's go all out."

"Wax, too?" Nell said. "A dollar ninety-five."

"Wax," Terry said. "Sure."

Nell leaned back and looked at the front of Terry's car. "I was going to say bug solvent — maybe not."

Terry said. "Got no bugs."

"You will," Nell said. "It's that time of year. Two-by-two, if you know what I mean. Can't go a mile without coming up covered in them."

Terry turned around and looked at me. "That's a heck of a thing, isn't it? Don't you think so?"

I nodded. "Bugs will be bugs," I said.

Terry smiled, folded her arms, and waited for Nell to finish her ticket, then headed for the waiting room. I stood around while Nell wrote up the Tercel, then took my receipt and went inside. There were just three of us in the glassed-in waiting room, each positioned on his or her own summery wrought-iron chair with its print pillow decorated with leaves and limbs. The television across the room was suffering through some daytime talk. After a minute I dumped my magazine back on the stack and moved closer to Terry.

She moved slightly away from me, gathering her skirt and smoothing it against her crossed legs. "You get your tires done?" she said.

I shook my head. "Nope." It was startling to be that close to her. To see her eyes so clearly, as if they were a photo blowup, crystal and perfectly focused. When she turned I could see the downy hairs on her face. Her lips were some color I'd seen only in glossy ads — some clay color.

"Hey!" she said, snapping her fingers. "Bob — it's Bob, right?"

"Exactly Bob," I said.

"You aren't married, are you?"

"Not now," I said. "You?"

"No. Sometimes I wear a ring to keep everybody honest, know what I mean? But, no."

"That's good," I said. "More for me."

The burly guy in the suit was wiggling a hand in our direction. Terry held her arms out to her side. "What?"

"The magazine," the guy said. "Could you hand me the magazine there?"

"This one?" she asked, snatching a copy of *Parenting* off the table.

"Thanks," he said, taking it. "I have two—girl twelve, boy nine."

"You've got trouble coming," Terry said.

The big guy grinned. "No, they're fine. Everybody says it just gets worse and worse and then they move out, but we'll be lucky. Cindy's got her first boyfriend. Had him two years. She cooks for him at our place. It's kind of cute."

Terry laughed and said, "There's a word you'll forget."

"Aw, c'mon, don't spoil it for me. You have children?"

"One," Terry said. "Eighteen. She says I'm, like, from Mars."

Big Fellow rolled his eyes as he flipped the pages of *Parenting*, snapping one page after another, left to right. "Well, maybe we're luckier than I know, huh?"

I leaned over and said, "I thought you weren't married?"

Terry whispered, "I didn't say I was *never* married."

▼

She took me home. She lived in a two-story house on a tree-lined street not far from downtown. The street was shaded and damp, thick with red BMWs and black Lexuses. Gentrified. Older houses with elegant modern touches in the furnishings. That's what Terry's was like. I didn't leave for two weeks except to teach my classes. I'd been at school long enough so I had a cushy schedule — you get that after a while. I went in one or two days a week, usually half days. I had work of my own—a thing about blacks in the army in the Second World War. There are some horror stories. I spent my time at Terry's reading and making notes, and I spent a lot of time looking out the window, waiting for her to come home.

The first couple weeks were typical—romance in the morning, romance in the evening. We got along famously. It was something new for both of us, more like a movie than anything else—lots of music-listening, wine-drinking, weather-appreciating. We took walks, did stuff people never do after they outlive the big moment. We ate, went to movies, rented movies, swapped favorite wines — we almost went to the zoo but caught ourselves just in time.

One Sunday night when we were eating sandwiches in her bedroom and watching *The Practice,* I said, "Let's get married."

She looked at me, her lips pursed, a smile lighting her eyes. She finished chewing and swallowed, took a sip of her wine, and said, "Uh, no."

"Marriage isn't silly," I said. Lara Flynn Boyle stood before the court in a prim black suit, very sexy, cross-examining a bear-hairy witness. "So I've got the jump on you," I said. "We don't have to get married right away. We could get married later, in the summer. I just want to plan ahead."

"Ask again later," she said, rotating her hand as if holding one of those eight-ball answer-anything toys.

▼

Spring semester we started hanging out with the students. There just wasn't anyone else. We were regulars at their parties, took people out to dinner, waded into the lives of the kids. Terry gave advice to the guys, I specialized in the girls. It was safe and fun, and we talked earnestly and at enormous length. It was exciting to have the students care about what I said, and I got close to the kids in a way I'd never done before. They called us up, asked us over for dinner, and we had them over, too, or joined them at clubs to hear local hero bands. I became a music expert overnight, dragging out old rock CDs from when I used to listen to music, making lists of the greatest rock songs of all time.

It was Terry who changed this for me. Throughout all my years of teaching I'd carefully avoided the students, I'd maintained a distance, a strict, professional, academic distance. I'd avoided any opportunity for misunderstanding, or error in judgment, or difficult circumstances — problems that routinely plagued and intrigued my colleagues. I guess the real reason was I was scared and didn't know what to say to them, and who wanted the trouble that was bound to follow if you got involved with them? Now I discovered that talking to them was like talking to children, and they knew it as well as I did. They had their world, I had mine. As much as I might wish I was in theirs, I wasn't. They let me pretend sometimes. The few people I was close to on faculty didn't have this problem. They loved the attention the students showered on them, loved being the cool professor, the mentor, the one who could party all night and teach all day. My friends on staff were comfortable with the students in a way I never was — teaching, holding forth, lecturing, and later, after drinks and dinner, satisfying themselves with whoever felt particularly racy or dangerous that night.

So there was envy. Outside the classroom or the conference I was stiff as a stick, giving only a nod, a wry smile, a wave — offering no invitation to intimacy, having nothing to share. I couldn't manage to treat the students as equals, or even as pretend equals. There was a gulf between us, our years, our cultures, our experience. Every idea they had I'd long since put to bed, when I was their age, when I was one of them, when I *was* them. Now I hated sitting and waiting for them to get over some idea, dishing out bogus encouragement, congratulations, feigned interest as they stumbled on. I hated the excitement in their eyes as they discovered some tired idea and jabbered about it endlessly, as if it were new. My colleagues enjoyed the advantage this gave them, but it just fatigued me.

I had been at the university for too long. The students were toys, not viable eventual replacements. They weren't even people, exactly — they were kids, and to take advantage of them, as some of my colleagues did, seemed ungenerous. Or maybe it was a fair exchange: you let them believe they're adults, they let you believe you're still alive.

I knew, of course, that it was their world. Mine had come and gone, and I hung on only as a consequence of their generosity or disinterest. Their ideas would replace mine — their cultural opinions would render mine harmless and old-fashioned. Time levels everything — the Ricky-Nelson-Was-an-Artist rule. In the classroom we could pretend I was the teacher and they were the students, but out of it, I was just so much inconsequential history.

So I was pleased, finally, with the changes wrought by my affair with Terry. I became, for a moment, the dangerous professor, the one who dared flaunt convention, the one who lived with the attractive young former runner, now triathlete, the one who came to their parties and drank too much, danced too hard, laughed too loud. An old, out-of-shape, loudmouthed know-it-all who smelled bad in his silly "stylish" duds. It was, at least, a role I could play blindfolded.

▼

Summer was good. We hit the beaches along the Gulf Coast. We spent time at Seaside, a grotesque but peculiarly affecting manufactured Gulf-side town. It was a scary place, always ironic while somehow showing its slip, eventually turning us all into yuppie robots in spite of our best efforts. There was no denying it was pleasant — the people were friendly and funny, the drinks were good, the beaches were handsome, and there were classy restaurants within minutes. We traveled, too, down the Florida coast to Tampa, Fort Myers, Sanibel, Captiva, eventually the crowded Keys, at every turn roasting ourselves mercilessly, running through bottle after bottle of aloe, turning unnatural shades of brown, feathering off the burned skin in great papery chunks.

When we returned in August, Terry said she needed some time alone. I was frightened by this, and she could tell. We were in the bedroom at her house, the TV silently rolling through its news day, story by story.

"It's not like that," she said.

"I didn't say a word," I said.

"You looked," she said.

"It's fine," I said. "I need to get ready for the semester anyway. More little hot-water bottles at our university. Don't want to stem the flow of hot-water bottles out into the culture. Lots of apartments to fill up, lots of young fathers and mothers needed."

"Don't be snide," Terry said.

▼

We went to a Halloween party given by grad students in the History Department, and I drank heavily and dirty-danced with an Indian girl who was new in town. I think she did not know what was going on. Later I caught a ride home with a woman named Freddie who drove one of the new VW Beetles in a startling blue. She had a tiny house in an older subdivision — a wood-framed house up on cement piers, a house with almost no furniture and a bed set diagonally in the bare bedroom. The place had that wonderfully austere college-student-lives-here feeling. I managed the usual tour of the bookshelf, the kitchen, the bathroom closet before I passed out. At first light I woke up in Freddie's bed.

She was there alongside me, her back bare and freckled, her hair shampoo-commercial pretty on the pillow. Her face was turned away. I shoved up a little, propping myself against the headboard, and studied the room. Facing the corner, it looked as if the room was whirling around me — no edges were parallel, everything vanishing into the corner. The room looked abandoned. In the gentle light the scarred walls and bare floors and curiously tilted door frame were otherworldly. The windows were paired, dust-whitened, and covered with vines. The sheets were crisp and smelled of jasmine.

For a few minutes I planned my escape, but I must've fallen asleep again, because when I next opened my eyes I saw Freddie, a deliberately thin girl with scrambled hair, wearing a black Chinese robe with red and emerald piping. She greeted me with a cup of coffee.

Leaning against the pillows, I sat up, pulled the sheet to my waist, and accepted the cup.

"I'm in your 523 class," she said. "You went a little crazy last night."

I nodded and sipped the coffee. "I did? That would be unusual."

"I know," Freddie said. "I talked to some people."

"What did some people say?"

"They said you're dull as a duck," she said. "They said you've been minding your business and behaving well for twenty years and in the last six months you've become Mr. Steamy. They don't get it."

"Me neither," I said.

"You were drinking last night. That's part of it."

"I must have found you very attractive," I said.

She gave me a get-real look. "That's probably not a stretch. I'm nineteen."

I smiled at her, watched her slit her eyes like a woman who knew exactly how attractive she was.

"You were very rude to the woman you were with," Freddie said. "Eventually, she walked. Nobody blamed her."

"Did we make love last night?"

"Hey! Have a little couth. You're killing me here," she said.

"OK," I said. The coffee burned the roof of my mouth. I rested my head against the headboard and stared at the ceiling where someone had pasted hundreds of light-reflecting plastic stars and planets. Either it had been a child's room once, or . . .

"You stumbled around and said how you wanted to live with me. You were willing to share me, some kind of turn-of-the-century thing."

"Your name is Freddie, and you're from — "

"Taos," she said. She was sitting on the edge of the bed with her knees up. She barely dented the mattress.

"I didn't used to hang out with students. Not until I met Terry."

"The last-night woman?" Freddie said.

"I met her at the car wash. She changed everything. When you're older you shut down, you stop playing the game. You get a routine and stick with it, and, no matter what, decline all invitations. She changed that."

"And now here we are," Freddie said. "Just the two of us."

"Exactly," I said. "That's a pretty robe."

"Is, isn't it? My mother's. She had it when she was my age. It's from China."

"Dragons," I said. "I see that."

"No, I mean it's sort of, you know, *authentic*," Freddie said. "Forties, I think."

"Very handsome," I said. "Suits you."

She patted the cuffs and straightened the lapels of the shiny robe. "It makes me feel like I'm in a movie," she said. "That's why I wear it sometimes."

"So you can feel like you're in a movie."

"Right. Old movie. I don't know. You want more coffee?"

I put the cup on the bedside table. "Nope. Just want to sit here and look at you."

She dropped her head, letting her hair screen her face. "You were doing some dancing last night," she said. "Somebody told me you were married."

"Was. I had a wife, and then she left. She got old, the pleasures got smaller, things weren't fresh. Sometimes, no matter how hard you try, you can't make things fresh."

"Yeah, I know what you mean," Freddie said.

"You pretend there are things that replace freshness, but there aren't, and after a while you don't even *want* to be swept away. Not by a woman, a season, an evening, or the sea. You live a tucked-in life, and you don't really remember anything."

Freddie got off the bed and walked to the window and finger-opened the blinds. "You know, I hear that from every old guy I run into," she said. "I was hooked up with Mr. Eisenbaum — in English? — last semester and I got the same thing from him. He couldn't believe my skin, he said. It was so beautiful, he said. He was like nuts about it, on and on. It's like you guys don't really get it anymore."

I sat up straight and looked at Freddie's back. "Well, we're just trying to stay in the game a little longer. Besides, he was right about your skin."

She turned around and pointed to the chair on the other side of the bed, smiled at me. "So — your clothes are there. Why don't you jump into them. I'm taking a shower and then I'll run you home. That OK?"

▼

Terry wrapped a towel around my head and patted my skull when I was done drying my hair. I'd found her at my apartment, a dingy guest house that I'd leased from the dean of the journalism school for the last nine years — two stories, fifties, lots of paneled glass, jalousie windows, a small brick patio, very private, with a brick wall on the alley. She'd been there twice in our time together.

I was sitting at the bamboo bar with coffee. She was on the sofa. "So what's the deal?" she said.

I noticed how much greenery there was in and around my apartment. It was cool already. The air that filtered into the room had the scent of rain on it. I looked at the brick wall out back and thought how pretty it was.

"I guess I got out of whack," I said. I brought the coffee to my mouth, let it warm my lip. "Nothing happened."

"You didn't make me the coolest bitch in town," she said.

"You don't need me for that."

"I don't know," she said, fingering some open magazines on the coffee table. "Is this work?"

"Was," I said. "I'm not sure I'm doing that anymore. So what are you doing here, anyway? I thought you were the personal-space girl."

"Yeah," she said, nodding. "I remember saying that. I wondered."

"Now you know."

"You're fourteen, under all those fancy degrees. That's great."

I shrugged at her, gave her open hands. She got off the sofa, came around to the other side of the bar. I was thinking I wasn't close to fourteen, and she knew it. I was thinking when you're our age there are different rules, and that it's too bad, but you can't do anything about it. You give up stuff, forget stuff. You're not in somebody's barn during a rainstorm. There is both more and less at stake, and the game is played with that in mind. The job used to be to cut the distance down to the point where your shirt was touching her shirt, but now it was about balance, distance and balance. There was news in that.

I took my coffee and went to the plate glass that overlooked the little patio. "Pretty out here," I said, touching the cup against the window. The touch sounded like a smack, and I pulled the cup away too fast, spilling a teaspoon of coffee over the lip and onto the ruddy wood of the windowsill.

"Need a rag?" she said, turning toward the sink.

"Got it," I said, rubbing the coffee into the wood. "The girl says she's in one of my classes. That's a first."

"I hope you enjoyed it," Terry said.

I gave her eyebrows and drawn lips. "I guess. I didn't expect you to walk on me."

"Me neither," she said. "I got caught up in the moment."

"It was kind of like the old days, wasn't it? All that high-powered stuff?"

"We don't see it too much," Terry said. "My husband nearly

killed me with it way back when. He was sure I was going around on him. Lost his job because he kept dodging the office to follow me. It was worse after we split up. Kept coming over, spying on me, looking in windows — the whole deal."

"I've done my share," I said. "No fun either end."

Terry got up on the stool I'd vacated. "So what was her name again?"

"Freddie." I smiled at Terry. "It's good, huh? Except they're way ahead of us. She had an English professor give her a bad impression of us, and I didn't do much better."

Terry popped open a box of sugar cubes, took a couple out and gave them a look. "Wish you could get the old ones," she said. She put a cube between her teeth and sipped the coffee through it, gave that up and crunched the sugar. Then started a new cube. "You know, when they were shaped like little matchboxes?"

I was suddenly thrilled by her, by her being there, crazy with her ease and resolve and control. She was radiant, lovely to look at, the rich complicated eyes, that sharp strict hair, skin laced with fine lines, and she was something else, too, a blessing, a prayer — tight, tough as teeth, and mine for the asking. A gift from God. I grinned and reached for the sugar cube she was holding out for me. "Matchboxes," I said. "Who could forget?"

THE AUTOBIOGRAPHY
OF RIVA JAY

I'M SIXTEEN, going on thirty. Everybody says that about me — social workers, truckers, drunks in bars, losers I corral in hotels. God knows what they think it means. My name is Riva Jay, and my parents got busted up in a convenience store robbery when I was eleven. They ran the place, or Mama did — Daddy was the janitor, is what I remember. Three Mexican boys with skinny little I-can't-really-grow-sideburns sideburns and tweezery moustaches came in, and Daddy, well, he decided he'd be a hero. The boys started poking their guns around, one of them went off, then the others, and pretty soon we had a full-fledged TV show in there. Then, the Mexicans were flying out of the joint in a starlight blue Pontiac Bonneville, leaving Mama and Daddy on the floor bleeding.

They recovered, but I had to take care of Daddy, and after a while Mama got upset about that. She found us playing around a little, me in shorts and stuff, and plugged him in the forehead with the gun they got after the robbery. Pop! Just like that. I was amazed at how little the hole was where the bullet entered his skull.

After that I lived at Gram's in Mobile, Alabama, for a while, but when I hit high school I looked too good. All the seniors loved me and I loved 'em right back, because that was new to me then, and I ended up two years in the Certification School for Troubled Youth. That was all kinds of ugly. One night in 1998 I busted out and hitched back to Quantum, the Florida Gulf Coast town where I'd been raised. Like everywhere else, kids had pretty much taken over, scaring their dull parents silly, so I had some pals. We climbed the water tower, loitered at the train station, swam the creeks, and laid out on the white satin beach running along the highway. We lived in the parking lots — there was a Ford dealership, a ratty mall, a Quad Cinema, and the Gerald R. Ford High School. Mama's grocery was long gone. North of town there was an unmarked army base people said was for "black ops," like anybody cared about anything but the buffed-out guys strutting through town all the time in full-combat shit, all red skin and new tattoos.

I got a room at the Get Up Motel and a burger job at Pattyland, which was Bob Rupert's idea of what to call his hamburger stand. Patty was his wife's name and another name for a hamburger. He was always telling the customers that.

First week I was there I met this guy Furlong. He was fifty, but he was a cocky motherfucker. He looked like the kind of scum might pay a pretty girl to pee on him, but he was nice to me. He came on easy when I was messed up on weed and Crown Royal, so I figured, Why not? Turned out he owned a titty bar called the Kit Kat Klub on the edge of town. So we started talking, and then he took me for a ride in his Cadillac, and that's when he told me he was "stung with my great pubescent beauty."

"Put a leash on that thing," is what I told him.

But he went on talking and took me for a look at his peach-colored building off the beach. "There she is," he said, stopping in the middle of the damn highway at three in the morning. "I'm upstairs. How do you like it?"

I hardly knew. I think I waved at the place. Left-handed.

And then he said we could live there together, and I was thinking how that was what I really *really* wanted, and then he was saying how he had a heart of gold where Little Riva Jay was concerned. "I'm ready to be whatever you want me to be," he said.

So I figured he was good for meals and a roof, and maybe I wouldn't have to do too much that was disgusting, so I said fine, lead me to your squalor. The place was a rathole, but you could see the Gulf out the window, so it was a step up.

"You might even do some work for me," he said, and suddenly I saw him and me in my Daddy's and Mama's clothes, the whole show all over again, saw us diving around knee-deep in groceries, trying to dodge Mexican bullets.

So I said, "Here's the deal—I'm not pulling your pop for you, I ain't cooking nothing, and I ain't cleaning shit. Is that clear?" And he bought it, and that's all there was. Deal done. We slipped back to the Get Up and copped my stuff, and then we were moving in together, stopping at the All-Night to pick up some groceries and a giant bag of pork skins.

I figured he thought he was going to keep me around a while and then fuck me silly when I wasn't looking, when my guard was down, only my guard never was. Besides, I was planning on being as mean to him as a witch.

The first couple of weeks we were like pool balls, bouncing off each other. So one night he got all careful and asked me how I felt about him, and I said, "You know, Furlong, I love you for the man you want to be, and I love you for the man you almost are," which he found so heartbreaking that he busted into tears.

We were still in the middle of things, and he hadn't seen the movie, apparently.

▼

A month later everything was so settled I felt like I'd been there twenty years. I was hanging at the club nights, making fun of him, telling his buddies he was a dead man, and that any one of them could have me for a nickel.

Furlong got a kick out of that. He got some grease for having a sixteen-year-old live-in. The buddies, they just rolled their eyes and fixed their rubbery asses on the stools, grinning like jack-o'-lanterns. That was exactly the respect Furlong wanted.

Truth was, he wasn't so bad. I mean, he liked TV. Sometimes I got a couple girlfriends from the high school, and we all got down to our panties and T's, and Furlong thought he'd gone to heaven. The girls liked to tease him, I don't know why. Just how they were. Otherwise he cooked breakfast and bought the smokes, all the time telling me how this thing was really working out well, really well.

I figured he wasn't far wrong. Living over that bar, going down at night, hitting the juke, going outside and finding that string of pale lights draped across the front of the club, wind whispering across the highway, that big Gulf of Mexico ratcheting in and out in the dark. Sometimes I stood out in the middle of that desolate highway for hours at a time, just so I could feel what weather was.

So I guess it went to Furlong's head. One night he told me I made him feel like a kid again, and that made me feel bad, like I was something small that left a trail wherever it went. It was about the worst thing he could have said. But he had found his voice, and he went on to confess that I was everything to him, I was his Blessed Virgin Mary, which also was not exactly what I wanted to hear. This was three months out, and what I wanted to hear, if I wanted to hear anything, was the usual — that he didn't know my name, that I was just more crap dirtying up his drawers, that I was the kind of white trash that decent men used for a rag sometimes. All the stuff I was *familiar* with.

When he went down to close up the bar suddenly I realized it had all gone wrong in some big way, the worst way wrong, and I was thinking maybe a fast shower and a shot up the coast with a cowboy trucker while Furlong wasn't looking, but he was too quick downstairs, and when he got back he was worse, blubbering, saying how much he loved me and how much he needed me and how much he wanted to marry me and make an honest woman out of me. So I sat him down in the kitchen, dropped a bottle on the table in front of him, and told him I was already right now just about twice as honest a woman as he would ever want to meet, and I asked him, did he have a gun?

FROM MARS

CALI'S CHEEK had a cut along the chin line the size of a small tropical fish. It opened like that. She was in the passenger seat, bleeding too much, swabbing the cut with a blue-jean jacket. I was driving as fast as I could trying to get us to the Urgent Care center to get the thing looked after. Cali is my nineteen-year-old step-daughter. She'd just had a fight with her boyfriend. She'd called me at three A.M. from a gas station where she holed up after she tumbled out of his car. He was a guy I didn't like, and her mother didn't like either, but Cali was nineteen and sure he was just the man for her. They spent all their time at bars called Tubby's and Wa-Wa and the Lagoon. I couldn't imagine what she found so interesting or why the bars let her in, but she did and they did and there was no way around it. The Lagoon was a black club that had "white nights" when middle-class white kids were more or less welcomed. The rest of the week a white kid couldn't get in for love or money.

Cali and Mitchell had been coming home from one of the bars, and had gotten into a fight about whether or not she had slept with his roommate, a guy Mitchell had known since grade school. He said yes, she said no. When I said I'd heard this story before, she just waved me off. "Just don't mess with it," she said. "OK?"

"Fine," I said, going back to driving full-time.

Cali was difficult. She wasn't mean, but she was a little out of control in a middle-class way, a girl who paid no attention to her mother or me or anybody else. She took everything that Ellen had to offer and then some, and offered nothing in return. Once in a while she'd clean up her room or bring the dirty dishes from her room to the kitchen, but more often she was loud, or snide, or rude. About par for the course, I was told. This is what teenagers are like nowadays, I was told. I didn't know better, so I went along with it and just stayed out of her way.

I had moved to Honey, Florida, from Dallas, after twenty-five years as an architectural employee. I had started off as a wunderkind at the age of twenty, no degree, no credentials, but I could draw fast, and everything I drew looked like it came out of *Progressive Architecture*. All the architects liked me for my presentation drawings, renderings, and perspective sketches. But that was twenty-five years ago. It didn't take long for that to wear off — then the business changed dramatically, so designers weren't the hot dogs anymore, and all the kids that came up were CAD freaks, and pretty soon I was booted down to graphics guy, then draftsman. Then, I was just the older guy sitting in the back, detailing toilet stalls, elevator shafts, doorjambs.

So I moved to Honey. I had money set aside. A few years ago I started investing on-line, just before it became all the rage, and I had the good luck of getting AOL and Amazon earlier than most. In a year and a half I made more than I had in the twenty previous years, which meant that I could live comfortably in Honey, for a while anyway. So that's what I did. I got a couple extra computers and set up a room in my house as an office. I networked the computers and got a DSL line for reliable connects to the broker, the research, and the real-time intraday charting service I used. I made a couple of trades a day, every day, trying for discipline, continuity, small gains and smaller losses. It had taken me a while to learn the business of selling before your losses exceeded your interest in the underlying stock, but I got it eventually. Mornings I sat at the house watching the market, sometimes buying pre-market so I could sell into the "amateur hour" pop, or shorting as the market went through ten A.M., anticipating the lunch slowdown. I didn't make a fortune, but I made a little every day, usually, and it added up.

I met Ellen Watts, a woman from El Paso who taught school in Honey. Ellen was almost forty and looked every minute of it, and was as handsome a woman as I'd ever been out with. She was divorced, with only the one child. We were comfortable together right away. We dated, had dinner, went walking on the beach, took weekend drives to resorts along the coast — simple pleasures. We liked each other. When I met her daughter, Cali, I wished she were my own.

Six months later we were ready to move in together and decided her place was the best choice. Spoils of her first and only marriage, it was a pleasant old white four-bedroom wood house in the better section of Honey, complete with carriage house, which I was delighted to use as my new "office." Day after day Cali and I passed each other in the house — in the living room, on the stairs, in the parlor — and nodded, or smiled, but that was it. I liked her because she was funny and attractive, but she so lacked interests that didn't immediately have to do with her — friends, clothes, makeup, guys, music, car — that it was hard to credit her with having a personality outside of those things. For a while I figured the distance between us was just a teenager's aversion to the stranger her mother happened to take up with. I figured she'd get over it, that maybe we'd have a conversation one day. I'd say, "How are you?" just like always, and, instead of "Fine," I'd get "Not too good," and I'd say,

"Why? What's up?" and she'd say something like she couldn't handle a class at the university, or that she didn't like her boyfriend, or that she missed her father, or that she wished she were a kid again — just about anything that would lead to more conversation.

But it didn't happen, it hadn't happened in the year and a half I'd been in the house. When Cali was around, which was none too often, I kept a low profile. I'd see her on the stairs, or hear her hair dryer flip on and off as she got ready to go out. Then she'd rush down, two steps at a time, and toss her mother a good-bye over her shoulder as she swept out the door. I'd be ready to wave, sometimes I even waved in anticipation, on the off chance that she might turn around at the last minute. When she was gone, I'd sit there and listen to the dead bolt close as she turned the key.

Days, if I was at home and not in my office, she would stay in her room, watching television, sleeping, talking on the phone. Nights she came home at two or three or four in the morning. I'd hear her come in, and while I was waiting to go back to sleep, I'd listen to her showering upstairs. I listened to the water running in the middle of the night, and I wondered, just as I did when she'd come banging in, rush upstairs, then come right back down into the laundry room to start a load of wash in the Maytag.

▼

In the summer she started seeing this guy Mitchell. Six o'clock one Saturday night he arrived at the door. He looked like a wrestler — short, olive-skinned, tight hair, some odd combination of sideburns and lower-lip patch. He was wearing cutoffs and a T-shirt, and a sleeveless shirt, and a basketball jersey. His baseball hat was, naturally, backwards.

Seeing him reminded me of a time when I was a kid and went to pick up some girl for our first date, and her father opened the door and immediately turned away and yelled back into the house that "the kid from the gas station" was there for the car.

"I'm Mitchell," Mitchell said. "I've come for Cali."

I shook Mitchell's hand and invited him inside, then called up the stairs for Cali. I sat with Mitchell in the living room for a minute.

"What are you guys going to do?" I asked.

"The usual," he said. "Hang out, check the clubs, maybe."

I nodded at him. "That's what you do most of the time?"

"Yeah, pretty much. Sometimes we go over my place, watch TV, maybe rent a Blockbuster. You know."

Mitchell's clothes suggested seventeen, but his face looked twenty-six. I didn't know which it was, but that's what it looked like. A few minutes later Cali came downstairs and stood in the door.

"Let's go," she said.

Mitchell was up and moving. I followed them to the door, but she didn't say a word to me. Over his shoulder he said, "Nice to meet you, sir."

"You too," I said, and then they were outside, going down the walk.

I heard her say, "Catch the lock, will you, Dad?"

"Got it," I said.

▼

Now, two months later, we were on our way to the twenty-four-hour Urgent Care center. Cali was crying and wiping at the gash on her cheek. I was driving full force—one foot on the gas pedal, the other on the brake, barely slowing at intersections, stoplights, stop signs.

"How're you doing over there?" I said, without looking in her direction.

There was silence, and then the screech of brakes as I dodged a panel van full of kids with lots of hair. I took a right on Holland Street and hit the horn to wake some guy out of a stupor as he was wandering around in the road.

Cali said, "I've been better."

"I know what you mean," I said.

"No," she said. "No, you really don't."

I had to stop at a light because a police car was going across in front of us. I watched the cop go by. "That's probably right," I said. "I wouldn't mind, though."

"Sure," she said, folding the jacket to get a clean spot to wipe her cheek.

"It's true," I said.

"I thought you just wanted me out of the house," she said. "Out of the way."

I turned around to look at her. I must have raised my eyebrows, because she raised her eyebrows right back. "I don't know where you got that," I said.

"You aren't exactly toasty warm," she said. "Never mind. It doesn't matter."

"Sure it matters," I said. "What are you talking about?"

She gave me a like-you-don't-know look.

I sighed. "I'm trying to be friendly here."

"Now he tells me. A year and a half later." She zipped down her window and reached into her purse, working with her left hand, looking for a cigarette. When she had it lit and going, one hand on her cheek with the jacket, the other holding the cigarette out in the center of the car, smoke curling up against the windshield, she said, "Let's have a moment here, you and me. Just the two of us."

"C'mon, Cal. We don't need this," I said.

She took a drag off the cigarette and spit out the smoke. "OK. Sorry. I guess it's never too late to start, huh?"

That was the moment for me. It came so quietly and so suddenly I almost didn't recognize it. There was just silence in the car. You could hear the wind at the window and the tires on the ground. I was trying to think of the next thing to say, when I realized what had happened, what she had meant. An open invitation. Just what I'd been looking for. My skin tightened.

346

"You're going to do fine. You're going to do OK." I made a little fist with my right hand and did a paper-scissors-rock thing into her palm. It felt strange to touch her. I hadn't done much of that. I didn't usually put my arm around her or hold her hand or give her a high five or move her hair away from her face. I didn't tug on her clothes in the idle way parents have of straightening their children's garments while they're talking to them. I didn't look at the bruises that she occasionally got or the scratches or the rashes on her skin. I didn't enter into the discussions when she came downstairs to ask Ellen what she should wear or whether this shirt looked better than that shirt. I didn't rub her back in front of the television or brush a fleck of mascara off her cheek or study her fingernails to see whether or not I thought the French finish looked right on her.

"Mitchell is a true creep," she said. "But I don't want him to go to jail, OK?"

"Whatever you say," I said.

"Do you think he ought to go to jail?" she said.

"Well, yes," I said. "I guess." I pointed to her cheek. "This is more than a polite disagreement between the two of you."

"I just think he needs some help," she said. "He needs to understand what his problem is."

"What is it?" I asked. We were pulling into the hospital parking lot. She had the bleeding under control, the jacket pressed against her cheek.

"He gets angry," she said. "He just loses it. Maybe he's fine. Maybe it's me."

"I don't think it's you, darling. Whatever it is, I think it's not you."

▼

Cali didn't look so bad after the doctor got through with her. There's something reassuring about bandages, and she had them in spades when we left the Urgent Care center. She had a little of the Invisible Man about her. I felt strangely excited and relieved.

We walked out into the parking lot, and I listened to the soles of our shoes scraping the blacktop and I felt terrific.

"So what now?" I said. "You want to eat something?"

"No," she said. She was fingering the gauze over her cut. "I could sit with you, though. I guess. I don't have anyplace else to go."

"Me neither," I said. "I have to call your mother and tell her something."

"No, you don't," Cali said. "Really."

"You kidding? She's going to see the bandages, the scars, the mess — what, you want me to tell her you fell out of a chair? Tripped over the coffee table?"

"I don't know what we can tell her," Cali said. "She's going to be super-pissed. She hated Mitch from day one."

"We all did," I said.

She gave me a withering look. "Sure, but he wasn't all that bad, not really, you know? He bought me that jacket, he took me to eat — usually he was fine. He just got bad when he drank too much."

"So what do you want to eat?" I said. We were in the car, rolling out of the tree-lined parking lot, heading into traffic.

The IHOP was empty. It reeked of maple syrup, air freshener, cigarette smoke. The workers, all refugees from better times, loitered at the serving counter, looking sticky. I steered Cali into a booth up front, away from smoking.

Our waitress was sixty, gray-haired, and sort of motherly. She swabbed the table with a spotty towel, leaving ridges of water on the Formica. The plastic menus she dropped on the tabletop stuck there. The waitress bent over way too close when asking what we were drinking. Cali got a Coke, and I got a coffee.

"So what's next?" I said. "A replacement?"

"Maybe later," she said. "I think I'm going to take a break. I don't absolutely have to have a boyfriend, do I?"

"Had enough good times, huh?" I flipped the cover of my menu open so I could see the food inside. Glossy pictures, strange enough for the museum.

"I'm going to Mardi Gras and drink until I'm paralyzed."

"Now, there's a good idea. Marvelously adult and life-affirming."

"What, you don't ever feel that way?" she said.

I shrugged, watching the waitress make her way back to us. "You know what you want?"

"Double-waffle," she said. "Two eggs."

I ordered and then listened to Cali explain in detail how she wanted her eggs. When the waitress had finished, I said, "I used to feel that way — the paralyzed deal. Not so much now. But I know what you're saying."

"Attaboy," she said, reaching across the table to catch an errant thread on my shirt.

She spun her knife as we waited for our food. I watched it spin, listened to it, and marveled a little at how she looked. Year by year I'd watched her go from full-blown teen to young adult, watched her skin tighten and take on a sheen, that little edge that comes with passing the outer edge of childhood. Also known as makeup, maybe. But now she was a full-fledged adult, sitting across from me, taut, wised-up, experienced, with bruises. I was thinking how strange this parent business was, that even though I wasn't her parent I *felt* as if I were.

"So what're you going to do, really?" I asked.

"What do you mean? With Mitch? He's so over."

"You said that about the last one — what was his name? Shelby? And then he got real nice, and then you guys got back together."

"That was different."

"Yeah?" I said. "How different?"

She swiveled her head around, looking toward the cash register and the kitchen. "I don't know, just was. Where's my waffle?"

The IHOP was all pink on the inside — pink plastic booths, pink tabletops, the waitresses in pink-and-white getups, the walls done in a floral print on a heavy vinyl-looking wallpaper. There were etched-glass partitions above the seatbacks and between the side-by-side booths. Everything in the place seemed slightly tacky to the touch. I didn't want to put my arms down on the tabletop. I was afraid to pick up my knife and fork.

"OK. So if I'm going to have a big talk with somebody, it might as well be you, huh?" Cali broke her silence just as our waitress arrived with the food on an armload of plates.

"I'm flattered," I said. Then I was afraid that might be too glib, so I said, "I am, really. Kind of."

She gave me a patronizing look and said, "Whatever. You going to eat that bacon? You shouldn't. I'd better eat it for you." She reached across the table and snatched two of the three strips of bacon curled on my oval plate.

"Help yourself," I said.

"Mmm — " She was already crunching. "See, I know this has already been worried to death, but this morning I was thinking about it again." She was pointing my second piece of bacon at me. "What if, like, our whole world, I mean everything — the planet, the solar system, the universe, the whole thing — what if it's all just like one molecule, one little atom or something in this much bigger world, like one tiny bit of DNA in this huge person's world, like our whole universe is a part of a whisker growing on this giant's face, and like the whole life of our universe, the millions of years, is different time for this huge guy, like just overnight, just long enough for this whisker to grow out, and what we're really waiting for here is not some big religious apocalypse, but just for this guy to shave tomorrow morning? Like, what if the world is one of infinite regress, and like in every little bit of material here on Earth there are tinier and tinier universes, each filled to the brim with, like, 'intelligent life,' and that when you, like, clip your nails you're really sending zillions of tiny little people to their deaths, and plunging their miniature universes into darkness, and raining wretchedness beyond imagination on whole civilizations? This could be happening, you know? Thousands of universes of millions of civilizations, on trillions of planets, exploded into oblivion every time we sneeze."

I forked a three-layer-high square of pancake into my mouth and nodded earnestly, thinking I hadn't heard this idea in more than a few years.

"I mean," she went on, still dangling the bacon, "just imagine that you could go up or down the chain, and you could actually get to the individual level in each universe, and you could talk to people, and they'd all be doing the same things we do, like football games, and first dates, and girlfriends who screw you over, people being rude, smart cracks — you know? The whole thing. Like right now in the millions of universes in my body, on billions of planets in those universes, those parallel universes, there are trillions of people eating pancakes at IHOPs, or places like IHOPs, you see what I'm saying? So you think about that and let that soak in, and this little deal with Mitch just seems like so much more Wonder Fluff. I mean, how could you ever pick out a pair of shoes if you thought of this? How could you answer the simplest questions, like what you want for dinner, or do you want to go to the movies? See? You couldn't. The weight of all this other stuff is just too much, too terrifying, and everything is so way useless if you think of it, I mean — shoes? You see what I'm saying?"

I kept nodding, added a grunt of agreement. "I know what you mean," I said, downing some coffee. "Makes everything seem kind of, I don't know, puny. Right?"

"Exactly," she said, finally parking the bacon between her teeth.

So then there was a commotion at the door, and I looked up and there's Mitchell pushing aside the waitress who was trying to show him to a booth. He was heading straight for us.

Cali saw me staring and turned to see what I was staring at, and when she saw it was Mitchell she held out her hand palm first, fingers splayed. "No way," she said. "Don't you be coming up around me."

"I gotta talk to you, Cali," he said. "Really. I'm so sorry."

"You should've talked to me before," she said. "I'm not hearing you. You're just more bad shrimp from where I sit."

Mitchell squeezed into the booth across from us, sitting side-ways so that he was facing Cali. His face was badly bruised.

"Take it easy there, will you?" I said. "What's with your face?"

"He hits himself," Cali said. "Whenever he fucks up. That's how you know he's being real."

Mitchell made fists of his hands and did a little mockery of punching himself in the face, then gave me a miserable look.

I nodded. "Got it," I said to him. "You OK?" He didn't look OK. He looked as if he'd been doing too much of this bruise therapy.

"I gotta talk to Cali," Mitchell said. "You explain to her, OK? Things just got a little out of hand. I forgot everything, is all. That happens. It's happened to you, hasn't it?"

I said, "Sure, I suppose," though I didn't remember it happening. He was miserable. You wanted to help him out.

"See there?" he said to Cali. "Really, baby, I am *so* sorry. You can't know how sorry I am." He pressed his face into his fists.

I thought he looked too much like that Dirk Diggler guy from *Boogie Nights*, and then, of course, as soon as I thought it, I wished I hadn't. "I think maybe you should just give us some time," I said. "Let's let things settle down a bit before we rush on."

"Oh, man," Mitchell said. "Oh hell, yes. Time. Man, I shoulda thought of that." He leaned across the narrow aisle between his booth and ours and put his forehead down on Cali's seat.

"Oh, get up, Mitchell," she said, taking a swipe at his head. She looked at me and said, "He is so twisted, you know?"

"No, I'm not, baby," Mitchell said. "I'm just yours, like, forever. I'm just really really so *yours*."

The motherly waitress arrived to see if we needed anything more but couldn't get past Mitchell, so she stood there quietly, tak-ing in the scene. She smiled at me as if to say "Aren't they cute," and I smiled back at her as if to say, something in return, but I had no idea what it was.

ELROY NIGHTS

THE YOUNG MAN who lived across the courtyard from me was always elegantly dressed in expensive clothes, good shoes, his hair well cut and his face cleanly shaven. He was, precisely, dapper. He drove an older Cadillac convertible in periwinkle blue, and seemed a little too intent on having his way. He appeared to be lonely. I rarely saw him with company. Mostly I saw him crossing the courtyard from the parking garage, carrying a handsome leather case, his heels clicking on the faded tile. Then I would hear the screech of the elevator doors and the tired whine of the car as it rose to our floor. My apartment was on the third floor as well, directly across the court from his, and while I used my windows a good deal, his blinds were never open.

We had a new tenant in the building, a woman named Eileen Wiesatch. I met her when the landlord introduced us on a Saturday morning in March. Eileen was a TV producer for the local NBC affiliate. She worked on the news, I gathered. She was an attractive woman in her early thirties, small, with close-cropped hair, and she wore casual clothes — jeans and mannish dress shirts, an elegant sports jacket. It may have been cut especially for a woman, but it did not look as if it had been. It occurred to me that she might buy her clothes in the boys' department at Saks. It was a nice look — comfortable, casual, and, at the same time, a little daring. She was hidden and exposed by these clothes.

I assumed Mrs. Bolton, who was our landlady, introduced Eileen to the other tenants, just as she had introduced her to me. I was Mrs. Bolton's oldest tenant in two senses — the one with the greatest tenure in the building, and the oldest. Mrs. Bolton and I were contemporaries, in fact, so occasionally we would have dinner together — a casual arrangement. I would see her in the courtyard or in front of the building, and she would invite me to dinner or I would invite her. We would have a pleasant hour and a half, with wine and salad and gossip.

It was one of these dinners at Mrs. Bolton's that Edward Works, the young man who took too much care of himself, interrupted when he arrived to complain about Eileen Wiesatch, who was, according to him, filling the hall outside her apartment, which was immediately adjacent to his, with boxes, packing materials, crates, and a general run of garbage that he thought ought to be taken immediately to the Dempsey Dumpster behind the building.

Mrs. Bolton invited Works into her home and introduced me. "Elroy Nights," I said, shaking his hand. I said I'd seen him before, and was pleased to finally meet him. As the grand old man of the building, I said, I was pleased to have him with us.

"And I am pleased to be here," Edward Works said. "Except for this little difficulty with the new tenant who doesn't seem to want to play by the rules."

"She just moved in," Mrs. Bolton said. "Don't you think we should give her a week or two to get settled? I'm sure we can have Rupert take that material out of the hall."

"We should have the young woman take care of it," he said.

"She should dispose of the mess as soon as it comes out of her apartment."

"Of course you're absolutely right," Mrs. Bolton said. "Still, a little tolerance is sometimes a kindness we can afford, don't you agree?"

He drew a large breath through his nose at this point.

Seeing Edward Works up close was interesting. Most often when you see a person that close, you see, among other things, the flaws in their presentation—the ties don't quite match the shirts, the shirts have hairline wrinkles in the collars, the belts are off center, the shoes are scuffed, the sewing on the trouser cuffs may have come undone. Any number of small details give us away, conspiring to suggest just how much of our "self" is manufactured, just how far we are from the person we want to present for public consumption. But in the world of Edward Works there were no errors, there was not a single hair out of place, no choice was even slightly mistaken, no bit of fluff or dander flawed his suit. His shirt was impeccably pressed and arranged. His trousers were creased to perfection, and his shoes, which looked very English, had a lovely warm polish. He looked so good that he was enormously out of place in Mrs. Bolton's living room, which was chintz and Naugahyde and small, thick with bad Impressionist prints in gaudy golden frames. In that setting Edward Works was a cutout, an image from a magazine, an exquisitely coiffed and prepared figure dropped into this too-comfortable, too-carpeted, too-worn apartment.

"I could help with the boxes," I said to Mrs. Bolton. "If they aren't too large."

"You'd do that?" Mrs. Bolton said. Then she froze a second, and then made a cartoon expression, blinking and twirling her eyes at the same time—the kind of thing a character does when hit over the head with a frying pan. "Of course you'd do that. Why am I even asking?"

I smiled and said, "Well? You never know, do you?"

"That's right," Mrs. Bolton said. "Exactly."

"So whatever you want to do," Edward Works said, snapping his wrist out so he could look at his very expensive, very small watch. "I have a meeting, so I guess I'll leave it to you." He rearranged his cuff and turned for the door. Over his shoulder he said, "I genuinely appreciate your help with this, Mrs. Bolton." He did not look back. He opened the door, walked out, and let the door close behind him.

Mrs. Bolton and I stood in the living room a moment before returning to the dining table where our food, looking a little forlorn, remained. As we sat down Mrs. Bolton said, "I think I've lost my appetite."

"No. No, you haven't," I said. "You are profoundly hungry. You will eat and eat until you can eat no more. I will help with Eileen, and Mr. Works will be happy again."

"He is a strange bird, isn't he?" Mrs. Bolton said.

"I've noticed," I said. "He seems altogether too well kept up."

"Exactly. Exactly my thought," she said. "Has he nothing better to do than dress and polish and do his nails?"

"I missed the nails," I said.

"They're gorgeous," she said. "You must have a look." She was grinning now, reaching for her fork, beginning to toy with the salad again. "When we finish here, let's take a walk up to Eileen's place and see just how bad the situation is."

"Excellent plan," I said. I was looking at my salad, where two halves of a boiled egg stared at me out of their leafy green pasture. I thought them very handsome — big yellow eyes, lovely milk-white flesh. Just looking at them reminded me of the peculiar taste of boiled eggs, a taste I'd savored since childhood. There was special pleasure in the damp dryness of the yolk held in that cooled, almost gelatinous white. I had discussed this with Mrs. Bolton on several occasions, and we had agreed that boiled eggs were best served slightly cooler than room temperature. Not cold, precisely, but slightly chilled. So whenever we dined together I could be sure the boiled eggs would have been held in the refrigerator for half an hour or so before serving. I took up my fork and inserted the tines into the yellow of one of the egg halves, then extracted the yolk whole, holding it at the end of my fork between us.

Mrs. Bolton raised an eyebrow and then smiled, closed her eyes, and nodded. "You go ahead," she said. I salted generously and popped the yolk into my mouth.

▼

Eileen was wearing a halter top and very short shorts, and she was in the hall arranging boxes that were lined up along the carpet, stacked four or five high. She had made a mess of things, there was no question. She greeted us warmly, shrugging at Mrs. Bolton as if to say, *You said I could stack my things out here*, as if she were apologizing and complaining about herself, all at the same time.

Mrs. Bolton said, "Yikes."

"Elroy Nights," I said, reminding her and extending my hand.

Eileen nodded. "Of course."

"I'm kind of across the courtyard here," I said, pointing in through her front door toward where my apartment was. As had been the case when I was first introduced to Eileen, I was a little stunned. She looked too much like somebody you'd see on television, like all the young women who operate MTV and VH1 and E!, who seem innocent and randy at the same time. Eileen had the look — all lovely skin, fresh hair, eyes that sparkled, perfect features, slender shoulders, small breasts, smaller waist. She was a type. Had I not known she worked for NBC, I would have thought she was a model. She took my hand when I extended it, and her grip was bony.

"Pleased to see you again," she said. "I've been trying to figure out which are your windows, actually. And I've talked with Mrs. Bolton about you as well." She said this with a certain flash in her eyes, a good joke.

"Oh, yes?" I said, turning to Mrs. Bolton. "And what has she said?"

"She maintains that you are the real deal," Eileen said, smiling and glancing quickly at Mrs. Bolton as if they shared a slightly different version of this.

"I'm sure I'm flattered," I said.

Mrs. Bolton patted my arm. "We've had a meeting with Mr. Edward Works," she said to Eileen. "Your neighbor. He seems to think there is too much, uh," she paused, looking at the debris in the hall, "*stuff* here. We were wondering if we might help you get it downstairs."

"We could do it together," I said.

"He's a little worm, isn't he?" Eileen said. "Edward Works."

Mrs. Bolton and I both regarded the ceiling at the same time.

"No, I don't want you to do it. I'll take care of it, don't you worry," Eileen said.

"But we want to help," I said.

"Sorry, it's not happening," she said. "I'll take care of it. Don't give it another thought, please. It is a mess. I wish it weren't, but I can take care of it. I'll speak to Mr. Go Down Moses as well."

"I should say in his defense that Mr. Works's mother died just two months ago," Mrs. Bolton said. "I think it hit him harder than he imagined it would."

"His mother died. That's right. I remember you telling me that," I said.

"That's a terrible thing to have happen," Eileen said. "I'm sorry to hear that."

"Losing your mother makes you feel disconnected from the world," Mrs. Bolton said.

"That's only true, of course, if your mother is someone with whom you are connected," I said. "Don't you think that's so?"

"Not at all," Mrs. Bolton said. "I think your mother tethers you to the world in a way that no one else does."

"How did she die?" Eileen said.

"It was a car accident," Mrs. Bolton said. "She was driving a car on one of the freeways — I believe she was on the way to meet Mr. Works for lunch — when her car was hit by a truck, one of those huge trucks that carry the great pine logs. She was decapitated. Like Jayne Mansfield."

"She wasn't really decapitated, I believe," I said.

Eileen made a face. "Well, in any case, I guess he has reason to be upset. It's too bad we have to live with such things."

"Exactly," I said. "I spend a great deal of time thinking about things that I would like to correct in my life, things I would change if I had the opportunity to do them over again."

Mrs. Bolton and Eileen both turned to me expectantly.

"Well, I do," I said. "I would like to go back in time and try again. Like my father's death. It's ten years ago now, but we were not as close as we had been. He lived in Atlanta, in a small house, alone. I talked to him on the phone often, but I don't think I was as loving as I might have been. He was quite sick the last years, and I don't think I did enough to help out."

"I'm sure you did fine," Mrs. Bolton said. "But I know what you mean. We all have our regrets."

"Count me in," Eileen said.

"Still," I said, "there are two or three times in my life that I would really like to go back and do over again. A moment when I wish I'd been somewhere I wasn't, or done something I didn't, a moment that might have significantly changed things. I just never paid sufficient attention. My dad's death was one. If I'd done it better, been there with him, helped out a little, well, his death might have been avoided, or at least made less terrifying for him. He might have had one of those good TV deaths where the person is ready. But he didn't. He was discovered by the plumber who was coming to the house to work on the toilets. Dad had a lot of complaints about toilets, had lots of trouble with them. So the plumber was called and when he arrived my father was dead, sitting in his chair staring at a television set tuned to the preview channel. The plumber told me. He was very specific. But I think if I had been there, if I had been with him, if I'd been kinder and tried harder, maybe he wouldn't have died that way."

"Well," Mrs. Bolton said, touching my arm. "Maybe it wasn't as bad as you imagine. Perhaps he just sat down to watch a little television and sort of dozed off."

"Yes," Eileen said. "Maybe he just stepped into the next world. Right as rain. The most natural thing in the world."

"I suppose it could have happened that way, but I do not think that it did. He was inclined to torment himself about almost everything. He found trouble wherever he looked. He found things done wrong, people doing things wrong, people not trying hard enough—he found things to complain about. And while the complaints were always directed at other people, I always had the sense that he was really complaining about himself. Cloaking his own inadequacies by pointing to the failures of others. He was easily exasperated."

Mrs. Bolton rearranged some of the boxes against the corridor wall. "Yes, many of us are easily exasperated. Mr. Works, for example. He's exasperated with our young friend here."

"And I'm exasperated right back," Eileen said, smiling.

"Oh, pish," Mrs. Bolton said, laughing at Eileen's joke.

"I would be exasperated with him," Eileen said, "if I were the exasperating kind. No, that's not what I mean."

"That's OK. We know what you mean, dearie," Mrs. Bolton said. She rubbed her gray hair, tucked in a tight bun. She loosed it as if to freshen herself.

"There are not many times in your life when you can make a real difference," I said. "Dad could have used some companionship, a friendly son to take care of him, to sit with him, to get what he was about, to like him in spite of himself. I mostly talked to him on the telephone. So I could get away quickly and easily. Shed of him, I didn't have to think about him all the time. That was easier. I called him often to chat about what was going on, to hear his medical problems, but see, by calling I didn't have to *see* the problems, didn't have to deal with them. We had a woman from Catholic Health Services — "

"I did that with my mother," Eileen said.

"What?"

"Took her to look at nursing homes, had people in to take care of her. Everybody does that."

"I just went along with whatever he wanted," I said. "Encouraged him, whatever he said. I didn't give it that much thought. I figured he wouldn't listen to me anyway."

"My mother always wanted to figure out her future," Eileen said.

"How old a woman was she then?" Mrs. Bolton said.

"Mid-fifties, I guess," Eileen said. "She still has a house in Baltimore."

"Oh, so you're from Baltimore?" Mrs. Bolton said. "Why didn't I know that?"

Eileen looked at her and raised an eyebrow. "Don't look now, Mrs. Bolton, but I believe you did."

"Well, of course," Mrs. Bolton said. "I must have misplaced it. Just one tiny bit of information misplaced. Nothing to worry about."

"He was kind of a tyrant," I said.

Just then the elevator clinked to a stop down the corridor and the doors hissed open, and Mr. Edward Works stepped out and started toward us down the carpeted hallway.

"Speak of the devil," Mrs. Bolton said, Groucho-Marxing her eyebrows.

"I think I'll just step back inside here," Eileen said, backing into the doorway of her apartment.

"Come right back out here," Mrs. Bolton said. "I want to introduce you."

"He was kind of a bore, too," I said. "He couldn't help it, but the truth was that's what he'd become. He was plenty ugly in those last years."

"Maybe that's what we all become," Mrs. Bolton said, eyeing me.

She turned around just in time to catch Mr. Edward Works by the elbow. "How are you, Mr. Works?" she said.

"I'm fine, thank you," he said, drawing his elbow away from her unsuccessfully.

"I want you to meet Eileen Wiesatch," she said. "She's new in the building. Just moving in, as you can see."

Mr. Works gave Mrs. Bolton a look as cross as any I'd seen in quite some time. Then he stepped forward and extended his hand to Eileen, who took it and smiled, saying, "Hi. How are you? Glad to meet you."

"Edward Works," Mr. Works said. "I'm just down the corridor here."

Eileen nodded, still holding his hand. "Yes, I know. I do want to apologize about all this mess I've made in the hall. I'll have it straightened away in a day or so. Do you think you can put up with it for that time?"

"Of course," Mr. Works said. "I hadn't even noticed it. I'll be happy to help if you need a hand."

"That's very kind of you," Eileen said.

"We were talking about things we would have done differently in our lives if we'd had the opportunity," I said. "Things we'd like to go back and correct."

"Go back?" Mr. Works said.

"Yes," I said. "Go back in time. How things might have been different if we were at a certain place in a certain time, and how now we might actually like to go back in time and be at those places at those times."

"Ah," he said, nodding.

"Time travel," Mrs. Bolton said.

"Yes, I see," Mr. Works said.

"I was talking about my father," I said. "I find that as I get older I think more and more about him, what his life must have been like after the children were grown into middle age and my mother passed away and he was living alone."

"Eileen's come to us from Baltimore," Mrs. Bolton said.

"That toddlin' town," I said.

Behind Mr. Works's back Mrs. Bolton gave me a vicious shake of the head and a grimace, as if telling me to behave myself. I shrugged at her and smiled. I thought what a lovely woman she was — generous, sweet, absent malice.

▼

At two o'clock in the morning I was sitting at my window. I'd been watching a movie on HBO and was now having a bowl of cereal and watching the tree limbs blow in the breeze. There was rain headed our way.

I looked down into the courtyard, and something there caught my eye. Mr. Works and Eileen Wiesatch were sitting together on a bench and smoking cigarettes. The breeze carried the smoke from the cigarettes away. They appeared to be laughing. They were kissing there on the bench, their arms strewn about, their knees propped up. They were in animated conversation.

I thought about a young man I had known some years before. He was a student at the university and lived in our building. I knew him only slightly, by Mrs. Bolton's introduction, hallway conversations, a rare chess game on a Saturday afternoon. He was on the sixth floor. One night, very late, he apparently had a wretched argument with his girlfriend. I heard the fight, but, like the others, ignored it. Two days later we discovered that he had committed suicide that night.

Sitting at my window, watching Mr. Works and Eileen in the courtyard, I thought about that young man, and I wished that I had gone out of my apartment that night many years ago. I wished that I'd gone down the hall and up the elevator and knocked on his door, and interceded somehow. I didn't know him well, but I knew him well enough. He was a friend of mine. Sitting at my window, watching the clouds go across the sky, spooning my cereal, what I thought was, I could have stopped him from killing himself. Practically anyone could have stopped him from killing himself. Of course, he might have done it later, but how can you know? How can you be sure that if you get him through one threatening nightmarish evening that he will ever get that close to suicide again? How can you be sure you have not saved him? One tiny joke, one gentle gesture, one little cuff on the back might have been enough to get him through the night, through the impulse. One of anything might have worked.